ADOBE® FLASH® CS4
PROFESSIONAL
HOW-TOs

100 ESSENTIAL TECHNIQUES

MARK SCHAEFFER

Adobe

Adobe® Flash® CS4 Professional How-Tos
100 Essential Techniques

Mark Schaeffer

This Adobe Press book is published by Peachpit.

For information on Adobe Press books, contact:

Peachpit
1249 Eighth Street
Berkeley, CA 94710
510/524-2178
510/524-2221 (fax)

Peachpit is a division of Pearson Education.

For the latest on Adobe Press books, go to www.adobepress.com

To report errors, please send a note to: errata@peachpit.com

Copyright © 2009 by Mark Schaeffer

Editor: Jill Marts Lodwig
Production Editor: Cory Borman
Technical Reviewer: Jeremy Rue
Compositor: ICC MacMillan
Indexer: Jack Lewis
Interior and Cover Designer: Mimi Heft

ISBN 13: 978-0-321-58004-7

ISBN 10: 0-321-58004-4

9 8 7 6 5 4 3 2 1

Printed and bound in the United States of America

Dedication

In memory of Brook, my devoted feline companion for nearly 19 years—writing all night is a much lonelier experience without her.

Acknowledgments

Although mine is the only name on the cover, this book is the product of many people's skillful and careful work. Chief among them are the editorial and production team at Adobe Press, who made the book as clear, accurate, and attractive as it is: project editor Rebecca Gulick, editor Jill Marts Lodwig, technical editor Jeremy Rue, production editor Cory Borman, compositor Gunjan Chandola, and indexer Jack Lewis. I'd also like to re-acknowledge the editors of last year's edition for CS3—Becca Freed, David Morris, Eric Schumacher-Rasmussen, and Kim Saccio-Kent—much of whose work persists in this new edition.

My good friend Karen Reichstein was the acquiring editor for this project; I'm thankful that such an otherwise perceptive person remains unable to hear the words "never again."

Gary Carter, dean of Arts and Humanities at Chabot College, offered me his support and encouragement. Lindsay Shuman, a former student of mine at Chabot, was a great help with organizing material for the book's early chapters.

I owe a huge debt of gratitude to my oldest and best friend, Brad Hartfield—the most brilliant person I know—for volunteering many hours of research, creative input, and editorial advice when I desperately needed those things. Having Brad offer to help with a how-to book is like having Buckminster Fuller offer to help with a garden shed.

As always, my deepest thanks go to my wife, Debra Goldentyer, whose love, patience, humor, intelligence, and way with food—not to mention editorial and managerial skills—are a continuing source of comfort, surprise, and delight.

Contents

Introduction

Adobe Flash is a single program with multiple personalities. It's an animation studio that's used not only to make small things move on computer screens, but also to create many of the full-length cartoons you see on TV. It's a multimedia authoring environment that combines text, photographs, sound, animation, and video into projects that may be artistic, entertaining, informative, or all three. It's a software development platform that allows programmers to create the powerful but easy-to-use applications that you see all over the Web. It's a friendly, intuitive program that was originally designed for anyone to use, but has evolved into a complex, professional-level tool for seasoned designers and developers.

No single publication can cover all those facets thoroughly, and this book isn't even going to try. It doesn't describe every feature or tell you what each keystroke and menu item does; you can get that information just as easily from the Help files that come with Flash. What it *does* do is introduce you, by means of clear explanations and carefully selected examples, to 100 fundamental skills that will allow you to work productively in Flash. Once you see how Flash "thinks" and how it approaches tasks, learning to use its multiple features and options becomes much easier.

Chapters 1 through 10 constitute a complete book on their own. If you're interested in animation and multimedia, those chapters are all you'll need. If you want to move toward more interactive, user-focused projects, move on to Chapters 11 and 12, which acquaint you with the versatile programming language called ActionScript.

Each chapter includes techniques of varying levels of difficulty. If you're new to Flash, you'll probably want to go through them in order. If you already have experience in Flash or related programs, feel free to skip around and pick up what you need. Scattered throughout, you'll find notes and sidebars that you may find interesting and occasionally amusing. As I tell the students in my Flash classes, "If you're not having fun, you're not doing it right."

CHAPTER ONE

Exploring the Flash Interface

If you're a first-time user of Flash, it may take you some time to get used to the program's idiosyncratic approach to drawing and animation. But even if you've used Flash before, you'll find that familiar tasks now have to be handled differently. In version CS3, Adobe took a first step toward giving all its Creative Suite products a similar interface. Now, in CS4, the developers have redesigned that interface to be simpler, more flexible, and more consistent among products and platforms.

This first chapter will guide you through launching Flash, customizing it, and preparing for a project. It's tempting to skip these steps and dive into creating a movie, but you'll find that taking the time to configure your workspace and organize your files helps you use Flash more comfortably and efficiently.

If you're new to Flash, it's helpful to keep in mind that Flash began as an animation program for the Web. Therefore, several of its interface elements have names drawn from the world of film: A Flash file is called a *movie* (regardless of whether anything in it actually moves); the area where the visual elements of the movie are assembled is called the *stage*; the incremental steps by which a movie's action takes place are called *frames* (like the frames on a strip of film); and long movies are sometimes divided into segments called *scenes*. Even if you plan to use Flash as a programming environment or as an interface-development tool, it's still important to see how these more advanced capabilities relate to the animation features.

#1 Starting Flash

The first time you launch Flash, you'll encounter a Software Setup screen (**Figure 1a**). To use the software, you have to enter your serial number no more than 30 days after installation. If the number you've entered is valid, a green check mark appears.

When you click the Next button, you're taken to the Activation screen. Your copy of Flash won't work unless you activate it. If you are connected to the Internet, Flash will handle this automatically; if not, you have the option of activating by phone.

If you've done a group installation of several Creative Suite products, you may not have to activate Flash individually. Activating one product in the suite automatically activates all of the others.

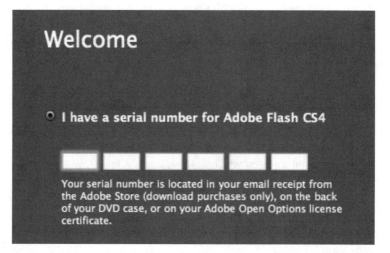

Figure 1a This setup screen appears the first time you launch Flash. If you don't have your serial number handy, you can use the program without one for up to 30 days.

Once Flash has been activated, the standard Welcome screen appears (**Figure 1b**). This screen offers shortcuts for tasks that users typically want to do when they start Flash, such as opening a previously saved file or creating various kinds of new files.

Don't Show Again check box   News from Adobe

Figure 1b This Welcome screen appears by default anytime you launch Flash, or anytime you have no files open in Flash.

To create a new movie, click Flash File (ActionScript 3.0), the first item in the Create New column. This command opens a new Flash document that's set up to use the latest version of the ActionScript programming language. Even if you don't intend to do any interactive scripting and are using Flash strictly for its animation capabilities, you should still choose to create an ActionScript 3.0-compatible file; otherwise, your animation won't be able to make use of advanced features, such as the 3D tools (see #16) and Inverse Kinematics (see #48). If you're an experienced Flash user who isn't ready to give up on the earlier version of ActionScript, you can opt for ActionScript 2.0 and continue scripting in the traditional way; however, all of the examples in this book assume that you've chosen ActionScript 3.0.

(continued on next page)

Two's Company; Three's a Crowd

Your license agreement with Adobe permits you to install Flash on two computers—for example, one desktop and one laptop, or one home computer and one office computer—as long as the program isn't used simultaneously on both computers. If you want to install Flash on a third computer, you'll first have to deactivate one of the two currently installed copies by choosing Deactivate from the Help menu.

4

Welcome Back

If you've dismissed the Welcome screen by clicking its Close button—and you haven't selected the Don't Show Again check box—you can bring the screen back at any time by closing all open Flash documents.

If you've clicked Don't Show Again and you decide later that you miss seeing the Welcome screen, you can bring it back by choosing Edit > Preferences (Windows) or Flash > Preferences (Mac), clicking the General category in the left column, and selecting Welcome Screen from the On Launch menu. While you're there, you may change your mind and decide to let Flash display a new document or a previously open document instead.

Flash now has the capacity to create standalone applications—interactive programs that will run on any computer—by means of a new technology called *AIR* (see #82). To create an AIR-compatible movie, click Flash File (Adobe AIR). To create Flash movies for handheld devices such as cell phones and personal digital assistants, which are not covered in this book, click Flash FIle (Mobile).

The Create from Template column is useful for those who aren't yet ready to build interactive Flash movies from scratch. It offers a variety of movie templates in which the design and interactive elements are in place, so that all you have to add are the text and graphics.

The content of the Welcome screen is dynamic, meaning that it's different at different times. Assuming your computer has a connection to the Internet, the rectangular area at the lower right will act as a billboard on which Adobe may promote particular Flash features, provide links to Flash-related services, and notify you of downloadable maintenance updates for Flash.

#2 Managing Your Workspace

The workspace in Flash consists of a variety of panels. The panels can be arranged in various ways, depending on the kind of project you're working on and the environment you're comfortable with. Four essential panels will almost always be visible: the Tools panel, the timeline, the stage, and Properties (formerly called the *Properties Inspector*). Although these panels have the same functions that they did in earlier versions of Flash, their appearance and layout have changed noticeably in Flash CS4 (**Figure 2a**).

Stage

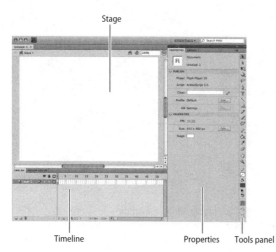

Timeline   Properties   Tools panel

Figure 2a These are the four most important panels in the Flash CS4 user interface, shown in their default layout.

The Tools panel contains the tools you'll need to create and edit the visual elements of a Flash movie. You can roll your pointer over each tool to find out the name of that tool and the keyboard shortcut that you can use to select it. A tiny, black triangle to the lower right of a tool indicates that there are other tools hidden beneath it. To see them, press and hold your mouse pointer over the currently visible tool.

The timeline is where you map out how the elements of your movie change over time. Above it is the stage, where you create, edit, and arrange the shapes, images, video clips, and elements that make up the visual portion of your movie.

Whenever you need to change options or settings for tools, frames, or an entire movie, the Properties panel is where you do it. This panel is *context-sensitive*, meaning that it displays different information depending on where on the screen you've most recently clicked the mouse (**Figure 2b**).

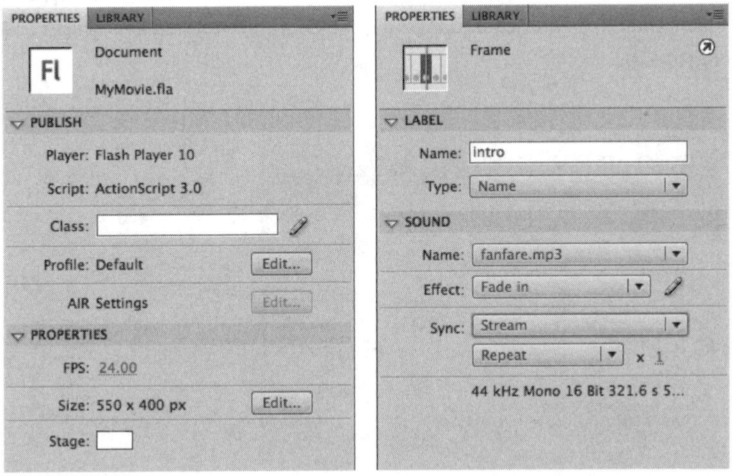

Figure 2b The changing face of the Properties panel: on the left, it displays information about the entire movie; on the right, it displays information about a single frame.

Smaller panels are usually fastened together in a rectangular container called a *dock*. Docked panels can be expanded or collapsed by clicking the medium-gray bar at the top of each panel (**Figure 2c**). By clicking the dark-gray bar at the top of any dock, you can reduce all the panels in that dock to icons.

If you need a panel that's not currently available, you can choose its name from the Window menu. If the panel was in a dock the last time it was closed, it will reappear in that dock. Otherwise, it will appear in a free-floating window. You can grab the panel by the dark bar at the top (**Figure 2d**) and drag it toward an existing dock.

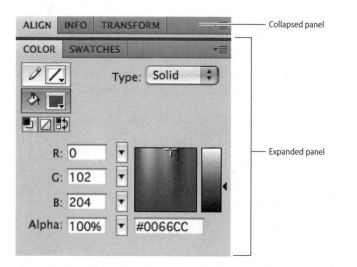

Collapsed panel

Expanded panel

Figure 2c Docked panels may be collapsed (e.g., the Transform panel) or expanded (e.g., the Swatches panel).

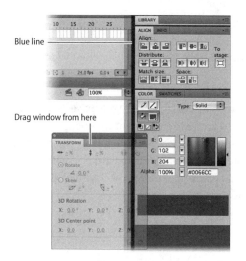

Blue line

Drag window from here

Figure 2d A floating window being dragged toward a dock

As you near the dock, a vertical blue line appears. If you drop the panel now, it will park itself in a new dock adjacent to the old one. If you continue to drag the panel onto an existing dock, one or more horizontal blue lines will appear. Each line shows where in the stack the dragged panel would land if you were to drop it immediately (**Figure 2e**).

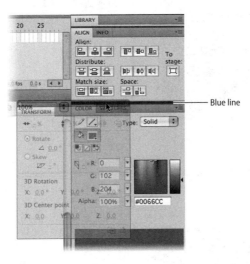

Figure 2e The window from Figure 2d, about to be dropped into an existing dock.

Any combination or arrangement of panels is referred to as a *workspace*. When you first launch Flash, its default workspace (shown in Figure 2a) is rather minimal, so you're likely to want to modify it. As you work with Flash, you may find that there are certain panels you want to have available all the time, or that a certain layout feels most comfortable. If you develop a workspace that you're fond of, you can save it by choosing Window > Workspace > Save Current.

At any time, you can retrieve that saved workspace by choosing it from the Window > Workspace menu. Flash comes with several predefined workspaces already available on that menu (**Figure 2f**).

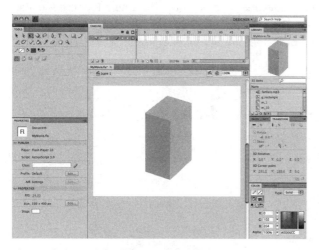

Figure 2f The predefined Designer workspace makes the Color and Transform panels readily available.

Secret Slider

Whenever you see a numerical value in Properties, verify whether it's shown in blue with a dotted underline. If so, you can change the value by sliding. Place your mouse pointer over the number and depress the mouse button; the pointer changes to a double-headed arrow. When you drag to the left, the value decreases; when you drag to the right, it increases.

10

#3 Setting Document Properties

When you create a new, blank Flash movie, the first thing you'll want to do is to set the Document Properties—a collection of fundamental settings that affect the entire movie. To set these properties, choose Document from the Modify menu to open the Document Properties dialog box (**Figure 3a**). The most important properties to set are Dimensions, Background Color, Frame Rate, and Ruler Units.

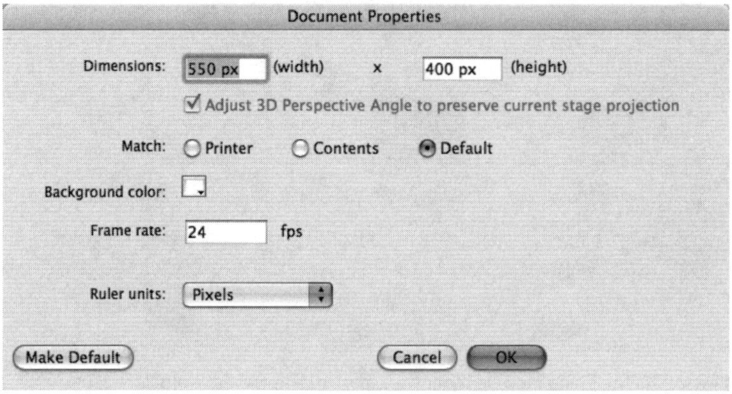

Figure 3a The Document Properties dialog box with its default settings.

Dimensions. This property determines the height and width of the stage. Since most Flash movies are designed to be viewed onscreen, it's common practice to specify movie dimensions in pixels rather than in print-oriented units such as inches or points.

The default dimensions of 550 by 400 pixels are arbitrary. Make your movie's dimensions as large or as small as are appropriate for your project. The only time you'll need to pay special attention to the dimensions is when you're using Flash to produce animation for video. In this case, the video editing program will specify what the dimensions of the movie should be—typically 1920 by 1080 pixels for high-definition video.

There are two shortcuts, represented by the radio buttons to the right of the Match label. (The third button resets the default dimensions.) Printer sets the movie's dimensions to match the printable area of your currently selected printer, and Contents makes the movie's dimensions match the dimensions of whatever's on the stage. Think carefully before you make your selection. Although it's simple to change the dimensions later, it's much more difficult to modify your movie to fit the new settings.

Background Color. This property determines what color the stage will be. Whatever color you choose will show through on all unoccupied areas of the stage. For information on choosing a color, see #8.

Frame Rate. Frame rate, which is discussed in detail in #31, is a measure of how fast your movie progresses. For now, it's enough to know that 12 to 15 frames per second (fps) is typical for Flash movies that are posted on the Web, and that 30 fps is standard for animation used in video. The default frame rate in Flash CS4 is 24 fps.

Ruler Units. This property doesn't affect the movie, but only affects how the movie and its contents are measured in Flash. If you've specified the movie's dimensions in pixels, it's usually good to set ruler units to pixels as well.

If you want to make these new document properties the default settings for future movies, click the Make Default button on the lower left of the dialog box.

#4 Using Function Keys and Keyboard Shortcuts

Because creating a Flash movie can be time-consuming, it's helpful to find ways to speed the process. One of the best ways is to master the built-in keyboard shortcuts that let you execute Flash commands with a single keystroke instead of having to choose each one from a menu.

The most common Flash tasks can be accomplished using function keys (those keys at the top of your keyboard labeled F1, F2, and so on). There are several function keys—F5, F6, and F7, for example—that are vital for creating animation and therefore should become a part of your vocabulary. (The specific uses of these keys are explained in Chapter 5, "Creating Basic Animation.")

Using the function keys in Flash is often a problem for Mac users. Mac OS X reserves some function keys for its own use, and those keys don't work properly in Flash. The most commonly affected keys are F9 through F12, which the operating system uses to control Apple features such as Dashboard and Exposé. This is especially frustrating in the case of the F9 key, which in Flash is used to open some commonly used panels.

There are two ways to get around this problem. The first is to navigate to Mac's System Preferences and remap the Dashboard and Exposé features to a different set of keystrokes. The second is to go into Flash and remap its F9 through F12 features. Since this is a book about Flash, not the Mac operating system, we'll look at the second alternative.

To remap keyboard shortcuts in Flash:

1. Choose Edit > Keyboard Shortcuts (Windows) or Flash > Keyboard Shortcuts (Mac). The Keyboard Shortcuts dialog box appears (**Figure 4a**).

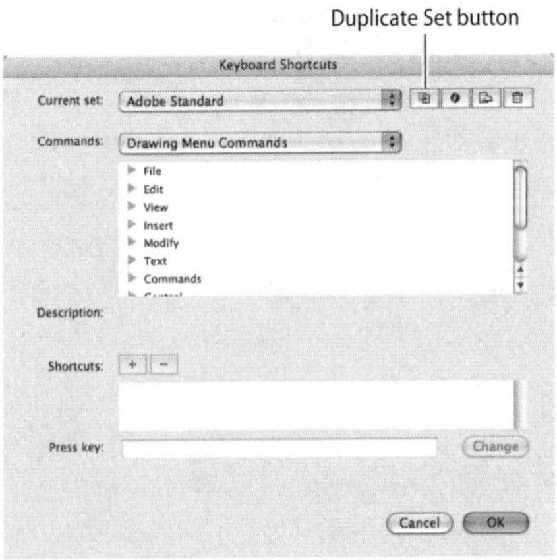

Figure 4a The Keyboard Shortcuts dialog box.

The Current Set menu should be set to Adobe Standard, which is the default set of keyboard shortcuts for Flash CS4.

2. To the right of the Current Set menu is a row of four buttons. Click the first button, Duplicate Set. (The original Adobe Standard set can't be modified.)

You'll see a Duplicate dialog box, with a default name (Adobe Standard copy) filled in.

3. Either accept the default name or type a new one, and click OK.

The Current Set menu now displays the name of your duplicate set.

4. If you know the name of the command whose keyboard shortcut you want to modify, locate it by choosing the appropriate list of commands from the Commands menu, then make your selection from one of the submenus (**Figure 4b**).

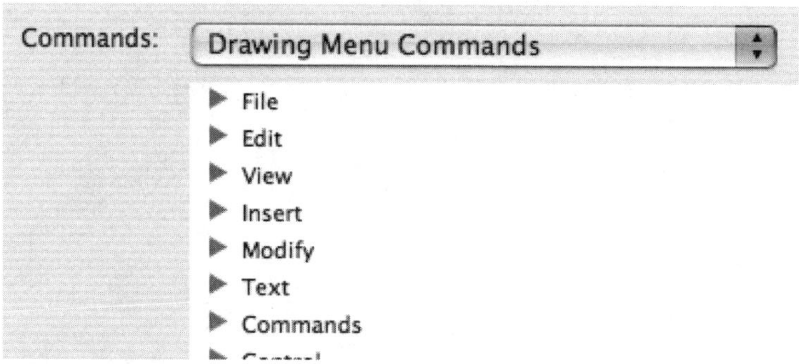

Figure 4b The submenus in the Keyboard Shortcuts menu correspond to the Flash menus on which those commands appear.

If you want to know which command a particular key combination is assigned to, you'll have to search through every submenu within the command lists. You're looking for a particular keystroke (for example, Shift-F9, which opens the Color panel).

5. Highlight the desired command.

The Description field defines the command, while the Shortcuts field shows the currently applied keystroke. The same keystroke appears in the Press Key field.

(continued on next page)

#4: Using Function Keys and Keyboard Shortcuts

6. Highlight the keystroke in the Press Key field, then press the key (or key combination) that you want to replace it with.

If the "This keystroke is already assigned…" error message appears, keep trying key combinations until you find one that's open.

7. Click OK.

The Keyboard Shortcuts dialog box closes, and the new keyboard shortcut takes effect.

If you're not interested in remapping keys, but just want to learn the existing keyboard shortcuts, look in the standard Flash menus. For each command that has a keyboard shortcut, the keystroke appears to the right of the command.

#5 Organizing Your Files

Flash is capable of saving and exporting a number of different file types, including QuickTime movie files, animated GIF files, projector files, and more. No matter which sort of work you're doing in Flash, there are two types of files you'll always use: FLA, usually pronounced *flah*, and SWF, usually pronounced *swiff* (**Figure 5a**).

Figure 5a FLA files and SWF files can be recognized by their icons. The icon for a FLA file is on the left; that for a SWF file is on the right.

FLA is a proprietary Flash authoring file format. A FLA file contains all the information Flash needs to create and modify your movie: vector shapes, symbols, uncompressed images and sounds, timeline information, text, uncompiled ActionScript code, and so on. For this reason, FLA files tend to be large, sometimes in the hundreds of megabytes.

To generate a FLA file, you open or create a movie in Flash and then choose File > Save (or File > Save As). The only way to view or edit a FLA file is to open it in Flash.

SWF is the Flash Player file format. All information not needed to display your movie has been stripped out of it, and the remaining information is highly compressed. Therefore, a FLA file of many megabytes may yield a SWF file of only a few kilobytes. Although the size of the FLA file doesn't matter (as long as it fits on your hard drive!), your goal in creating a Flash movie should always be to end up with as small a SWF file as possible. You'll learn some tricks for decreasing the size of SWF files in Chapter 2, "Using the Drawing Tools."

You generate a SWF file by opening a FLA file in Flash and either testing the movie (see #35) or publishing the movie (see #78). To modify a SWF file, you'll have to open its corresponding FLA file in Flash, make your changes, and generate a new SWF file to replace the old one. With some minor exceptions, SWF files can't be edited; they can only be played.

Y SWF?

FLA as the file extension for a Flash file makes sense . . . but where did SWF come from?

Long ago, before Flash existed (for that matter, before the World Wide Web existed), people created digital animation and inter-active environments using a Macromedia product called Director. When the Web sud-denly blossomed, Macrome-dia had to figure out a way to put Director movies online, and it came up with Shock-wave. (A Shockwave file was to a Director file what an SWF file is to a FLA file.)

When Flash came along, Macromedia wanted to take advantage of the well-promoted Shockwave trademark. Therefore, the files that Flash generated for online use were called "Shockwave Flash Files," or SWF for short.

As Flash became more popu-lar and Director less so, the Shockwave name began to seem more like a liabil-ity than an asset. As a result, Flash Player files ceased to be called Shockwave files; but the SWF extension lives on.

SWF is an open format: Although it originated with Flash, many programs other than Flash can create SWF files, and some non-Adobe programs can play them.

To include Flash movies on a Web site, you upload SWF files. FLA files are strictly for your own use (**Figure 5b**).

SWF file playing in browser

Figure 5b When a Flash movie appears on a web page, what you're seeing is a SWF file, not a FLA file.

As with all computer data, you should save your FLA files frequently while you're working on them. Saving SWF files isn't nearly as important; you can always generate a new SWF file from a working FLA file.

Instead of choosing File > Save each time you save your FLA file, it's a much better idea to choose File > Save As, and give each new version of the file an incremental name (for example, mymovie01.fla, mymovie02.fla, and so on). By doing so, you'll avoid overwriting earlier versions of your files, and you'll have a variety of different stages of development to which you can return if you become dissatisfied with the current version of your movie.

Because Flash projects almost always comprise multiple files, good file management is essential. Flash includes a Project panel that allows you to handle basic file-management tasks, such as creating and deleting files, and organizing files into folders, without leaving the Flash environment (**Figure 5c**). To open this panel, choose Window > Other Panels > Project.

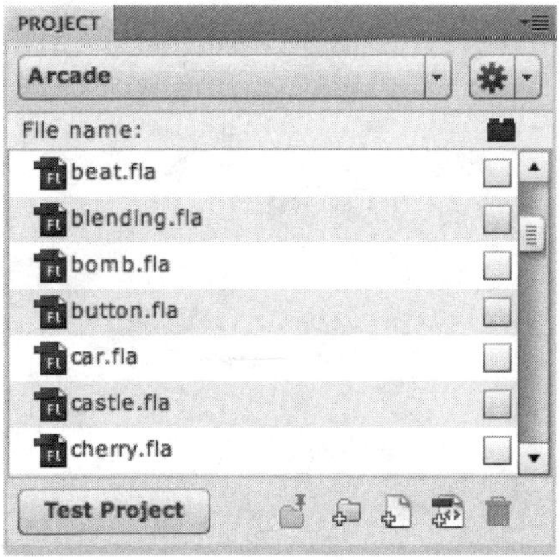

Figure 5c The Project panel makes file management easier.

CHAPTER TWO

Using the Drawing Tools

Before the introduction of Flash, most popular graphics programs were designed to create and edit bitmap graphics. A bitmap graphic (also known as a *raster graphic* or simply a *bitmap*) is made up of small squares called *pixels*.

Flash was one of the first popular programs to rely primarily on vector graphics instead of bitmaps. Vector graphics are essentially mathematical formulas that tell the computer what to draw. One of the innovations in Flash was a new set of tools that made creating vector graphics as simple and intuitive as creating bitmap graphics.

Since then, other programs such as Adobe Illustrator have further simplified the process of making vector graphics, but their tools often work differently from those in Flash. You need to become familiar with the unique ways in which Flash handles vector graphics.

#6 Getting Familiar with Paths

The most basic element of a vector drawing is a path. A path can be defined as a series of anchor points connected by either straight lines or curves. Think of the anchor points as a skeleton that gives the path its structure; and think of the connecting lines or curves as skin stretched over the skeleton.

Paths can be open or closed. An open path has a beginning and end, marked by anchor points known as endpoints. A closed path completely encloses an area; it has no beginning and no end (**Figure 6a**). You create paths by using drawing tools such as the Pen tool, the Pencil tool, and the Brush tool, all of which you'll learn about later in this chapter.

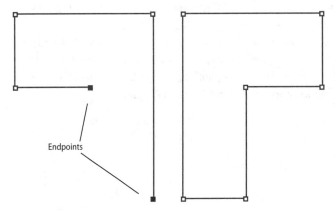

Endpoints

Figure 6a On the left is an open path; on the right is a closed path. Anchor points are represented in Flash by small squares.

To do anything to an existing path—such as edit, move, or delete it—you must tell Flash which path you want to work with by selecting it with a tool. The two most important such tools are the Selection tool, represented by a black arrow, and the Subselection tool, represented by a white arrow (**Figure 6b**).

To use these tools, click the item you wish to select. The fundamental difference between them is that the Selection tool is used to select an entire path, while the Subselection tool is used for individual anchor points within a path. A selected anchor point is represented by a filled-in circle; an unselected anchor point is represented by a hollow circle (**Figure 6c**).

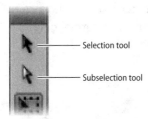

Selection tool

Subselection tool

Figure 6b The Selection tool and the Subselection tools are probably the most frequently used items on the Tools panel.

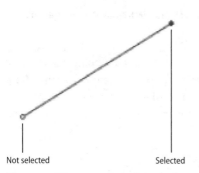

Not selected   Selected

Figure 6c When you use the Subselection tool to select one or more anchor points in a path, all the anchor points in the path—whether selected or not—become visible.

One of the innovations in Flash was allowing a user to work with vector paths without always having to pay attention to anchor points. For example, if you wanted to change a straight line into a curve in a traditional vector drawing program, you'd have to select the anchor points at each end of the curve and manipulate them. (You can still do this in Flash if you want to; you'll see how when we look at the Pen tool in #12.) In Flash, however, you can turn a line into a curve simply by dragging a portion of the line outward with the Selection tool.

(continued on next page)

To do this, position the pointer anywhere between two anchor points. A small curve appears next to the pointer, alerting you that dragging from this point will reshape the line or curve (**Figure 6d**).

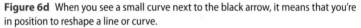

Before   After

Figure 6d When you see a small curve next to the black arrow, it means that you're in position to reshape a line or curve.

If you position the Selection tool over an anchor point, a small right angle appears next to the pointer (**Figure 6e**). This alerts you that dragging from this location will change the position of the anchor point itself, rather than reshaping the line or curve that connects two anchor points.

Before   After

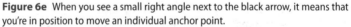

Figure 6e When you see a small right angle next to the black arrow, it means that you're in position to move an individual anchor point.

To use either of these techniques, you have to make sure the path that you want to edit isn't currently selected. (To deselect a selected path, click somewhere outside it with the Selection tool.)

#7 Working with Strokes and Fills

Strictly speaking, a path is a mathematical abstraction: Anchor points have no size, and the lines or curves that connect them have no thickness. To make a path visible, we have to give it either a stroke, a fill, or both.

A stroke is an outline, such as you might find in a paint-by-number set. A fill is what occupies the space enclosed by the stroke; it's equivalent to the paint that you'd apply within the outlined areas. A stroke has both weight (thickness) and color; a fill has only color (**Figure 7a**).

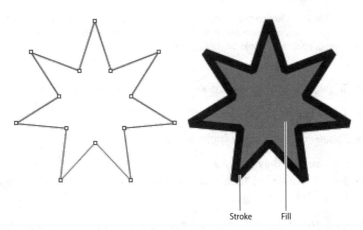

Stroke   Fill

Figure 7a A plain path is on the left; on the right, the same path has a stroke and fill added.

Drawing tools handle strokes and fills in different ways; for example, the Pencil tool and the Line tool create only strokes, and the Brush tool creates only fills. Most other drawing tools are designed to create a stroke and a fill simultaneously.

Even when a stroke and a fill are created at the same time with the same tool, Flash considers the stroke and the fill to be separate objects that can be selected and edited individually. To indicate that a stroke or fill has been selected, Flash covers it with a dot screen (**Figure 7b**).

Using the Selection tool to select strokes and fills requires that you remember various combinations of mouse clicks, most of which are unique to Flash:

- To select the portion of a stroke between the two nearest anchor points, single-click the portion of the stroke you want to select.

(continued on next page)

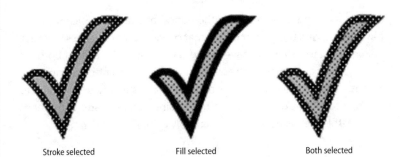

| Stroke selected | Fill selected | Both selected |

Figure 7b The selection dot screen (shown here in a magnified view) appears black when it's superimposed over a light-colored stroke or fill, but appears white when it's superimposed on a dark-colored stroke or fill.

- To select an entire stroke, double-click anywhere on the stroke.

- To select a fill, single-click the fill.

- To select a path's entire stroke *and* fill, double-click the fill.

- If a path has only a stroke and you want to add a fill, click the Paint Bucket tool on the Tools panel, and then click anywhere in the area enclosed by the stroke.

- If a path has only a fill and you want to add a stroke, click the Ink Bottle tool (hidden beneath the Paint Bucket on the Tools panel), and then click the fill.

Another interface feature that's unique to Flash is the way strokes and fills interact with each other. When you select a path, move it so that it over-laps another path, and then deselect it, the following things happen:

- If two stroked paths overlap each other, a new anchor point forms at each place where the strokes intersect.

- If two filled paths overlap each other, the fills are exactly the same color, and the top path has no stroke, the two paths merge into a sin-gle path.

- If two filled paths overlap each other and the top fill has a stroke, the top path deletes the portion of the bottom path that's directly beneath it. This occurs regardless of the color of the fills.

- If two filled paths overlap each other and the fills are different colors, the top path will delete the portion of the bottom path that's directly beneath it. This occurs regardless whether the top fill has a stroke.

Once you get used to them, these interactions can be useful. For example, the ability of one fill to erase a differently colored fill beneath it makes it easy to cut a hole in a filled path, something that's more difficult in a traditional vector drawing program such as Illustrator (**Figure 7c**).

Figure 7c On the left, two fills of different colors overlap each other. On the right, the top fill is moved away, revealing the eaten-away area underneath.

There may be times, however, when you don't want strokes or fills to interact in these ways. You can prevent these interactions by doing one of the following:

- Group each stroke or fill path individually before placing it on top of the other. (Grouping, which is a way of making several objects selectable as a single item, is covered in #17.) Although a group is designed to contain multiple objects, it's perfectly okay for it to contain just one.

- Place each stroke or fill path on a separate layer. (Layers are covered in #21.)

(continued on next page)

Seeing All the Options

Despite the standardization of interfaces across Adobe's product line, one Flash oddity has remained: a context-sensitive zone at the bottom of the Tools panel known as the *options area*. When you select a tool in the Tools panel, you generally need to set the tool's properties to make it suitable for the task at hand. Most of those settings can be made in Properties, but some are made by means of menus and icons that appear in the options area. The location of a particular control isn't always predictable—for example, the thickness of a pencil stroke is set in Properties, but the thickness of a brushstroke is set in the options area—so it's always a good idea to look in both places.

- Before creating each path, click the Object Drawing icon in the options area of the Tools panel (**Figure 7d**). Doing so causes the drawing tool to create a special type of path called a *Drawing Object*. Like the paths found in traditional vector programs, a Drawing Object has a stroke and fill that are inseparable.

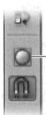 ———— Object Drawing icon

Figure 7d When a drawing tool is selected, this icon appears in the options area at the bottom of the Tools panel. Selecting it causes the drawing tool to create a Drawing Object rather than a standard path.

#8 Choosing Colors and Gradients

A stroke or fill, by definition, must have a color. To choose the color for a stroke, click the Stroke Color control on the Tools panel. To choose the color for a fill, click the Fill Color control (**Figure 8a**).

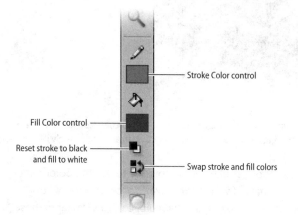

Fill Color control

Reset stroke to black and fill to white

Stroke Color control

Swap stroke and fill colors

Figure 8a The Stroke Color and Fill Color controls are near the bottom of the Tools panel. (A similar set of controls can be found in the upper left of the Color panel.)

When you click the small rectangle on either color control, a pop-up window appears (**Figure 8b**). Within it, you can choose a color in any of the following ways:

- Click one of the color swatches.

- Delete the contents of the Hex Edit box and type in a hexadecimal color number.

- Click the System Color Picker icon, which produces a window displaying an assortment of color-selection controls. (These controls vary according to your computer's operating system.)

Once you've selected a stroke or fill color, it will be applied to all subsequent paths you create, until you choose another color. (If any paths are selected when you choose a stroke or fill color, the new color is applied to them as well.)

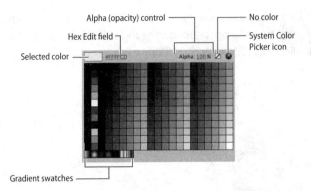

Figure 8b The pop-up window for selecting colors. (The No Color icon doesn't create a colorless stroke or fill; it instead causes Flash to omit the stroke or fill entirely.)

Another way to choose stroke and fill colors is to use the Color panel (**Figure 8c**). (If it's not part of your current workspace, choose Window > Color.) The upper left of the Color panel has color controls similar to those on the Tools panel, but the rest of the panel offers two color-selection tools not found elsewhere in Flash.

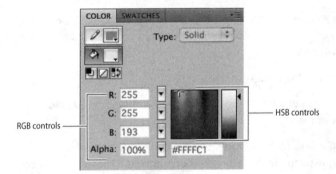

Figure 8c The Color panel allows you to specify colors by either of two systems: RGB and HSB. You can use the RGB controls either by typing a value into one of the fields, or by clicking the black triangle next to the field to access a slider.

The first tool is a set of RGB sliders for mixing varying amounts of red, green, and blue to get the color you want. (Red, green, and blue are known as the additive primary colors. They can be combined to form any color your computer is capable of displaying.)

The second tool is a set of controls for specifying colors by hue, satu-ration, and brightness (HSB). To use them, choose a hue and saturation by clicking anywhere in the multicolored square. (Moving horizontally across the square changes the hue; moving up and down increases and decreases the saturation.) Then choose a brightness for the selected color by clicking anywhere in the vertical rectangle to the right of the square.

A final way to choose colors is to use the Eyedropper tool in the Tools panel. When you select the Eyedropper in the Tools panel and click a stroke, the Stroke Color controls in the Tools panel and Color panel display the color of the stroke you clicked. When you click a fill, the Fill Color controls change similarly.

A *gradient* is a series of colors that blend smoothly into one another. They're often used to give flat objects the illusion of depth (**Figure 8d**). To create a gradient, you need at least two colors: a starting color and a destination color. (If you wish, you can add one or more intermediate colors.)

Flash supports two kinds of gradients: linear and radial. A linear gradient proceeds in a straight line from the starting color to the destination color; a radial gradient proceeds outward in a circular pattern, with the starting color at the center of the circle and the destination color at the edge.

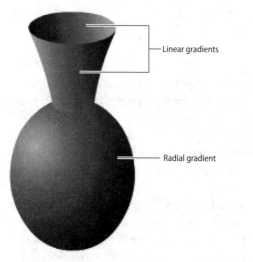

Linear gradients

Radial gradient

Figure 8d This simple vase has two kinds of gradient fills.

The simplest way to create a gradient stroke or a gradient fill is to choose one of the gradient swatches from a pop-up window in the Stroke Color or Fill Color control. (See Figure 8b.)

In most cases, the simple black-and-white or primary-colored gradient that you choose from the window won't suit your needs. You'll want to modify the colors, or perhaps add some intermediate colors. You use the Color panel (Figure 8c) to do either.

If a gradient fill or stroke is currently selected, or either the Fill Color or Stroke Color control is currently set to a gradient, the Color panel displays that gradient. Otherwise, you can create a new gradient in the Color panel by choosing Linear or Radial from the Type menu (**Figure 8e**).

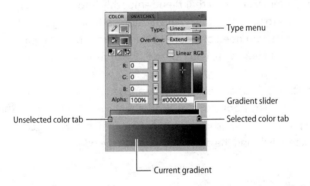

Unselected color tab

Current gradient

Figure 8e When Linear or Radial is selected on the Type menu, the Color panel displays these controls.

Initially, the gradient slider has two color tabs, one at each end, representing the starting and destination colors. (By default, the starting color is black and the destination color is white.) To change either of those colors, click the square part of the appropriate color tab and use any of the controls on the Color panel to choose a color for that tab. Alternatively, you can double-click the color tab and choose a color swatch from the pop-up menu.

To add a new color to a gradient, click the point in the gradient slider at which you want the new color to appear; an additional color tab will appear at that position. To delete a color from a gradient, drag its color tab away from the gradient slider. To change the position of any color, drag its color tab to the appropriate point along the gradient slider.

In many cases, you'll not only want to customize your gradient; you'll also want to change how the gradient is applied to a selected path. If so, choose the Gradient Transform tool from the Tools panel and click the stroke or fill that you want to change. (If the Gradient Transform tool isn't visible in the Tools panel, hold down your mouse button over the Free Transform tool and choose Gradient Transform Tool from the menu that appears.)

When you click a stroke or path with the Gradient Transform tool, a set of controls appears around the gradient. For linear gradients, the controls allow you to change the extent and direction of the gradient; for radial gradients, the controls also allow you to change the shape and the center point of the gradient (**Figure 8f**).

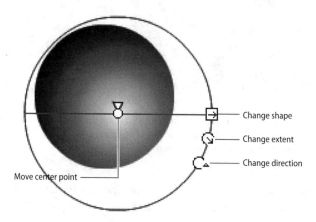

Move center point · Change shape · Change extent · Change direction

Figure 8f When a radial gradient is selected with the Gradient Transform tool, these controls become available. You can drag the controls to change different characteristics of the gradient.

That's Nice, But Do You Have It in Peach?

If you're like most people, you draw things in one color and then decide later that you'd prefer a different color. To change the color of an existing stroke or fill, select the element, and then choose a new color via the Tools panel or Color panel.

To change one color to another throughout your movie, you can use the little-known Find and Replace Color feature. Choose Edit > Find and Replace; and then set the For menu to Color. Specify the current color and its replacement by choosing them from pop-up windows. You can now find and replace colors the same way you'd find and replace text.

#9 Setting Options for Drawing Tools

Option controls appear in the options area of the Tools panel and in the Properties panel (**Figure 9a**). If a tool is selected in the Tools panel, these controls affect how the tool operates; if an existing path is selected, these controls change the characteristics of that path.

Aside from the Stroke Color and Fill Color controls, these are the option controls you're most likely to use regularly:

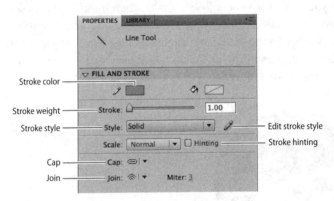

Figure 9a This set of option controls appears in Properties when the Line tool is selected in the Tools panel. Using other drawing tools, or selecting existing fills or strokes, will cause some of the options to change.

- **Stroke weight.** To adjust the weight (the heaviness or thickness) of a stroke, use the Stroke Weight controls in the Properties panel. You can type a number directly into the field, or you can choose a weight interactively by using the slider. Note that Flash isn't consistent in its terminology; stroke weight is also called *height* or *thickness* in other parts of the program.

- **Stroke style.** A stroke can appear solid, dotted, or dashed; it can have a hand-drawn or painted look; it can be straight or wavy. To make basic adjustments to the style of a stroke, use the Stroke Style menu in Properties. To make more elaborate changes, click the Edit Stroke Style icon to the right of the menu. A dialog box appears in which you can separately adjust the type, pattern, wave height, and wave length of a stroke. (You can adjust the stroke weight—here called *thickness*—in the same dialog box.)

- **Stroke caps and joins.** The Cap and Join menus in Properties let you decide whether the ends of a stroke will be rounded, squared off, or unmodified. The Join menu applies to the points where two segments of a stroke meet: You can decide whether the corners will be mitered, rounded, or beveled (**Figure 9b**).

Mitered   Rounded   Beveled

Figure 9b These three paths show the difference between a mitered corner, a rounded corner, and a beveled corner.

- **Stroke hinting.** Although the objects that you create with the drawing tools are vector objects, they are displayed on a computer screen as bitmaps. In some cases, a stroke may fall into gaps between pixels, making it appear faint or blurry on the screen. Selecting the Stroke Hinting check box on the Properties panel prevents this from happening.

- **Smoothing.** This control appears only for the tools that require freehand drawing—that is, the Pencil and the Brush. Drawing smooth lines and curves is difficult even with a graphics tablet, but it's almost impossible with more common input devices such as a mouse or trackball. Smoothing automatically makes a rough hand-drawn path more regular and gentle. The degree of smoothing can be set anywhere from 0 (no smoothing) to 100. Note that with the Brush tool, a high smoothing setting may distort the shape of the brushstroke, making it appear uneven.

- **Snap to objects.** This option is represented by a horseshoe-magnet icon in the options area of the Tools panel. If the icon is selected, it makes a path "magnetic," meaning that the path will automatically try to line up with other objects when you drag and drop it. Other kinds of snapping (to a grid, for example) can be selected from the menu at View > Snapping.

#10 Using the Primitive Shape Tools

Like all vector drawing programs, Flash offers a variety of shape tools such as ellipses and polygons. In most other programs, these simple shapes are called primitives, but Adobe reserves the term *primitive objects* for a particular type of shape whose characteristics can be changed dynamically by controls in the Properties panel.

Both the standard and primitive shape tools are listed in a single menu in the Tools panel. (You can see this menu by holding down your mouse button when the pointer is hovering over the Rectangle tool.) The standard shape tools available in that location are the Rectangle tool, the Oval tool, and the Polystar tool, the last of which can be used to create either polygons or stars. The primitive shape tools are Rectangle Primitive and the Oval Primitive; as of yet there is no Polystar Primitive tool.

To see the difference between these two types of tools, let's look at the procedure for drawing a rectangle with rounded corners:

1. Select either the Rectangle or the Rectangle Primitive tool in the Tools panel. A set of option controls appears in Properties (**Figure 10a**).

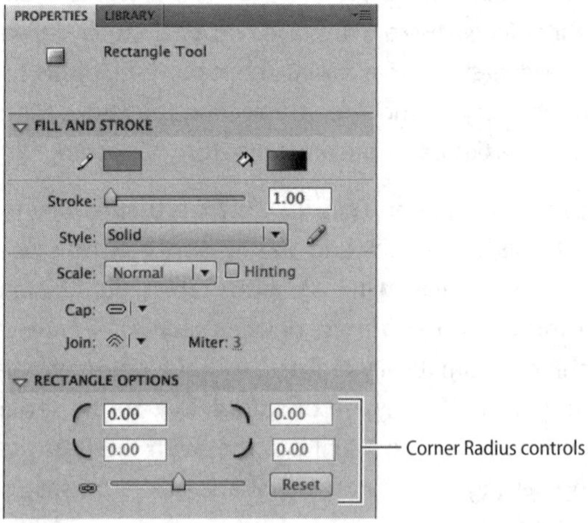

Figure 10a These controls appear in the Properties inspector for both the Rectangle tool and the Rectangle Primitive tool.

2. Set a Corner Radius value, either by typing it into the appropriate field in Properties or by using the slider. The higher the number, the more round the rectangle's corners will be. (The default is for all the corners

to be equally round, in which case you only have to enter one value. If you want the corners to have different degrees of roundness, click the lock icon and then enter a value in each of the four fields.)

3. Click and drag the mouse on the stage to draw the rectangle. The corners are automatically rounded to the degree you specified.

These steps are the same, regardless of whether you use the Rectangle or the Rectangle Primitive tool; but the resulting rectangles have several significant differences:

- **Editability.** Let's say you don't like the setting you used for the corners—you want them to be more rounded. If you drew the rectangle with the Rectangle tool, you can't change the roundness of the corners; you have to delete the rectangle and draw it again with a new Corner Radius value. If you drew the rectangle with the Rectangle Primitive tool, you can simply enter a new value in Properties and see the corners change instantly.

- **Flexibility.** Let's say you want to reshape the rectangle in some way, such as turning the straight sides into curves or cutting a hole in the middle of the fill. If you drew the rectangle with the Rectangle tool, you can do these kinds of things easily. If you drew the rectangle with the Rectangle Primitive tool, you can't. The *only* characteristics of a primitive object that can be changed are those that are controlled from the Properties inspector, such as the object's width, height, and location on the stage.

- **Convertability.** You can convert a primitive object to a drawing object by double-clicking it with the Selection tool and then choosing OK. The reverse is not true: You can't convert any type of object into a primitive object.

(continued on next page)

Turning the Corner

When you create a rectangle with rounded corners, the maximum Corner Radius value that you can use is one-half the shortest dimension of the rectangle. (For example, if the rectangle is 75 pixels wide and 50 pixels high, the Corner Radius value must be 25 or less.) You can enter larger values, but they won't have any effect.

If you want to create a rectangle with standard sharp corners, use 0 for the Corner Radius value.

For an attractive cut-out corner effect, try using a negative number for the Corner Radius value.

The Oval Primitive tool works like the Rectangle Primitive tool, except that it allows different characteristics to be set: The Start Angle and End Angle values allow you to create pie-shaped wedges (or pies with wedges cut out of them); and the Inner Radius setting allows you to create donut-shaped objects (**Figure 10b**).

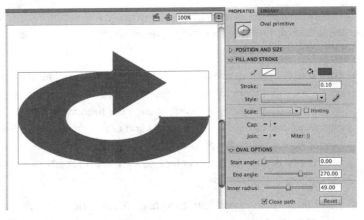

Figure 10b The curved shaft of this arrow is an oval primitive object, with settings as shown on the Properties panel. The arrowhead is a three-sided polygon made with the Polystar tool.

Tip

To create a perfect square, hold down the Shift key while drawing a rectangle with the Rectangle tool or the Rectangle Primitive tool. Similarly, to create a perfect circle, hold down the Shift key while drawing an ellipse with the Oval tool or the Oval Primitive tool.

The shape tools, whether standard or primitive, can be handy for making things other than geometric shapes. In many cases, you'll find that the easiest way to draw something is to start with a simple shape and modify it. For example, the vase in Figure 8d (see #8) is constructed entirely from two ellipses and a modified rectangle.

#11 Using the Pencil Tool

If you're accustomed to drawing with pen or pencil on paper, you'll find the Pencil tool to be intuitive. Simply select it in the Tools panel and draw with your mouse (or other input device). Depressing the mouse button creates a new path; releasing the mouse button ends the path.

The pencil line you've created is a standard vector path with a stroke applied. You can modify it in the same ways you'd modify any other path—for example, by changing the stroke's weight or color, or by dragging anchor points with the Subselection tool.

When you select the Pencil tool in the Tools panel, a Pencil Mode menu appears in the options area (**Figure 11a**). The menu gives you three choices:

Figure 11a This menu appears in the options area of the Tools panel when the Pencil tool is selected.

- **Straighten.** Select this option to convert a curved line into a series of straight-line segments. It also activates a shape-recognition feature that allows you to hand-draw smooth geometric shapes. For example, if you use the Pencil tool to draw a path that's approximately oval-shaped, Flash will convert the path automatically to a perfect oval.

- **Smooth.** This setting leaves your path fundamentally as you drew it, but makes it smoother and more elegant. This is the option most people prefer: Instead of displaying the path you actually drew, it gives you the path you *wanted* to draw. The Smoothness control in the Properties panel (see #9) is available only when this option is selected.

(continued on next page)

A Hole in the Bucket

Because the Pencil tool is imprecise, drawing a closed path is sometimes difficult. You may *think* you've closed the path, but there could be a gap between the starting and ending anchor points that's too small to notice.

This gap becomes a problem only if you decide to fill the path. Because the Paint Bucket's default behavior is to fill only closed paths, you may click repeatedly inside your path without being able to fill it.

You could zoom in very closely on the suspected gap and try to close it with the Pencil tool. An easier way is to use the Gap Size menu, which appears in the options area of the Tools panel whenever the Paint Bucket tool is selected.

The Gap Size menu determines how big a gap the Paint Bucket will overlook. You'll almost always want to choose Close Large Gaps; what Flash calls a "large gap" is what most of us would consider to be very small. When you make this choice, the more tolerant Paint Bucket is likely to fill the path.

- **Ink.** If you want your path to appear exactly the way you drew it, use this option. Since most input devices (with the possible exception of a stylus and pressure-sensitive tablet) are ill-suited for drawing, you're not likely to use this setting very often (**Figure 11b**).

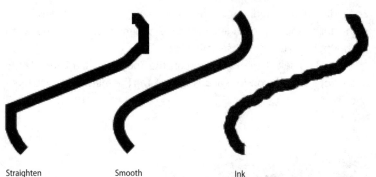

Straighten   Smooth   Ink

Figure 11b The same path has been drawn with three different options.

The Pencil tool creates only strokes, without fills. (The Fill Color control is unavailable when the Pencil tool is selected.) If you create a closed path with the Pencil tool and then want to fill it, you can select the Paint Bucket tool and click in the enclosed area of the path.

Note
The Brush tool is similar to the Pencil tool, except that the "brushstrokes" it creates are actually fills rather than strokes. If you want to add a stroke to a path created by the Brush tool, select the Ink Bottle tool and click the path.

#12 Using the Pen Tool

The Pen may be the most unintuitive tool you'll ever encounter. And if you're willing to master it, you'll also come to appreciate the degree of control that it provides. No other drawing tool can create lines and curves as precisely.

To draw with the Pen tool, there's one basic rule you must remember: *You can't draw with the Pen tool.* More specifically, you can't use it in the way you'd expect, by dragging your mouse around the stage.

The Pen tool lets you create anchor points. As you create each new anchor point, Flash automatically connects it to the previous one with a line or curve. You can create three different kinds of anchor points with this tool (**Figure 12a**):

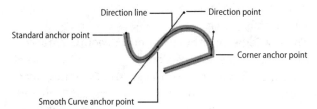

Figure 12a This path contains anchor points of all three types.

- **Standard.** To create a standard anchor point with the Pen tool, place the mouse pointer where you want the anchor point to be, and click—that is, press and immediately release the mouse button. If you then create another anchor point (by moving the pointer and clicking again), Flash connects it to the previous one with a straight line. By making several anchor points sequentially, you can create a path consisting of a series of line segments.

Tip
To end a path, click the Pen tool icon in the Tools panel after creating the last anchor point. When you make a new anchor point, Flash won't connect it to the previous one.

- **Smooth Curve.** To create this kind of anchor point, press the mouse button, but don't release it—instead, drag it outward. As you do so, you'll see a pair of thin lines, called *direction lines*, extend outward from the anchor point. These direction lines distinguish a Smooth

(continued on next page)

Hooray for Bézier

The curves you make with the pen tool are called *Bézier* (pronounced *bays-YAY*) curves, after the French engineer who popularized them. They don't look different from ordinary curves; what's distinctive about them are the direction lines and direction points that allow you to resize and reshape them efficiently.

Bézier curves are becoming an increasingly useful part of the Flash interface. They now give you precise control not only of visible objects on the stage, but also of those objects' motion paths (see #42) and properties (see #44). Working with them may take some getting used to, but any effort you devote to mastering Bézier curves will almost certainly be rewarded.

Curve anchor point from a standard anchor point. Each direction line is capped with a diamond-shaped handle called a *direction point* . When you create a second Smooth Curve anchor point, Flash automatically connects it to the previous one with a curve. You'll find out later how to use direction points to control the shape and size of the curve.

- **Corner.** A Corner anchor point is the place where two curves—or a line and a curve—meet. It's essentially two anchor points in one; that is, it presents one face to the anchor point before it and another face to the anchor point after it. A Corner point may be half standard anchor point and half Smooth Curve anchor point, or it may be a hybrid of two Smooth Curve anchor points. You can recognize a Corner point easily because it has only one direction line, or because it has two direction lines that point in different directions.

  You can make a Corner point by modifying a Smooth Curve anchor point. To do so, choose the Subselection tool from the Tools panel. Then, while holding down the Alt key (Windows) or Option key (Mac), drag either of the two direction points that are attached to an existing Smooth Curve point. In doing so, you convert the Smooth Curve point (with two direction lines moving in tandem) to a Corner anchor point (with direction lines moving independently of one another). If you want one "face" of the Corner point to be a standard (non-curve) anchor point, use the Subselection tool to drag its direction point into the Corner point.

To change the size or shape of a curve—regardless of whether it passes through a Smooth Curve point or ends at a Corner point—simply drag its direction points. (Make sure to do this with the Subselection tool, not the Pen tool.) Each direction point acts like a magnet: When you move it away from the curve, the curve bends to follow it; when you move it toward the curve, the curve moves away from it (**Figure 12b**).

If you hold down the mouse button as the pointer is hovering over the Pen tool icon in the Tools panel, you'll see a menu showing several related tools:

- **Add Anchor Point.** This tool allows you to add a new anchor point between any pair of existing anchor points.

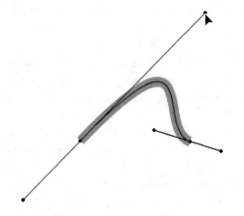

Figure 12b You can change the size or shape of a curve by dragging its direction points.

- **Delete Anchor Point.** This tool allows you to delete any anchor point from an existing path.

- **Convert Anchor Point.** This tool allows you to convert a Smooth Curve point into a standard anchor point by clicking it. You can also convert a standard anchor point into a Smooth Curve point by dragging outward from the point.

#13 Using the Pattern Tools

Flash CS4 includes two new drawing tools: the Spray Brush and the Deco tool. They allow you to add effects to your animation that were not possible before.

The Spray Brush is hidden beneath the Brush tool. With its default settings, it works like a can of spray paint, scattering tiny dots in a random cloud. The Brush controls in the Properties panel let you change the size and angle of the cloud.

The standard stroke and fill colors have no effect on the Spray Brush. To change the color of the dots it sprays, use the pop-up color menu in Properties.

The Spray Brush isn't limited to spraying dots; it can spray multiple copies of nearly anything you can create in Flash (**Figure 13a**). To make an object suitable for spraying, you have to convert it to a symbol (see #22). With the Spray Brush selected in the Tools panel, deselect the Default Shape check box in Properties. A dialog box appears, allowing you select the symbol that you want to spray.

Figure 13a The Spray Brush can make multiple copies of any symbol. For variety, this example uses the Random Scaling and Random Rotation options in Properties.

The Deco tool allows you to fill large areas with decorative patterns. Its three effects—Vine Fill, Grid Fill, and Symmetry Brush—can be chosen from the Drawing Effects menu in Properties (**Figure 13b**).

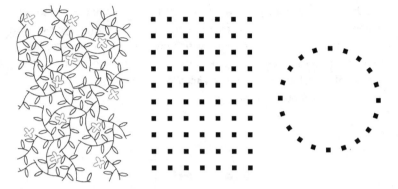

Figure 13b From left to right: examples of Vine Fill, Grid Fill, and Symmetry Brush, using default settings for each.

Vine Fill. This is the default effect. It causes a winding vine to grow outward from the pointer when you click the mouse. Press the Esc key to stop the growth; otherwise, the growth will stop automatically when the stage is filled. Controls in the Properties panel allow you to change the colors of the leaves and flowers, or to replace them with other symbols.

Grid Fill. This effect causes the Deco tool to fill the stage with an array of squares. You can change the color, size, and spacing of the squares, or substitute a symbol of your own.

Symmetry Brush. With this effect selected, you can use the Deco tool to make a variety of symmetrical patterns out of default squares or your own symbols. An Advanced Options menu allows you to choose what kind of symmetry you want—for example, Rotate Around (the default) creates a circular design, and Grid Translation creates a perspective effect.

(continued on next page)

Pattern Makes Perfect

When you deselect a newly created pattern, it becomes a group (see #17). You can choose either Ungroup or Break Apart from the Modify menu to split the group into a collection of individual objects. Don't do this unless you really have to, since turning one object into many objects will add significantly to the file size and potentially slow down your movie.

Once created, a pattern isn't editable. If you try to modify an existing pattern with the Deco Brush, all you do is create a new pattern on top of the old one. Instead, delete it and recreate it.

Using the Symmetry Brush effect is tricky: Move the pointer to the stage and press—but don't release—the mouse button. A light-green axis, or pair of axes, appears along with a preview of your pattern. Dragging the mouse pointer around the stage causes the pattern to change its size, angle, and frequency (**Figure 13c**). When it looks the way you want it to, release the mouse button.

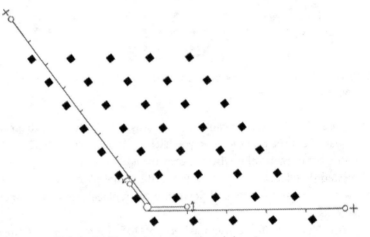

Figure 13c With the Grid Translation option selected, dragging the mouse allows you to change the perspective of a grid.

CHAPTER THREE

Editing and Transforming Objects

The essence of animation is change. Flash has always offered numerous ways to change an object's size, color, position, orientation, and other characteristics. A new addition to Flash CS4 is the ability to transform objects in 3D space, which you'll learn about in #16.

This chapter also covers techniques that make working with objects easier, such as simplifying them, grouping them, and placing them on different layers. Getting familiar with these nuts-and-bolts procedures will provide a solid foundation for the creative work you do in Flash.

#14 Using the Selection Tools

You already know that the Selection tool (the black arrow) is used to select an entire path, and the Subselection tool (the white arrow) is used to select individual anchor points within a path. Now it's time to get more specific. Here are other ways in which you might use selection tools:

- **Selecting more than one path.** Drag the Selection tool to outline a rectangular area on the stage. When you release the mouse button, any paths within that area are selected. If a path is partly inside and partly outside the rectangular area, only the inside portion is selected.

- **Selecting more than one path on a crowded stage.** You can use the Lasso tool to outline an irregularly shaped area surrounding the paths that you want to select. When you release the mouse button, any paths that are within that irregular area are selected (**Figure 14a**). If a path is partly inside and partly outside the area, only the inside portion will be selected.

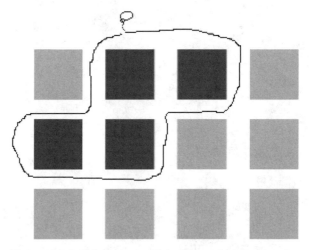

Figure 14a Outlining an area with the Lasso tool selects any paths (or portions of paths) that are within that area. The Lasso tool can't select individual anchor points.

- **Selecting more than one anchor point.** Drag the Subselection tool to outline a rectangular area on the stage. When you release the mouse button, any anchor points within that area are selected, regardless of whether they belong to one path or several.

Tip

To select only one anchor point, draw a rectangle around it with the Sub-selection tool. Doing so is often easier than trying to click directly on the point.

- **Adding to an existing selection.** If one or more paths or anchor points are already selected, hold down the Shift key while clicking additional paths (with the Selection tool) or anchor points (with the Subselection tool). Those paths or anchor points will be added to the selection.

- **Subtracting from an existing selection.** If multiple paths are already selected, hold down the Shift key while you use the Selection tool to click each path that you want to subtract.

- **Selecting everything.** Use the Selection tool to draw a rectangle around the entire stage, or choose Edit > Select All.

- **Deselecting everything.** Use any of the selection tools to click an empty area of the stage, or choose Edit > Deselect All.

#15 Using the Free Transform Tool

Transforming an object means changing its position, orientation, or proportions. Paths, groups (see #17), and symbol instances (see #23) can be transformed using the Free Transform tool.

You can use any of the methods described in #14 to select the objects that you want to transform. Alternatively, you can select objects directly with the Free Transform tool, either by clicking them or stretching a rectangle around them.

When you click the Free Transform tool in the Tools panel, any currently selected objects become framed by a black rectangle. The rectangle has eight black squares (or *handles*) around its perimeter—four at the corners, and four midway between them—that you can use to perform the transformations (**Figure 15a**).

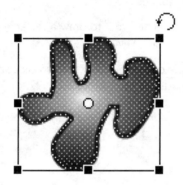

Figure 15a The object surrounded by this black rectangle is ready to be transformed. The pointer looks like a curved arrow, which means that dragging the mouse will rotate the object.

You can transform the selected object or objects in several ways:

- **Scaling.** Position your pointer directly on any of the eight handles. The pointer becomes a vertical, horizontal, or diagonal double-headed arrow. Depending on the orientation of the arrow, you can drag a particular handle vertically, horizontally, or both. (The top and bottom center handles adjust height, while the left and right center handles adjust width; the corner handles can adjust both dimensions at once.) To scale the object without changing its ratio of width to height, hold down the Shift key while dragging a corner handle.

- **Rotation.** The white circle in the center of the rectangle is called the *transformation point*; it's the point around which the rotation will occur. (Think of it as a pushpin in the middle of a sheet of paper.) If you want to rotate the object around some point other than the center, move the transformation point to the desired spot. Then place your pointer a few pixels outward from any of the corner handles. The pointer becomes a curved, double-headed arrow, indicating that you can now rotate the object by dragging clockwise or counterclockwise.

- **Skewing.** Skewing an object means changing the angles at the corners of the selection rectangle, making one pair of angles narrower and one pair wider, while keeping the sides of the rectangle parallel to each other. (The same transformation is called *shearing* in Adobe Illustrator.) Place your pointer on the perimeter of the selection rectangle, midway between any two handles. The pointer turns into two overlapping half-arrows, indicating that you can now skew the object by dragging along the axis indicated by the arrows.

- **Distortion.** Distorting an object means moving each of its corner handles independently of the others. You can do this by holding down the Control key (Windows) or Command key (Mac) while dragging each corner handle individually. For a perspective distortion effect, do the same thing while holding down the Shift and Control keys (Windows) or Shift and Command keys (Mac) (**Figure 15b**).

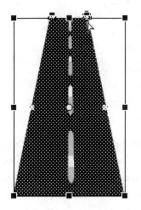

Figure 15b Tapering an object, otherwise known as distorting it in perspective, causes two sides of the selection rectangle to converge while the other two remain parallel.

#16 Transforming Objects in 3D Space

3D effects are being used with increasing frequency in illustration and animation. In recent years, Adobe has added 3D capabilities to Photoshop and Illustrator; now it's begun to add them to Flash as well.

There are two 3D tools: the 3D Rotation tool, which is initially visible on the Tools panel, and the 3D Translation tool, which is hidden beneath it. These tools can be used only on Movie Clip symbols (see #28), and only in FLA files that were created using the ActionScript 3.0 option (see #1).

3D transformations take place in relation to three axes labeled X, Y, and Z. The X and Y axes are the familiar ones; they correspond to the horizontal and vertical dimensions. For the Z axis, imagine a line that's oriented with one end toward you and the other end away from you (**Figure 16a**). This is the axis that adds depth.

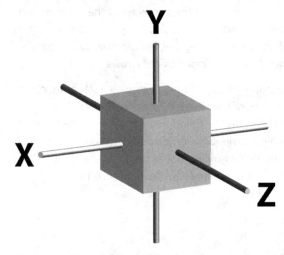

Figure 16a These three axes define three-dimensional space. (Note that this diagram cheats by using a perspective effect. If it were drawn accurately, the Z axis would have to extend outward from the page.)

When you select a suitable object and choose a 3D tool, Flash places the center of the object at the intersection of the three axes. The 3D Rotation tool allows you to turn the object around one or more of the axes, changing its orientation. The 3D Translation tool allows you to relocate the object in 3D space, moving it closer or farther away in any direction (**Figure 16b**).

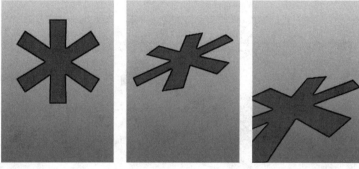

No transformation   3D Rotation   3D Rotation and
3D Translation

Figure 16b An object in three stages: with no transformation, transformed by the 3D Rotation tool, and further transformed by the 3D Translation tool.

You use both 3D tools the same way: Select the object you want to transform and choose the desired tool. Lines appear on the stage representing the three axes: red for X, green for Y, and blue for Z. Drag along any of the axes to turn or move the selected object in the corresponding direction.

The Z axis is the most challenging, since it can't be represented accurately as a straight line. The 3D Rotation tool displays it as a blue circle; dragging around the circle changes the angle of rotation (**Figure 16c**). The 3D Translation tool displays it as a blue dot; dragging the dot causes the object to move forward or backward.

(continued on next page)

The Transformation of "Transform"

In addition to introducing two 3D tools, Adobe has added 3D controls to the Transform panel in Flash CS4. In previous versions of Flash, this panel allowed you to scale, rotate, and skew objects—the same kinds of transformations for which you'd usually use the Free Transform tool (see #15). Now, the Transform panel also provides controls for rotating movie-clip instances in 3D space—a numerical equivalent of the 3D Rotation tool.

Regardless whether you're doing 2D or 3D transformations, the Transform panel allows you to do something you can't do elsewhere: You can click the Remove Transform icon to restore an object's original appearance, with all scaling, rotation, and distortion removed.

3D Lite

The 3D features in Flash are minimal. Flash won't allow you to create objects in three dimensions, change their texture and reflectiveness, map images onto their surfaces, or use simulated lighting to bring out their highlights and shadows. Perhaps Flash will have these capabilities in future versions—Illustrator already has them—but for now, don't expect to achieve anywhere near the same level of realism that you can get from a real 3D animation program such as Maya or 3D Studio Max.

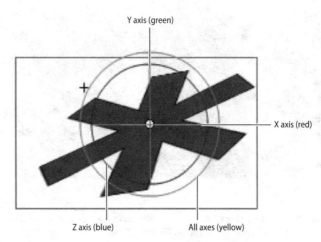

Figure 16c The 3D Rotation tool displays the axes by means of colored lines and circles. The outermost circle allows you to rotate the object in all three dimensions at once.

One important difference between the 3D Translation tool and the 3D Rotation tool is that the former calculates positions relative to the stage, while the latter calculates positions relative to an arbitrary location in space called the *3D center point*. By default, the 3D center point is in the middle of the stage, but you can drag it anywhere you like.

Whenever a 3D object is selected, you have access to 3D Position and View controls in the Properties panel. Unlike the 3D Translation and 3D Rotation tools, which move the 3D object in space, these controls allow you to change the perspective from which you're *looking* at the object—the equivalent of relocating the stage in 3D space. As with most numerical controls in Flash, the easiest way to use these is to drag left or right across the numbers to make them decrease or increase.

#17 Grouping Objects

In #7 you found out how two identically colored fills can merge if they're allowed to overlap. Combining multiple objects into a single object is often desirable, but the problem with that method of merging paths is that it isn't reversible. When two or more paths are turned into one, they permanently lose their identities as separate objects.

There are many occasions when you want to treat several objects as a single unit—for convenience in selecting them, for example—but want to retain the option to separate them again. In these situations, grouping is the answer.

To combine any number of objects into a single group, select them all and choose Modify > Group. Grouping the objects doesn't change their appearance, but it does allow them to be selected with a single click (**Figure 17a**).

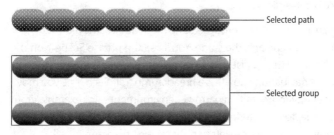

Figure 17a Unlike a path, which displays a dot-screen overlay when it's selected, a selected group is indicated by a blue rectangle.

A group doesn't behave like a path. Selecting a group and trying to change its fill color or stroke weight doesn't work. But if keeping the objects grouped becomes inconvenient, you can easily reverse the process by choosing Modify > Ungroup. All of the formerly grouped objects regain their independent identities, and they can once again be edited or transformed individually.

Often, you'll want to modify an object within a group, but you won't want to go through the trouble of ungrouping, making the modifications, and then grouping again. In such cases, you can edit objects within a group without ungrouping them.

To do this, choose the Selection tool and double-click the group on the stage. Some odd things occur: The paths within the group now sport dot screens to indicate that they're selected and editable, and everything else on the stage becomes dim (**Figure 17b**). What's happened is that Flash has entered group-editing mode. Think of it as an alternate universe where the group is the only thing that exists.

Figure 17b On the left, a group selected on the stage. On the right, the same group after it's been double-clicked.

To confirm that Flash is in group-editing mode, look at the narrow divider between the timeline and the stage. You'll see the phrase Scene 1 on the left, and the word Group just to the right (**Figure 17c**). These words represent a type of navigation known as a breadcrumb trail. Each time you move from a wider environment to a narrower environment—for example, from the main stage, to the interior of a group, to a symbol inside the group—your progress is charted from left to right on the breadcrumb trail.

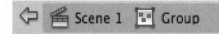

Figure 17c You know that you're in group-editing mode because the word Group appears at the end of the breadcrumb trail.

While you're in group-editing mode, you can make whatever changes you want to the objects in the group. Then, to find your way back to where you came from, you follow the trail in reverse—that is, from right to left. In this case, if you want to exit group-editing mode, you can click the phrase Scene 1 (which represents the movie as a whole). The word *Group* disappears from the end of the breadcrumb trail, the *group* once again acts like a group, and all of the other objects on the stage become accessible again.

Knowing how to follow the breadcrumb trail will become even more important when we get to #24, "Editing Symbols."

#**18** Simplifying Objects

Keeping the size of a Flash file as small as possible is crucial, because the effectiveness of a SWF file depends partly on how quickly it can be downloaded from the Web.

"The fewer the anchor points, the smaller the file" is a good rule of thumb in working with vector graphics. If you can get rid of unnecessary anchor points, your animation will look better and play more snappily.

When you work with the shape tools and shape primitives, extraneous anchor points are not a problem. But when you use tools such as the Pencil or Brush, you're likely to have many more anchor points than you need (**Figure 18a**). Every time your hand-drawn path jiggles or changes direction slightly, Flash creates another anchor point. Even if you use the Pen tool, you're often tempted to put in extra anchor points because it's easier than making smooth curves.

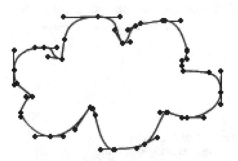

Figure 18a This path, drawn with the pencil tool, has many more anchor points than it needs.

There are several ways to reduce the number of anchor points in a path:

- **Delete the anchor points manually.** If you're comfortable working with Smooth Curve points, Corner points, and direction lines, you can look for unnecessary anchor points in your path and use the Delete Anchor Point tool to remove them. Doing so is time-consuming, but it gives you full control over the appearance of your paths.

- **Smooth your path.** You saw in #9 and #11 that the Smoothing control in Properties can make hand-drawn paths look much cleaner. In most cases, Flash removes unnecessary anchor points as part of the smoothing process. A smoothed path not only looks better; it also yields a smaller file size.

If you didn't use the Smoothing option when you first created your path, you still have an opportunity. Select the path with the Selection tool, and then click the Smooth icon in the options area of the Tools panel (**Figure 18b**). You can click this icon repeatedly, and each time you do, the path gets a little smoother. (Another way to do the same thing is to select Modify > Shape > Smooth; you can do that repeatedly as well.)

- **Optimize your path.** The automated way to simplify a path is to select the path and then choose Modify > Shape > Optimize. The resulting dialog box allows you to choose a degree of smoothing from 0 to 100. As you change the amount of smoothing, you can preview the result on the stage. When you click OK, Flash does the optimization and reports how many curves—which essentially means anchor points—were eliminated.

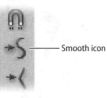 —— Smooth icon

Figure 18b Each time you click this icon, your selected path gets smoother.

#19 Working with Text

Most of your Flash movies will contain text of one kind or another. If you've ever used a word processor, you should be comfortable with the way Flash handles text.

To add text to the stage, select the Text tool from the Tools panel. The Properties panel fills up with options, the most important of which is the Text Type menu at the top. Make sure the menu says Static Text. (The other options—Dynamic Text and Input Text—are only for specialized ActionScript applications.)

Use the Text tool to drag a rectangle across the stage. Make the rectangle as wide as you want your text block to be, but remember that you can adjust the width at any time by dragging the white square on the upper right of the rectangle (**Figure 19a**). A blinking cursor appears inside the rectangle, indicating that Flash is ready to accept your text entry.

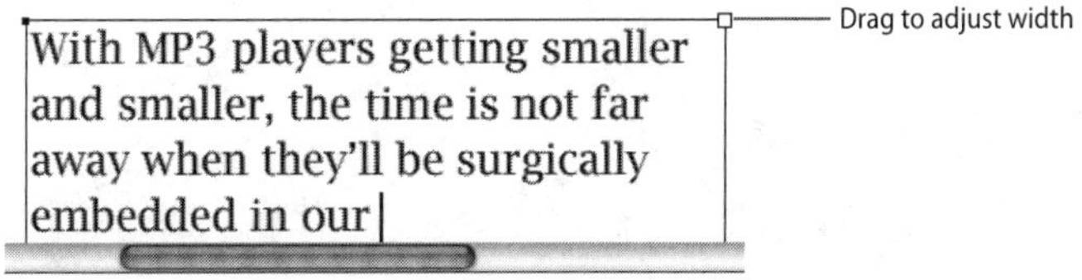

Drag to adjust width

With MP3 players getting smaller and smaller, the time is not far away when they'll be surgically embedded in our

Figure 19a As you type, the text automatically wraps to a new line whenever it reaches the right side of the rectangle.

When you include text in a Flash movie, it's important to understand how Flash handles fonts. You can use a particular font in your movie only if that font is installed on the computer you're using. When you test or publish your movie, a subset of the font is automatically embedded in the SWF file, so anyone who watches the movie will see the text in the correct font and size. However, *no* font information is embedded in a FLA file. If you give your FLA file to colleagues or clients, be sure their computers have the necessary fonts installed. Otherwise, they'll be prompted to choose replacement fonts when they open the FLA file.

Anti-aliasing is the process used by Flash and other programs to make text and images look smoother on the screen. The Properties panel includes a Font Rendering Method menu that lets you set anti-aliasing options for each text field you create. If the text you're creating is intended

The Fine Print

Keep in mind that Flash text has to be easily readable on a computer monitor. You may have a super-sharp flat-panel monitor, but the people who watch your movie may be doing so on an old, blurry CRT. Out of courtesy to your audience, try to avoid ornate typefaces, tiny font sizes, and large or dense blocks of text.

If your Flash movie is intended for use on the Web, consider removing text from your movie and putting it in the HTML portion of the page. Doing so will allow users to search for and copy the text, which they can't do with text in a SWF file. It will also allow Google and other search engines to index the page more reliably.

to be put into motion, you'll generally want to choose Anti-Alias for Animation. If the text is intended to be static, you'll get better results with Anti-Alias for Readability. If you use extremely small text, it will probably be most readable with no smoothing at all. In that case, you'd choose Bitmap Text (No Anti-Alias).

#20 Breaking Apart Text

A block of text in Flash is known as a *text object*. As the name implies, it's a self-contained unit. If you move, resize, or delete a text object, all of its text is affected.

Sometimes, however, you may not want your text to behave as a single object. For example, you may want to animate an explosion, scattering all the text randomly. To do this, you have to convert your text from a single object to many; in fact, every character needs to be a separate object.

The Break Apart command on the Modify menu is ideal for situations like this. As you'll see in the next few chapters, Break Apart does different things in different situations. In this case, when applied to a text object that contains two or more characters, the Break Apart command automatically breaks each character into a separately selectable object (**Figure 20a**).

Figure 20a From left to right: a selected text object, the same text object with Break Apart applied once; the same text object with Break Apart applied twice.

You can apply the Break Apart command a second time to the same text. Applying it once breaks the text object into individual characters; applying it a second time converts each character into an editable vector path. Using Break Apart in this way has advantages and drawbacks.

- **Advantages.** When text characters have been converted to standard vector shapes, the computer no longer needs to have a specific font installed in order to display the text. You can save your FLA file and

(continued on next page)

pass it on to anyone else with assurance that your text will display correctly. Also, these converted text characters can now be edited like any other vector paths, allowing you to experiment with interesting typographical effects (**Figure 20b**).

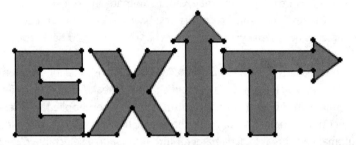

Figure 20b After being broken apart twice, text characters can be edited like ordinary vector paths.

- **Drawbacks.** Breaking text apart is irreversible; individual characters can't be turned back into an editable text block. If you need to change the content, the spelling, the typeface, the anti-aliasing, or any other characteristic of the text, you'll have to input it all over again. Also, converting each individual character to a freestanding vector path may add an excessive number of anchor points, bloating the file size.

#21 Using Multiple Layers

Every new FLA file begins with a single layer. You can see it in the left column of the timeline, labeled Layer 1.

Practically speaking, you need only one layer to create a vector drawing. That's because every time you create a new object, Flash stacks it on top of the previous objects in the same layer. The position of an object in relation to the others in the stack is known as its depth level.

To change the depth level of a particular object, use the commands under Modify > Arrange. For example, let's say a cloud is behind a building, and you want it to be in front. You could accomplish this by selecting the cloud and choosing Modify > Arrange > Bring to Front (**Figure 21a**).

Background Check

If you want the background of your movie to be a solid color, there's no need to put a colored rectangle on a background layer. Instead, click anywhere on the stage where there isn't a selectable object; doing so brings up the Document Properties in the Properties panel. Use the Background menu to choose a background color for the stage. Unlike using an object as a background, choosing a color from the Background menu is "free"—that is, it doesn't add to the size of the SWF file.

Figure 21a The Bring to Front command lets you bring an object up to the highest depth level.

The other commands on the Arrange submenu are Bring Forward, which moves a selected item up one depth level at a time; Send Backward, which moves the item down one depth level at a time, and Send to Back, which moves the item to the lowest possible depth level.

Using the Modify > Arrange commands can be tedious, especially if you have many objects with many different depth levels on one layer. So you may choose to distribute your objects among different layers.

Unlike Photoshop and Illustrator, each of which has a dedicated Layers panel, Flash displays all of its layers in the timeline. To create a new layer

Good Housekeeping

If you're accustomed to working in Photoshop or Illustrator, you probably use layers freely, creating a new layer every time you want to add something new to your graphic. It's possible to do the same thing in Flash, but it's not common practice.

Because Flash is an animation program, objects often have to go on one layer or another for technical reasons. Using an unneeded layer makes editing your movie more confusing, so consolidate your objects onto a single layer whenever possible. For example, if you have stationary objects in the background of your movie, it's tidier to put all of them on a single layer (labeled Background) instead of spreading them out over several layers.

Another way to simplify your timeline is to group related layers together. Like Photoshop, Flash allows you to move layers into folders that can be expanded or collapsed as needed. To create a new layer, click the New Folder icon to the right of the New Layer icon.

in the timeline, click the Insert Layer icon (**Figure 21b**). Each new layer is numbered by default, but you can change a layer's name by double-clicking the layer name and typing a new one.

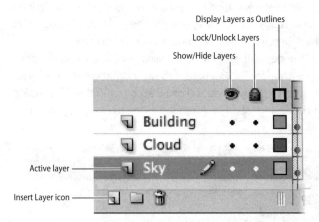

Figure 21b Layer names are displayed in the leftmost column of the timeline.

Once you have multiple layers in the timeline, you have to keep track of which layer is active at any given time. The active layer is highlighted in blue. Any object that you create is automatically placed on the active layer. If you want a new object to be on a different layer, you should first select your preferred layer in the timeline to make it active.

If an object is on one layer and you want to move it to another, you can select the object and choose Edit > Cut. Then select the layer to which you want the object to be moved and choose Edit > Paste in Place (if you want the object to have the same position on the stage as it did before) or Edit > Paste in Center (if you want the object to appear in the middle of the stage).

Layers that are higher up in the timeline appear in front of layers that are lower down. You can drag any layer up or down.

To the right of the layer names in the timeline are three columns that affect the way the objects in each layer are displayed. Each column has an On and an Off setting; you can toggle between the settings by clicking in the appropriate column and row.

The first column, with the eye icon at the top, controls the visibility of each layer. A dot in that column means that the corresponding layer is visible; a red X means that the corresponding layer is hidden.

The second column, with the padlock icon at the top, controls the security of each layer. A dot in that column means that the corresponding layer is unlocked; a padlock symbol means that the corresponding layer is locked. No objects can be copied from, pasted to, or edited on a locked layer.

The third column, with the empty square at the top, controls the display mode of each layer. A filled square in that column means that the layer is set to display strokes and fills; an empty square means that the layer is set to display only unadorned paths. If you have a slow computer, turning off the display of strokes and fills may make the screen refresh faster and thus speed up your work.

Clicking the icon at the top of each column turns the corresponding setting on or off for all the layers.

CHAPTER FOUR

Using Symbols and the Library

Most of the power of Flash comes from its ability to create and manipulate symbols. A symbol is a master object that resides in one place—a panel called the *Library*—but can generate multiple copies of itself that can be used anywhere in Flash. Symbols offer a variety of advantages, including:

- **Economy.** If you have a visible object that's intended to appear more than once in a Flash movie, you can convert it to a symbol. You can then place any number of instances (copies) of that symbol on the stage without any significant increase in the movie's file size.

- **Adaptability.** Whenever you make a change in a symbol, that change is instantly reflected in all instances of the symbol.

- **Flexibility.** Every symbol has its own internal timeline. As a result, a symbol can contain its own animated content that plays independently of the animation in the main timeline.

- **Nestability.** Symbols can be embedded in other symbols, which can be embedded in still other symbols. By nesting symbols in this way, you can animate complex movements easily—for example, you could embed a symbol of a propeller turning inside a symbol of an airplane flying.

- **Scriptability.** Two kinds of symbols—buttons and movie clips—can be controlled using ActionScript. Movie clips can even include scripts of their own, allowing them to control other movie clips or the movie that contains them.

This chapter shows you the basics of creating, modifying, and organizing symbols. More advanced use of symbols is covered in Chapter 5 (Creating Basic Animation) and Chapter 11 (Introducing ActionScript).

#22 Converting Objects to Symbols

Any object (or group of objects) that can appear on the stage can be made into a symbol. Here's how to do it:

1. Select one or more objects on the stage. The selected objects may include paths, text objects, bitmaps, or even other symbols.

2. Choose Modify > Convert to Symbol, or press the F8 key. The Convert to Symbol dialog box appears.

   (While this book usually doesn't mention keyboard shortcuts, F8 is an exception because Convert to Symbol is such a frequently used command.)

3. Enter a name for the symbol into the Name field.

4. Click the radio button for the type of symbol you want to create: a movie clip, button, or graphic. (For the differences between these symbol types, see #27 and #28. If you're experimenting with symbols for the first time, the simplest choice is Graphic.)

5. Click one of the small squares in the diagram next to the word Registration. The square you click will determine the symbol's registration point (**Figure 22a**).

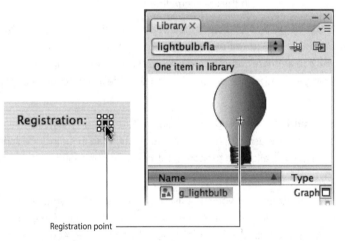

Registration point

Figure 22a Click the square corresponding to your preferred location for the symbol's registration point. Later, when you view the symbol in the library or in symbol-editing mode, your registration point will be indicated by crosshairs.

Technically, Flash lets you assign to a symbol whatever name you like. In practice, however, there are two issues you may want to take into account when you name a symbol:

- **Convenience.** Symbols listed in the library can be sorted by name or by type, but it's much more convenient to have them sorted by name and by type without needing to switch between the two sorting modes. For this reason, many Flash developers like to give each symbol a prefix such as b_ for button symbols, g_ for graphic symbols, and m_ for movie clip symbols.

- **Descriptiveness.** The more precise your symbol names are, the easier it will be to find the one you want among dozens or hundreds of symbols. If your movie contains graphic symbols of a beagle, a poodle, and a schnauzer, don't name the symbols g_dog1, g_dog2, and g_dog3. Instead, name them g_dogBeagle, g_dogPoodle, and g_dogSchnauzer.

Think of the registration point as the handle by which Flash will hold the symbol when it's in motion (see #42). When you're in doubt, the center is usually a good choice.

6. Click OK.

You can find the symbol you just created in the library. (If the library isn't part of your current workspace, choose Window > Library.) When you click the symbol's name in the library list, you'll see the symbol in the viewing pane above the list (**Figure 22b**).

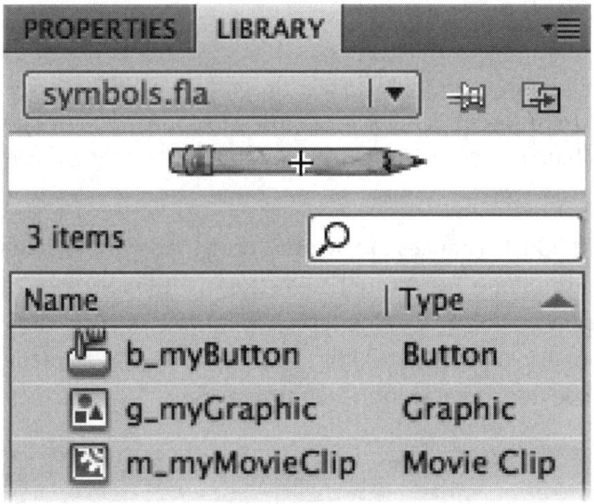

Figure 22b Each symbol is listed in the library next to an icon representing the symbol type. You can click the name of a symbol to see what it looks like.

It's also possible to create a symbol from scratch, without starting with an object on the stage. To do so, choose Insert > New Symbol. You'll see a Create New Symbol dialog box, which is identical to the Convert to Symbol, except for the lack of a Registration diagram.

When you complete the dialog box and click OK, Flash enters symbol-editing mode (see #24). If you wish, you can create some visual content for the symbol; if you'd rather wait until later, click Scene 1 in the breadcrumb trail to return to normal mode. If you don't create any content for the symbol, it will still be listed in the library, but the viewing pane will be blank when you click the symbol's name.

Group or Symbol?

Let's say you have several objects on the stage that you want to make selectable with a single click. Should you group them, or convert them to a symbol? Here are some criteria to help you decide:

- **Impermanence.** If you want just to bring the objects together temporarily, and you plan to separate them later, it's quicker to use a group than a symbol.

- **Uniqueness.** If a set of objects will appear only once in the movie, it's more efficient to group them than to convert them to a symbol.

- **Movement.** If you plan to animate a set of objects, convert them to a symbol. (As you'll see in #42, both symbols and groups can be motion-tweened, but motion-tweening symbols is preferable.)

#23 Working with Symbols and Instances

When you convert an object to a symbol, as you did in #22, the original object seems to remain on the stage. Although that object may look exactly as it did originally, it has become something quite different: It's now an *instance* of the symbol in the library.

An instance is a marker that points back to a symbol in the library and tells Flash, "display that symbol here." That's why multiple instances of a symbol don't significantly affect file size: The symbol in the library contains all the information that defines it, and therefore takes up space in the file, but each instance contains barely any information other than a pointer to the symbol.

Note
Flash developers often refer to instances as symbols, as in "Let's remove that symbol from the stage," but that's just shorthand. Strictly speaking, a symbol can be only in the library; any copy of it on the stage is an instance.

To create additional instances of a symbol, drag the symbol out of the library and onto the stage. The symbol itself stays in the library; what gets dragged is actually an instance of the symbol (**Figure 23a**). Another way to create additional instances is to duplicate an instance that's already on the stage—by copying and pasting, for example.

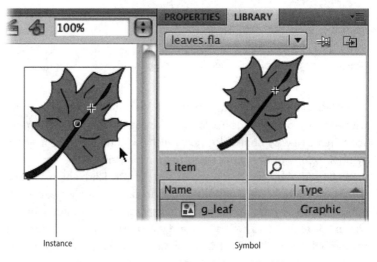

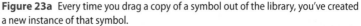

Instance   Symbol

Figure 23a Every time you drag a copy of a symbol out of the library, you've created a new instance of that symbol.

At first, all instances of a symbol look exactly the same as that symbol. It's possible, however, to change the appearance of an instance in two ways (**Figure 23b**):

- **Transformation.** By using the Free Transform tool, you can transform an instance in most of the same ways that you would a path: You can rotate it, scale it, or skew it (see #15). If an instance contains only vector paths, you can distort it as well.

- **Color effects.** When you select an instance on the stage, a menu labeled Style appears in the Color Effect section of Properties. You can change the instance's brightness, tint, or opacity by choosing the appropriate item from the menu (see #25).

Figure 23b All of these objects are instances of the same symbol. The one at the upper left is unaltered; the others have all been transformed or have had color effects applied.

When you alter an instance, you affect only that instance. The other instances and the symbol in the library remain unchanged. In contrast, when you edit a symbol, the changes you make are reflected in all instances of that symbol (see #24).

Instance or Group?

Symbol instances and groups behave similarly on the stage: Each allows you to select multiple objects with one click, as if they were a single object; each is surrounded by a blue rectangle when it's selected; and each becomes editable when it's double-clicked. If you're not sure at first glance whether you've selected an instance or a group, there are two quick ways to tell: look for the registration crosshairs (an instance has them; a group doesn't), or look at the Properties panel (it will say *Group* if a group is selected, or it will display the symbol type—Graphic, Button, or Movie Clip—if an instance is selected).

#24 Editing Symbols

There are two ways to edit a symbol. The first is to find the symbol in the library and double-click either its name in the list or its image in the viewing pane. When you do so, everything on the stage disappears, and the symbol you're editing becomes the only visible object. This is a good way to edit if you don't want to be distracted, but it prevents you from seeing the symbol in context with the other items on the stage.

The second way to edit a symbol, called *editing in place*, is to double-click any instance of a symbol on the stage. Flash goes into a symbol-editing mode that looks just like the group-editing mode described in #17: Everything other than the selected instance is dimmed, and the elements of the symbol become the only objects you can select and edit (**Figure 24a**). What's unusual about editing in place is that when you double-click the instance, the master symbol temporarily takes its place. Any changes you make to the symbol will affect not only the instance you double-clicked, but all other instances as well.

While you're in symbol-editing mode, using either editing method, you'll see a small white circle with crosshairs. That circle represents the symbol's registration point. The crosshairs can't be moved, but if you want to change the symbol's registration point, you can drag the contents of the symbol to a different position relative to the crosshairs.

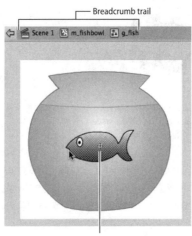

Breadcrumb trail

Registration point

Figure 24a Flash is in editing-in-place mode for a graphic symbol called *g_fish*, which is inside a movie clip called *m_fishbowl*. The breadcrumb trail leads back to the original contents of the stage.

If you have symbols nested within symbols, you can drill down one level at a time by editing the outermost symbol, then double-clicking a symbol embedded in it, and so on. You can return to any earlier level by clicking the appropriate link in the breadcrumb trail (see #17). Clicking the leftmost link, called *Scene 1* by default, takes you back to the main stage and exits symbol-editing mode.

Any changes you make to a symbol affect not only the symbol in the library, but all instances of that symbol, even if they were placed on the stage before you edited the symbol (**Figure 24b**).

Figure 24b Editing a symbol affects all instances of that symbol, even if they've been transformed or had color effects applied to them. (To see how these instances have changed, compare this screenshot to Figure 23b.)

The Domino Effect

When you make changes to a symbol, those changes affect all instances of the symbol. The effects may be especially far-reaching if some of those instances are embedded in other symbols.

Say, for example, that an instance of Symbol A is embedded in Symbol B, and that an instance of Symbol B is embedded in Symbol C. If you make a change to Symbol A, the instances of *all three* symbols will reflect that change.

#**25** Using Symbol Color Effects

Let's say you want to change the color of an individual instance of a symbol. You can't use the Color panel to change its stroke or fill, because a symbol instance isn't editable. You can't double-click the instance and change its color in symbol-editing mode, because doing so would change the color of *all* instances of that symbol.

The solution is to select the instance and look on the Properties panel for a section labeled Color Effect. Below that label is the Style menu, from which you can choose the type of effect you want to apply. Depending on which option you select, a different control (or set of controls) will appear next to the menu. The available options are:

- **Brightness.** The brightness control is a slider ranging from –100% to 100%, with 0% as the default. Choosing a positive number brightens the instance; choosing a negative number darkens it.

- **Tint.** There are several tint controls. The first, to the right of the Style menu, is a standard color menu that allows you to choose a tint for the instance in the same way you'd ordinarily choose a color for a stroke or fill (see #8). Farther down are three sliders—labeled Red, Green, and Blue—that allow you to adjust the level of each primary color on a scale ranging from 0 to 255.

None of these tint controls discriminates between strokes and fills. As a result, tinting an instance causes the stroke and fill to appear exactly the same color, even if they had contrasting colors to begin with.

To avoid this problem, you can use the Tint slider. This control acts as if the tint were a separate object overlaying the instance: If the slider is set to 100%, only the tint is visible; if slider is set to 0%, only the unchanged instance is visible. At intermediate settings—such as 50%, the default—the tint is treated as if it's partly transparent, allowing some of the underlying instance to show through. As you lower the tint amount, the original contrast between the stroke and fill colors becomes more apparent, but the tint looks increasingly washed out (**Figure 25a**).

Figure 25a The effects of the Tint slider can be seen in these three different views of the same instance. On the left, the tint is set to 0%, leaving the original instance unchanged. In the center, the tint is set to 100%, completely covering the instance with a uniform color. On the right, the tint is set to 50%, allowing the instance to partially show through the tint.

- **Alpha.** Alpha is synonymous with opacity. When the Alpha slider is set to 100% (the default), the instance is completely opaque; when it's set to 0%, the instance is completely transparent (invisible). If the background behind the instance is white, the effect of lowering the alpha is indistinguishable from that of raising the brightness.

- **Advanced.** This option lets you control tint and alpha at the same time. There are four controls—one each for Alpha, Red, Green, and Blue—with settings that align in columns (**Figure 25b**). By changing the values in the left column, you can vary the amount of alpha and of each primary color by percentage. (Note that a setting of 100% in this column indicates the level of alpha or color that's *already* in the instance. For example, if the instance originally contains 30 percent blue, a setting of 100% would maintain that level of blue; a setting of 50% would bring it down to 15 percent blue.)

By changing the values in the right column, you can add or subtract absolute amounts of alpha, red, green, and blue, in increments ranging from 255 to –255. Because these controls apply their calculations

(continued on next page)

individually to each color in the instance, they preserve the differences between stroke and fill colors. Therefore, if you wish to apply a color effect to an instance, you'll usually get better results with the Advanced option than you would with the Tint option.

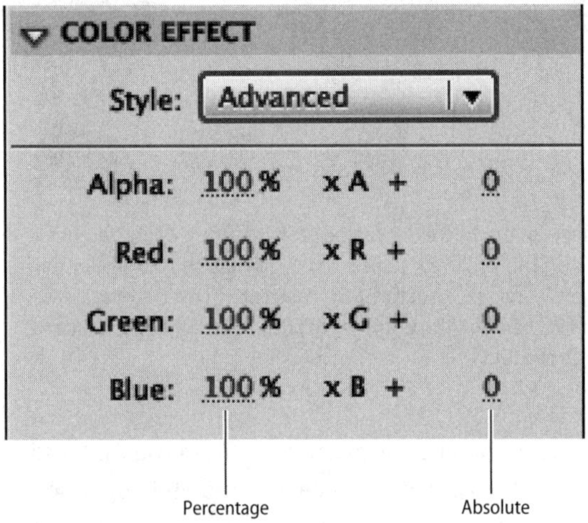

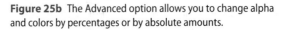

Percentage   Absolute

Figure 25b The Advanced option allows you to change alpha and colors by percentages or by absolute amounts.

#26 Breaking Apart Instances

As you've seen in #23 and #25, there are several techniques for modifying individual instances without changing the original symbol. Those techniques are limited, however. What if you *really* want to change the appearance of an instance—for example, by cutting a hole in it or changing its shape?

The answer is, you can't—at least not while the object you want to change is an instance. But it's possible to break the connection between an instance and a symbol, turning the instance into an independent, editable object. To do so, select the instance and choose Modify > Break Apart (**Figure 26**).

Figure 26 On the left, an instance of a symbol; on the right, the same instance after being broken apart. The dot screen indicates that it's now an editable object.

Keep in mind that using the Break Apart command has some negative consequences. When you break apart an instance, any color effects that you've applied to it disappear (since color effects work only on instances of symbols). Once an instance has been broken apart, it will no longer reflect changes you make to its parent symbol. And, most significantly, breaking apart an instance increases your movie's file size, since the former instance now contains real information instead of pointing to a symbol in the library.

Think twice before you break apart an instance, because the process isn't reversible. Turning an editable object into an instance of an existing symbol isn't possible, although you can convert the object into a new symbol (see #22).

Breaking "Breaking Apart" Apart

In ordinary English, the phrase *break apart* can have several meanings: to disintegrate, to divide an object into pieces, or to sever the connection between two objects. In Flash, the Break Apart command is equally vague: It means different things in different situations.

As you saw in #20, breaking apart text divides it into individual characters; breaking it apart again converts it to editable paths. Breaking apart a group has the same effect as ungrouping it. Breaking apart an instance of a symbol severs its connection to the symbol, allowing it to stand independently. Finally, as you'll see in #55, breaking apart a bitmap allows you to modify parts of the bitmap or use the bitmap as fill.

What does breaking apart do to an editable path? Nothing: The Breaking Apart command is dimmed when a path is selected.

#27 Creating Button Symbols

A button is typically used in an interactive environment (such as a Web page) as a way for the user to make something happen. As interactive design has matured, users have developed additional expectations. When they move the pointer over a button, they expect it to respond in some way—by getting brighter, for example. This change in a button's appearance when a user rolls over it is known as a *rollover effect*.

When users click a button, they expect some feedback showing that their input has been recognized. This feedback may take the form of an audible beep or click, an appearance change, or both.

Flash has made it easy to create buttons that provide all of these responses. Here's the usual procedure for making a functional button:

1. Use the drawing tools to create the button's normal appearance.

2. Select the paths that constitute the button and choose Modify > Convert to Symbol, or press F8. The Convert to Symbol dialog box appears.

3. Type a name for the symbol (preferably with a prefix such as *b_*) into the Name field.

4. Below Type, choose Button.

5. Click a square to choose the registration point. (For a button, the center position is typical.)

6. Click OK. The button symbol appears in the library, and the button on the stage becomes an instance of the symbol.

7. Enter symbol-editing mode, either by double-clicking the button symbol in the library or by double-clicking its instance on the stage.

You'll notice that the timeline changes from its standard layout to a series of four cells labeled Up, Over, Down, and Hit (**Figure 27a**). The labels Up, Over, and Down refer to three variations, or states, of the button. The Up state is the button's appearance when the user isn't interacting with it; the Over state is the way the button looks when the user rolls the pointer over it; and the Down state is the way the button looks when the user is clicking it (**Figure 27b**).

The black dot in the Up cell indicates that the symbol that's currently on the stage will represent the Up state of the button.

TIMELINE	MOTION EDITOR						Up	Over	Down	Hit
			👁	🔒	☐					
	⌐ Layer 1	🖉	•	•	☐		•			

Figure 27a This is how the timeline looks when a button symbol is being edited.

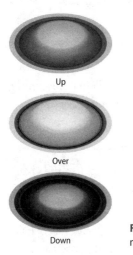

Up

Over

Down

Figure 27b These examples show how a button might look in each of its three states.

Mystery Button

You may have noticed that the buttons in Figures 27b and 27c don't have any labels on them. It's certainly possible to include text in a button symbol, thereby giving the button a label. Nevertheless, most Flash developers choose not to do so. If a button symbol contains text, the button can be used only for one purpose: the one expressed by its label. If there's no text in a button symbol, the button can be used repeatedly for a variety of purposes simply by placing different text on top of each instance.

8. Click in the cell below the Over label. The cell darkens to indicate that it's selected.

9. Choose Insert > Timeline > Keyframe, or press F6. (To understand what's happening in this step, see #30.) A black dot appears in the Over cell. Make sure this keyframe is highlighted (selected) for the next step.

(continued on next page)

10. Change the button's appearance to how you'd like it to look in its Over state. (The changes you make won't affect the button's appearance in the Up state.)

11. Repeat Steps 8 through 10 in the next cell for the button's Down state. You can ignore the Hit cell for now.

12. Click Scene 1 in the breadcrumb trail above the stage. Flash exits symbol-editing mode.

13. Choose Control > Enable Simple Buttons. (If the Enable Simple Buttons command already has a check mark next to it, skip this step.)

14. Roll your pointer over the button instance on the stage. You'll see it change to its Over state.

15. Click the button instance on the stage. While your mouse button is depressed, you'll see the button in its Down state.

While those are the basic steps for making a multi-state button, there are other things you might want to do to enhance it. For example:

- **Add audio.** You can add sounds as well as images to the Over and Down states. To find out how to attach an event sound to a keyframe, see #64.

- **Add motion.** A button doesn't have to be static; any or all of its three states can be animated by means of embedded movie clips. To find out how to accomplish this, see #36.

- **Add a Hit frame.** Some buttons are difficult for a user to click—for example, because they're too small or irregularly shaped (**Figure 27c**). You can make the button more user friendly by giving it a larger or more uniform "hot zone." To do so, return to editing the button, and repeat Steps 8 through 10 for the Hit cell. The variation of the button you use for the Hit frame won't ever be seen on the stage, but it determines the size and shape of the clickable area around the button.

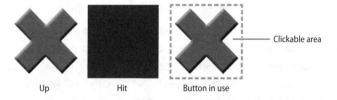

Up   Hit   Button in use

Clickable area

Figure 27c A button's Up state is on the left, and its Hit frame is shown in the center. The stroke and fill colors don't matter for the Hit frame; all that matters is the shape of the filled path. That path determines the button's clickable area, indicated by a dashed line on the right.

Although this button may be attractive and easy to use, it's still missing one important feature: It doesn't *do* anything. To make the button functional, you'll have to control it with ActionScript, which you'll find out about in #88.

#28 Distinguishing Between Graphic Symbols and Movie Clips

While button symbols are used for a single, specialized purpose, graphic symbols and movie clips have broader applications. Although *graphic symbol* sounds like something that contains a still image, and *movie clip* sounds like something that contains motion, the truth is that either type of symbol can have either type of content. The differences lie elsewhere.

If you're creating a symbol, and you don't know whether to make it a graphic symbol or a movie clip, consider these issues:

- **Dependent or independent?** Any instance of a graphic symbol is dependent on the pace of the movie it's placed in. If the symbol contains animation that takes 52 frames to complete, then you'll probably want the instance to remain on the stage for exactly 52 frames. If the movie ends before those frames have elapsed, the action in the symbol will appear to be interrupted in the middle.

  In contrast, a movie clip runs independently of the movie it's in. As long as a movie clip is on the stage, its animation will continue, even if the main movie ends (**Figure 28a**). For that matter, when the action in the movie clip reaches its end, it will start playing all over again from the beginning and loop repeatedly—unless you deliberately stop it with ActionScript.

Figure 28a The rotation of this pinwheel is contained in a movie clip. Even after the animation of the child is over, the pinwheel will continue to turn.

- **Passive or interactive?** ActionScript can't control instances of graphic symbols—in fact, it doesn't even recognize that they're there. For that reason, graphic symbols are useful mostly for traditional animation—the kind that the user watches, but doesn't interact with.

In contrast, a movie can use ActionScript to control the movie clip instances within it, and any of those instances can use ActionScript to control any of the others. (In fact, many interactive movies are only one frame long. The action of the movie takes place not in the timeline, but in sequential commands issued to movie clips by ActionScript.)

The fact that a movie clip instance *can* be controlled by ActionScript doesn't mean it has to be. It's fine to have a movie clip that simply plays animation. However, in a situation in which a graphic symbol or a movie clip would serve equally well, it makes sense to go with the graphic symbol. Because of their more limited capabilities, graphic symbols take up less space in the SWF file and make fewer demands on the computer's processor.

Tip

If you create a symbol as a movie clip and decide later that it should have been a graphic symbol—or vice versa—it's not too late to change your mind. Select the symbol name in the library list and click the Properties button (a lowercase I in a circle) at the bottom of the Library panel. A Symbol Properties dialog box appears, in which you can rename the symbol and assign it a different symbol type.

#29 Using the Library to Manage Symbols

Symboloids

Although the library is often described as a place to store symbols, Flash stores some items in the library that are symbol-like but that don't fit the usual definition of symbols. They include:

- **Font symbols.** When Flash creates a SWF file, it automatically embeds font information for all the text characters that appear in the movie (see #19). But sometimes you'll want to embed font information for characters that *don't* appear in the movie, such as text that will be generated on the fly by ActionScript. To do so, you can right-click (Windows) or Control-click (Mac) anywhere in the library list, choose New Font from the context menu, and select a font from a list of all the fonts installed in your computer. The font then appears as an item in the library.

(continued on next page)

The library is more than a repository for symbols; it's also a place where you can actively organize, modify, and track symbols. Many of the library's features are hidden away—either represented by small, unlabeled icons, or listed on menus that are not immediately obvious (**Figure 29a**).

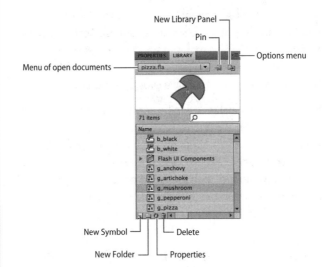

Figure 29a Some of the Library panel's less obvious controls are pointed out here.

Let's look first at the four icons at the bottom of the Library panel. They are, from left to right:

- **New Symbol.** Clicking this icon brings up the Create New Symbol dialog box (see #22).

- **New Folder.** Just like the files on your computer's hard drive, the items in the Flash library can be sorted into folders. Clicking the New Folder icon creates an empty folder into which you can drag any number of library items (including other folders). To expand a folder—that is, to see the folder's contents—double-click the folder in the library list; to collapse the folder, double-click it again.

- **Properties.** When you select any item in the library (other than a folder), clicking this icon opens a dialog box that lets you modify the item's properties. The name and contents of the dialog box depend on what type of item you've selected. For example, if you've selected a symbol, the Symbol Properties dialog box appears; if you've selected a sound file, the Sound Properties dialog box appears.

Tip

For library items that can't be edited in Flash (such as bitmaps and sounds), another way to bring up the Properties dialog box is to double-click the item's icon in the library list.

- **Delete.** You can delete any item in the library by selecting it and clicking the Delete icon or pressing the Delete key. Be careful, however: If you delete a symbol, all instances of that symbol will vanish from the movie. If you delete a folder, Flash will delete everything contained in the folder without giving you a warning or asking for confirmation.

If more than one document is open, the panel displays the library contents of whichever document is in the foreground. To see the contents of another document's library, you can select the document's name from the pop-up menu above the viewing pane.

The Pin icon to the right of that menu allows you to "pin" the current library in place—that is, to keep the current document's contents visible in the Library panel even if you bring a different document to the foreground. Click the icon once to "pin" the library; click it again to "un-pin" it.

The next icon to the right is the New Library Panel icon, which opens another copy of the current library in a separate panel. Doing this can be useful if you want to drag items between panels to copy them.

Tip

If you copy an instance from the stage of one FLA file and paste it to the stage of another, the instance's parent symbol will automatically appear in the second file's library.

Most of the library's other features can be found in the Options menu, which you open by clicking the three-line icon on the upper right of the panel. You can get an almost identical contextual menu by right-clicking (Windows) or Control-clicking (Mac) anywhere in the Library panel.

Some of the menu items, such as New Folder and Delete, are alternative ways to access features we've already looked at; others, such as Rename and Select Unused Items, are self-explanatory. Two menu items that need special explanation are those that deal with use counts.

- **Components.** Flash comes with a collection of components, or specialized objects that you can use to add interactivity to a movie (see Chapter 11). Components are initially stored in the Components panel, but once you drag a component into a movie, it appears in the library as well. A component is a symbol, but it can't be edited or modified the way ordinary symbols can; you can alter its appearance and behavior only by means of ActionScript or the Component Inspector.

- **Multimedia assets.** When you import sounds, video clips, and bitmap images into a FLA file, those assets are stored in the library. They behave somewhat like symbols, but you can't modify multimedia assets inside Flash.

Among the features that become visible when you widen the Library panel is the Use Count column (**Figure 29b**). For each item in the library, the *Use Count* column tells you how many instances of that item have been used in the movie. By default, the numbers in this column are refreshed only when you right-click (Windows) or Control-click (Mac) the Library panel and choose Update Use Counts Now from the contextual menu. If you want the use counts to be updated automatically, you can choose Keep Use Counts Updated; however, this option can place a drag on the program's performance.

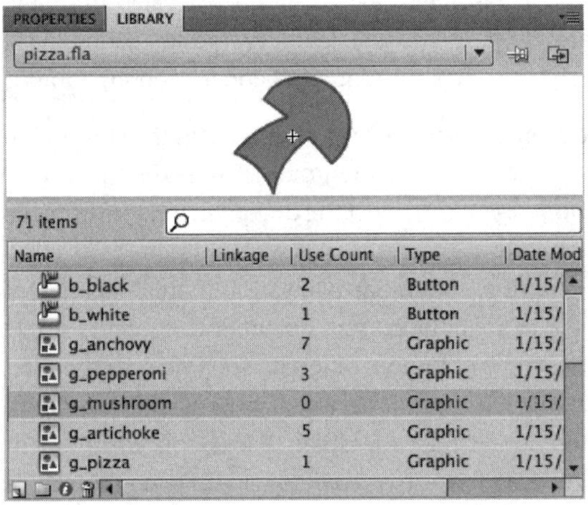

Figure 29b Widening the Library panel reveals previously unseen columns, including Use Count.

CHAPTER FIVE

Creating Basic Animation

If you've created artwork in Photoshop or Illustrator (or on paper, for that matter), you're accustomed to drawing in visual space. What you may not be used to is drawing in *time*.

Time is what makes animation possible. Animation isn't just cartoon characters running around; it's any incremental change in visual elements over time. Text moving across the stage is animation; so is a black-and-white photo that blossoms into color.

If you're planning to use Flash strictly as an ActionScript programming environment—for example, to make dynamic Web interfaces—you may think it's not important to know how to create animation. In Flash, however, Web interfaces or online applications *are* animation. (After all, the user's interaction with the computer takes place over time.) Whether you're an aspiring animator, game developer, or interface designer, you'll need to be familiar with the techniques in this chapter.

#30 Getting to Know the Timeline

The timeline is where you control how the objects on the stage change over time. The vertical red line that crosses the timeline is called the *playhead;* it marks the passage of time as it sweeps across the timeline from left to right (**Figure 30**).

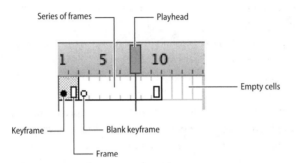

Figure 30 These are the features of the timeline you'll use most often for animation.

The timeline is divided into *cells*, each of which represents a unit of time. (The duration of that unit varies according to the frame rate—see #31—but it's usually somewhere between one-twelfth and one-thirtieth of a second.) The contents of each cell (or each column of cells, if the timeline has more than one layer) determine what's happening on the stage at the moment the playhead passes over it.

The cells in the timeline are empty by default, but you can fill them with either a keyframe or a regular frame:

- **Keyframe.** A keyframe signals to Flash that you want something in your movie to change. When the playhead passes over a keyframe, it updates the stage to display whatever is new in that keyframe. (A keyframe can also mark changes that aren't visible on the stage, such as the start or end of a sound.)

To insert a keyframe into the timeline, select the cell in which you want the keyframe to appear and choose Insert > Timeline > Keyframe, or press F6. A small black circle appears in the cell.

On some occasions, you may want everything that was in the preceding keyframe to disappear, without being replaced by anything. You can make this happen by choosing Insert > Timeline > Blank Keyframe, or by pressing F7. A blank keyframe is represented in the timeline by a white circle instead of a black one.

- **Frame.** A frame (which we'll sometimes refer to as a *regular frame,* to distinguish it from a keyframe) signals to Flash that you want to maintain the status quo. When the playhead passes over a regular frame, it tells the stage to continue displaying whatever was in the most recent keyframe.

To insert a frame into the timeline, select the cell in which you want the frame to appear and choose Insert > Timeline > Frame, or press F5. A white rectangle appears in the cell.

To insert a *series* of frames, select the empty cell in which you want the series to end. (Flash will assume that you want the series to begin in the cell immediately following the most recent keyframe.) When you choose Insert > Timeline > Frame or press F5, a white rectangle appears in the last cell in the series. The intermediate frames don't contain white rectangles, but the dividing lines between the cells disappear; the absence of dividing lines is what allows you to distinguish a series of frames from a series of empty cells.

Note that you can't have empty cells in the middle of a movie. If you insert a keyframe, skip a bunch of cells, and then insert another keyframe, Flash automatically fills the intervening cells with a series of regular frames.

Note also that there may be different things happening on different layers. When the playhead reaches any given point in the timeline—let's say it's frame 12—Flash looks at the entire column of cells and follows the instructions on each layer. For example, if frame 12 on Layer 1 is a keyframe, Flash will replace whatever was previously on that layer with whatever is new in that keyframe. If frame 12 on Layer 2 is a regular frame, Flash will continue to display whatever was in the previous keyframe in that layer. If frame 12 on Layer 3 is a blank keyframe, Flash will clear whatever was previously on that layer. All of these changes happen simultaneously when the playhead reaches a given frame, regardless of how few or how many layers there are.

Do It in Your Sleep

The three most commonly used function keys in Flash are almost certainly F5, F6, and F7, which insert a regular frame, a keyframe, and a blank keyframe, respectively. It's possible to accomplish these tasks via the Insert > Timeline menu options, but—apart from the newest of Flash beginners—nobody ever does. Particularly when you're doing frame-by-frame animation (see #32), which may require inserting dozens or hundreds of keyframes, you'd be downright crazy to use the menu. Get accustomed to those function keys now, and you'll never have to think about them again.

#31 Setting the Frame Rate

Every Flash movie has a *frame rate*, a measurement of how quickly the playhead moves through the timeline. Frame rates are expressed in frames per second, usually abbreviated as *fps*. Flash permits frame rates ranging from 120 fps (the fastest) to 0.01 fps (the slowest), which is equivalent to 100 seconds per frame. For comparison, the standard frame rate for a theatrical film is 24 fps.

A movie's frame rate is displayed on the horizontal strip at the bottom of the timeline (**Figure 31a**). The default frame rate is 12 fps, but you can change it by double-clicking the frame-rate display or by choosing Modify > Document.

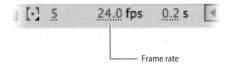

Frame rate

Figure 31a The frame rate of your movie is displayed here.

The smoothness of animation increases as the frame rate increases. For example, let's say the process of opening a door takes 1 second. You might animate the door opening in 10 frames at 10 fps, or you might animate it in 30 frames at 30 fps. Both animations would have a duration of 1 second, but the latter would be smoother, because there would be less movement in each frame (**Figure 31b**).

Figure 31b If both of these sequences are played in the same amount of time, the bottom one will have a higher frame rate and thus will look smoother. If both sequences are played at the same frame rate, they'll look equally smooth, but the bottom one will have a longer duration.

A higher frame rate requires more frames, and hence a larger SWF file; it also puts more of a demand on the computer's processor. Therefore, you'll often want to use a lower frame rate to gain efficiency at the expense of smoothness. If you're doing frame-by-frame animation (see #32), a lower frame rate also requires less work for you in creating the movie.

Keep in mind that the frame rate you set for a movie is only a target. For example, it's unlikely that a typical computer will be able to play a movie at 120 fps. The lower you set the frame rate, the more likely it is that any given user will be able to see the movie as you intended. A frame rate of 12 fps is generally considered to be the minimum for acceptably smooth motion; most animation on the Web has a frame rate of about 15 fps.

When you set a frame rate, you set it for the entire movie; if you change it, you change it for the entire movie. You can't start a movie with one frame rate and end it with another (at least not without some tricky ActionScript). If you want to slow down a particular sequence in your movie, the optimal solution isn't to lower the frame rate, but to add more frames to the sequence.

Don't Be a Processor Hog

Since most computers are powerful enough to play animation at relatively high frame rates, why is the standard frame rate for Web animation no more than 15 fps? It's because the computer's processor usually has other things to do. For example, if you have three SWF files on a web page, and each one has a frame rate of 20 fps, the load on the processor is equivalent to that for playing a single SWF file at 60 fps.

The load factor is especially important to keep in mind if you're designing a Flash movie that users won't freely choose to see—for example, a banner advertisement. The frame rate for an ad should be 12 fps or lower, in order to leave lots of processor cycles available for the Web page's "real" content.

#32 Animating Frame by Frame

Flash Isn't Creative; You Are

Before there were computers, animation was done by drawing one frame at a time. You'd think that using powerful software such as Flash would relieve animators of that drudgery, but the reality is that most animation—at least most character animation—is *still* made one frame at a time. In fact, much of an animator's job is the same as it's been for more than a century: watching how people and things move in the real world, breaking down that motion into incremental steps, and trying to reproduce it convincingly in a series of images.

If you look at old photos of the Disney or Warner Brothers animation studios, you'll see that they always had mirrors on the wall. Those were to allow the animators to model the movements they were animating. If a character had to jump, the animator would jump in front of a mirror to see how his body moved. He might even use a stopwatch to time how long the jump took. He'd

(continued on next page)

As you'll see in Chapter 6, Flash can automate mechanical kinds of motion through a process called *tweening*. But animation is most interesting when its motion *isn't* mechanical—when characters express their personality through the way they move (**Figure 32a**). To achieve that sort of expressive movement, you have to animate your characters one frame at a time.

The basic procedure for frame-by-frame animation is short and simple:

1. In the timeline, select the cell in which you want the animation to begin.

2. Press F7 to insert a blank keyframe.

3. Draw the first frame of animation on the stage.

4. Press F6. Flash inserts a new keyframe immediately after the first one, and it copies the contents of the first keyframe into the new keyframe.

5. Modify the drawing on the stage to represent the next incremental movement.

6. Repeat Steps 4 and 5 as many times as necessary.

Figure 32a A character's idiosyncratic way of moving can be captured only by drawing it frame by frame.

Naturally, elements that stay the same from one frame to the next don't have to be redrawn in each new keyframe. Instead, put them on a separate layer in the timeline (**Figure 32b**).

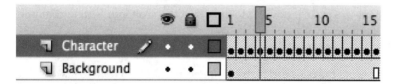

Figure 32b Because the drawing in each frame is slightly different from the previous one, frame-by-frame animation appears in the timeline as a series of keyframes. Background images that don't change from frame to frame should be put on a separate layer.

Each time you draw a new frame of animation, you'll want to make sure it flows smoothly from the frames that precede it. To do this, you can grab the pink rectangle at the top of the playhead and drag it back and forth through the timeline at varying rates of speed—a procedure called *scrubbing*. As you scrub, the corresponding frames of animation will play back on the stage. Scrubbing often reveals slight glitches in the animation that you can then go back and fix.

Once you have enough keyframes in place, you'll want to preview the animation at its proper frame rate, in any of these ways:

- Press Enter (Windows) or Return (Mac) to start the playhead moving through the timeline. Press the same key again to stop it. To rewind—that is, to move the playhead back to the beginning of the timeline—press Control-Alt-R (Windows) or Command-Option-R (Mac).

- Make the Controller panel visible by choosing Window > Toolbars > Controller. The Controller offers a standard set of buttons for playing, stopping, and rewinding the movie.

- Use the menu commands Control > Play, Control > Rewind and Control > Go to End.

In none of these cases do you have to stop the playhead manually. As soon as the playhead passes through all the frames and encounters empty cells, it knows it's at the end of the movie, and it stops on its own.

Another way to test your movie is to generate a sample SWF file (see #35).

then go back to his drawing table and sketch it out. Animators observed dancers and animals to see how they achieved their graceful ways of moving.

Frames of animation no longer have to be pencil-sketched, traced in ink, and hand-colored the way they once were; Flash and other animation programs allow those tasks to be done on a computer. But the humor, interest, and excitement of animation still come entirely from human creativity, frame by frame by frame.

#**33** Onion Skinning

Even the most experienced animators often need help in creating smooth motion. The help in this case is a technique called *onion skinning*, which lets you draw each new frame of animation directly on top of images of previous frames. (The images are dimmed—more so for the earlier ones—to make it possible to draw over them without getting confused about what's new and what's old.)

To use this feature:

1. Move the playhead to the keyframe in which you want to make a new drawing.

2. Click the Onion Skin icon to turn onion skinning on. The playhead is now bracketed by two markers—Start Onion Skin and End Onion Skin—with a dark gray area between them (**Figure 33a**).

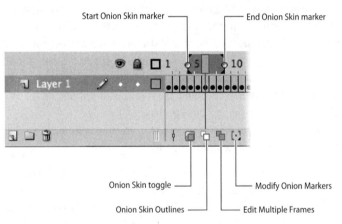

Figure 33a The onion skinning controls are above and below the timeline.

By default, the Start Onion Skin marker is two frames behind the playhead, and the End Onion Skin marker is two frames after the playhead. (If there are fewer than two frames available in either direction, the markers move in toward the playhead as necessary.) To see more or fewer frames, slide the markers.

The frames bracketed by the markers are visible on the stage, with increasing degrees of dimness depending on their distance from the playhead (**Figure 33b**).

Figure 33b This is how the stage looks when onion skinning is turned on. The black stroke in the center is what's in the current frame. The dimmer strokes indicate what's in the two frames before and the two frames after.

3. Create or modify the drawing in the current keyframe, using the dimmed images for reference.

4. Press F6 to insert a new keyframe, or move the playhead to another existing keyframe. The Start Onion Skin and End Onion Skin markers move with it, keeping the same distance from the playhead.

5. Repeat Steps 3 and 4 as many times as necessary. When you're finished, click the Onion Skin marker again to turn onion skinning off.

Here are some possible variations:

- To see just the paths in the onion-skinned frames, without seeing strokes and fills, click the Onion Skin Outlines icon.

- If you want the ability to edit all the frames between the markers—not just the one that the playhead is positioned on—click the Edit Multiple Frames icon.

- To change the behavior of the markers—for example, to keep them visible even when onion skinning is turned off—click the Modify Onion Markers icon and choose one of the listed options.

The Skinny on Skinning

The term *onion skinning* has nothing to do with peeling vegetables. It comes from the early days of animation, when animators used to do their pencil sketches on semi-transparent paper called *onionskin*. To draw each new frame of animation, the animator would lay a sheet of onionskin paper on top of the previous one. The transparency of the paper allowed him to line up the new drawing with the old one and to trace portions when necessary. To test the animation, the animator would lift the corner of the stack of onionskin sheets and slowly release them with his thumb, watching the animation play frame by frame as each sheet of paper dropped into place.

#34 Editing in the Timeline

Once you've created and previewed an animated sequence, you'll almost always decide to go back and modify it. You may want to make parts of it longer or shorter, change its position in the timeline, add more action to it, or take some action away.

This book doesn't provide an exhaustive list of menu commands and keyboard shortcuts for editing; you can get that information from the Help menu. Instead, here are some general hints to help you deal with the less intuitive aspects of working in the timeline. (Note that any hints dealing with F6 apply to F7 as well.)

- If you want to insert a new keyframe between two sequential keyframes, don't select one of the keyframes and press F6. (All that happens is that the playhead moves to the next keyframe; there are no changes at all in the timeline.) Instead, select the first of the two keyframes and press F5 to insert a regular frame after it. The second of the two keyframes, and everything beyond it, moves one frame to the right. Then select the newly inserted frame and press F6 to turn it from a regular frame to a keyframe.

- If you want to delete a selected keyframe, don't choose Modify > Timeline > Clear Keyframe. (That menu command and its keyboard shortcut, Shift-F6, will turn the keyframe into a regular frame instead of deleting it and closing the gap.) Instead, choose Edit > Timeline > Remove Frames, or press Shift-F5, to delete the selected keyframe.

- If you want to move a keyframe to another location in the timeline, don't try to click it and drag it in one motion. (Although this technique works in most programs, it doesn't work in the Flash timeline—all you'll end up doing is selecting a series of frames). Instead, click the keyframe to select it, release the mouse button, and then click again to drag the keyframe.

- If you want to cut and paste (or copy and paste) frames from one part of the timeline to another, don't use the standard Edit > Cut, Edit > Copy, and Edit > Paste menu commands or their keyboard shortcuts. (Those commands work only for objects on the stage, not for frames in the timeline.) Instead, use the special commands Edit > Timeline > Cut Frames, Edit > Timeline > Copy Frames, and Edit > Timeline > Paste Frames.

- If you have a series of regular frames at the end of your movie, and you want to extend the series farther into the timeline, don't select the last frame in the series and drag it. (If you do, Flash will insert a keyframe after it.) Instead, click the cell where you want the series to end, and press F5. The series of frames will extend to meet the cell you selected.

- Similarly, if you want to shorten a series of regular frames (that is, have it end sooner), don't select the last frame in the series and drag it backwards. Instead, find the frame that you want to end the series, click the frame immediately following it, and Shift-click the current last frame in the series. Then choose Edit > Timeline > Remove Frames, or press Shift-F5, to delete the selected frames.

- If you want to extend a portion of a movie and still keep all of its layers in sync, select a block of frames by clicking the frame on the upper left and Shift-clicking the frame on the lower right (**Figure 34a**). Then drag the whole block of frames at once.

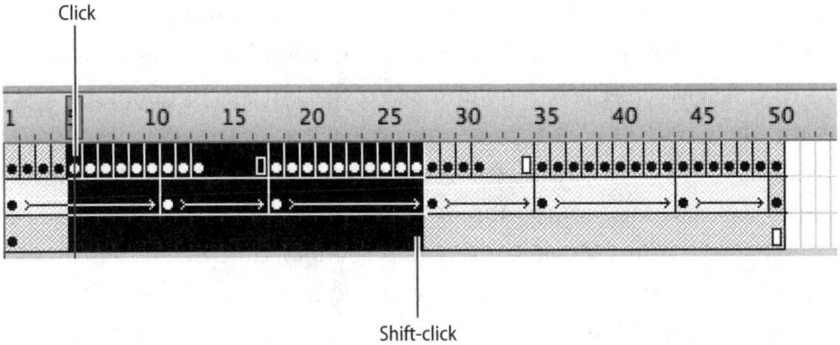

Figure 34a You can select a block of frames across multiple layers.

Speaking Span–ish

If you choose Edit > Preferences (Windows) or Flash > Preferences (Mac), select the General category, and look below the timeline, you'll see one of the more obscure options in Flash: "Span based selection." If you turn it on, the timeline treats any series of regular frames (including tweens) as a single unit called a *span*. Clicking any frame within the span selects the entire span.

This was how the timeline worked in early versions of Flash, and many users found it confusing, because there was no obvious way to select a single frame. (The answer: Alt-click [Windows] or Option-click [Mac] the frame.) Beginning with Flash 5, the timeline changed to its current default behavior, but span-based selection remains an option for those who appreciate the convenience of selecting multiple frames with a single click.

#35 Testing the Movie

In #32, you learned several ways to preview your movie in Flash. All of these techniques have a drawback, however: They don't show you what users' experience will be when they watch your movie. When you watch a movie in the Flash authoring environment, it usually runs more slowly than it would outside, because Flash has to do so many other things at the same time (such as animating the playhead as it moves across the timeline). Also, you see things in the Flash environment that your users can't see, such as where objects go when they leave the stage.

In contrast, the people who see your movie most likely won't even own Flash; they'll be playing it in their Web browsers using the Flash Player plug-in. To see the movie the way your users will see it, you too will have to preview it in the Flash Player. There are two ways to do this—one is more convenient, the other is more authentic.

The more convenient way is to choose Control > Test Movie, or press Command-Enter (Windows) or Control-Return (Mac). Flash generates a SWF file and opens it in a separate window representing the Flash Player. It's not *really* the Flash Player, at least not the one your users will have—it's actually a Flash Player module that's built into your Flash application—but it still gives you a reasonably good idea of what your users will see.

The more authentic way is to choose File > Publish Preview > Default. As with Test Movie, Flash generates a SWF file, but then it opens it in your computer's default Web browser and plays it with the real Flash Player plug-in. In this case, you're seeing the same SWF file your users will see, under basically the same conditions.

Because the Test Movie command is so much quicker, you'll probably want to use it when you're first developing a movie. It's only when you bring your movie into its final stages, and begin to refine and polish it, that the difference between Test Movie and Publish Preview becomes important.

Loopy Behavior

When you preview your SWF file, no matter which method you use, you'll notice that your movie doesn't play just once—it repeats indefinitely, snapping back to the first frame as soon as it gets to the last. The looping is useful in that it gives you the opportunity to observe your movie carefully, but it's also a reminder that the movie will be looping when your users see it. (There are ways for you to prevent it from looping—an unreliable way using Publish Settings, covered in #76, and a reliable way using ActionScript, covered in #87—but the default behavior is to loop.) If you really want to improve the users' experience, look for a creative way to smooth out the transition between the end of the movie and the beginning.

#36 Putting Animation Inside Symbols

Whenever you're in symbol-editing mode (see #24), you might notice that all of the information in the timeline disappears. That's because when you edit a symbol, you stop seeing your movie's timeline and start seeing that *symbol's* timeline. Every symbol in Flash has its own internal timeline. (As you saw in #27, the timeline inside button symbols is greatly simplified, but it's a timeline nonetheless.)

The significance of symbol-specific timelines is that they allow you to put animation *inside* a symbol. Because instances of symbols appear in a movie's timeline, and because instances of other symbols may appear in a symbol's timeline, it's possible (and actually common) to have several different levels of animation going on at once.

For example, suppose you want to animate a person running across the stage. If you had to do this frame by frame, it would take you forever, but the use of animated symbols streamlines the process.

Here's all you have to do:

1. Create a new movie-clip symbol and give it a descriptive name such as *m_running*.

2. Go into symbol-editing mode and animate the person running inside the symbol m_running. (That is, use the symbol's internal timeline, not the main movie's timeline.)

   You need only animate one cycle (that is, left foot forward and right foot forward). Make the cycle smooth enough that it can loop repeatedly without it being apparent where the cycle begins and ends (**Figure 36a**).

Figure 36a This frame-by-frame animation was created inside a movie-clip symbol.

3. Drag an instance of m_running onto the movie's stage.

4. Motion-tween the instance to make it travel across the stage.

(continued on next page)

98

A Movie in a Button

When you design buttons that provide user feedback (see #27), it's sometimes appropriate to include animation—for example, to make a button flash on and off when a user rolls over it. In theory, that should be easy: You could just put animation inside the button symbol. The problem is that buttons don't contain ordinary timelines. They have a specialized timeline containing only four frames, which isn't suitable for animation.

The solution is to put the animation inside a movie clip, because, as described in #28, once a movie clip starts playing, it loops indefinitely. If you put the movie clip into a single frame of a button's timeline—the Over frame, for example—the movie clip will start to play when the user rolls over the button, and it will keep playing until the user clicks the button or rolls off it.

5. Test or preview the movie. You'll see two levels of animation going on at once: the animation within the symbol of the person running in place, and the animation outside the symbol of the running person moving across the stage (**Figure 36b**).

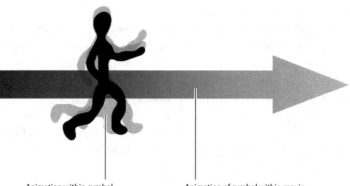

Animation within symbol   Animation of symbol within movie

Figure 36b As this person runs across the stage, two levels of animation are going on at once.

Placing animation inside symbols is powerful and convenient, especially if you're creating an interactive movie in which the action is different every time. The timeline for many interactive movies is only one frame long, because all of the movie's possible animation is contained within the symbols in the library.

CHAPTER FIVE   Creating Basic Animation

#37 Masking

A *mask* is something that hides part of an object and exposes another part of the object. Creating a mask is simple:

1. Place the object to be masked on one layer, and the object that will act as a mask on the layer just above it.

   The mask can be a path, a group, an instance of a symbol, a block of text, or just about anything else. Its stroke and fill colors don't matter (**Figure 37a**).

Figure 37a Top, a mask (the text) and an object to be masked. Bottom, the same objects after the Mask command has been applied.

2. Right-click (Windows) or Control-click (Mac) the name of the layer containing the mask, and select Mask from the context menu.

   Flash converts the upper layer into a mask layer and the lower layer into a masked layer. The object on the stage appears masked.

   Note
   Flash locks the mask layer and the masked layer because that's the only way the mask effect can be seen within Flash. If you unlock either layer, the masking effect disappears. In the SWF file, the masking effect is always visible, regardless of whether the layers in the FLA file are locked or unlocked.

A mask on its own is no big deal. What makes masks interesting is that you can animate the mask, the masked object, or both, thereby achieving complex effects quickly (**Figure 37b**).

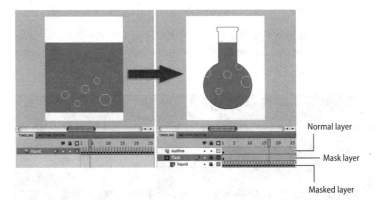

Normal layer
Mask layer
Masked layer

Figure 37b On the left: The bubbles in the water are animated frame by frame. On the right: A flask-shaped mask is added, making the bubbly liquid appear to be contained within the flask.

It's possible to have one mask layer affect multiple masked layers. If there's a layer that you want to put under the control of an existing mask, drag and drop the layer between a mask layer and a masked layer in the timeline (**Figure 37c**). The masked layers can be arranged in any order, so long as the mask layer is above them all.

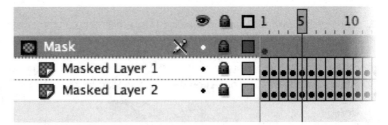

Figure 37c In this timeline, one mask layer is affecting two masked layers.

#38 Using Blending Modes

A blending mode is a tool for creating striking color effects quickly. Many design and animation problems can be solved simply by choosing the right blending mode.

To understand blending modes, consider what happens when you place one object on top of another: The upper object (assuming it's opaque) blocks the view of the lower object. By applying a blending mode to the upper object, you can cause it to reveal all or part of the bottom object in multiple ways (**Figure 38a**).

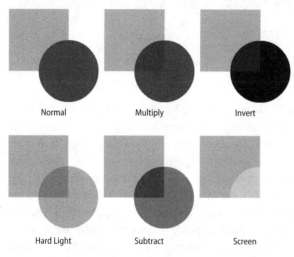

Normal   Multiply   Invert

Hard Light   Subtract   Screen

Figure 38a Here is a sampling of the blending modes available in Flash. Only five are shown; most can't be represented effectively in black and white.

Blending modes are usually described as an interaction between a *blend color* (the one on top) and a *base color* (the one underneath). If the overlapping objects are multicolored, each area of blend color interacts with the base color directly beneath it. Each blending mode is essentially a mathematical formula that determines how the two colors interact.

To apply a blending mode, select a movie-clip instance on the stage, preferably one that has another movie clip partially or totally beneath it. A pop-up menu labeled Blending appears in the Display section of the

Color by Numbers

Many of the blending-mode formulas require colors to be added, subtracted, or multiplied. The Multiply blending mode, for example, "multiplies the blend color by the base color" according to Flash Help. But how is it possible to do math with colors?

Remember that every color on your computer is made up of three primary colors: red, green, and blue. The amount of each primary color can be specified as a percentage, with 100% representing the maximum amount of that color. A standard pea-green, for example, can be made by mixing 50% red, 75% green, and 25% blue.

When Flash calculates blends, it does simple arithmetic with each primary color individually. For example, if the pea-green above is multiplied by neutral gray (50% red, 50% green, and 50% blue), Flash would calculate 50% × 50% = 25% for red, 75% × 50% = 37.5% for green, and 50% × 25% = 12.5% for blue, yielding a color that's half as bright as the original.

Properties panel (**Figure 38b**). Choosing a blending mode from the menu applies it to the selected object.

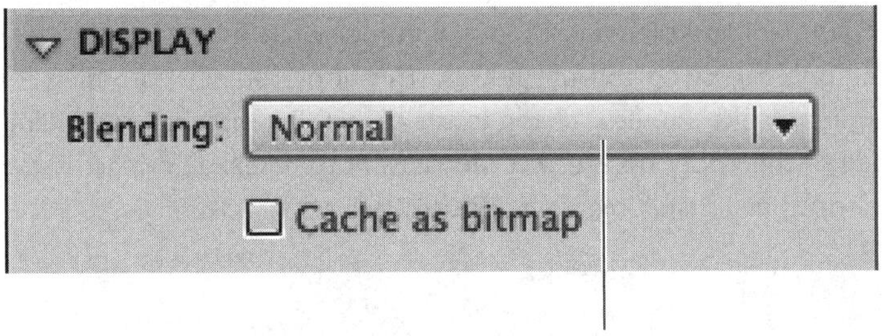

Blending menu

Figure 38b This menu appears in Properties only when a movie-clip instance is selected on the stage.

Blending modes work equally well whether the two objects are on different layers or are stacked on the same layer. The only limitation is that both objects *must* be instances of movie clips—if they're not, the Properties panel won't display the Blending menu. (If you want to blend a different kind of object—text, for example—convert it to a movie clip.)

Each blending mode has a precise technical description that you can read in Flash Help. However, only the most technically minded people find these descriptions useful in predicting what a blend will look like. Instead, when a blend is needed, most people try out all of the blending modes and see what happens with each. As you get more experienced with blending modes, you'll begin to know which modes are most likely to be useful for a particular pair of objects.

The Alpha and Erase blending modes deserve special attention because they're designed especially for masking. The masking feature in Flash (see #37) is limited to masks with hard edges, but the Alpha and Erase blending modes allow you to make masks with soft edges.

The following instructions assume that you know how to create symbols and convert objects to symbols (see #22). The symbol names here are just suggestions; you can call them whatever you want:

1. Create a movie-clip symbol and put something in it—for example, animation, a drawing, a bitmap, or text. This is the content that's going to be masked, so name the symbol *m_masked*.

2. Drag an instance of m_masked from the library to the stage.

3. Select the instance of m_masked and choose Modify > Convert to Symbol. (Obviously m_masked is already a symbol, but this step nests the instance inside a new symbol.) In the Convert to Symbol dialog box, click the Movie Clip radio button, name the symbol *m_sandwich*, and click OK.

4. Double-click the symbol m_sandwich in the library to put it into editing mode. The symbol's timeline should have one layer and one keyframe containing an instance of m_masked. Lock the layer.

5. Add a new layer above the existing layer on m_sandwich's timeline. Flash inserts a blank keyframe.

6. With the blank keyframe selected, use the Rectangle tool to make a rectangle slightly larger than the content in m_masked. Fill the rectangle with the standard black-and-white radial gradient (the one that appears on all of the color menus in Flash). The filled rectangle will cover up the instance of m_masked, but that's okay.

7. Select the rectangle's fill. The radial gradient is now available for editing.

8. Open the Color panel (if it's not already open) and click the white color tab on the gradient slider.

9. Just above the gradient slider is an Alpha control set to 100%. Use the slider or type in a value to bring Alpha down to 0%.

10. Deselect the rectangle on the stage. You can now see m_masked through the transparent portion of the gradient.

(continued on next page)

11. Using the gradient slider and/or the Gradient Transform tool, modify the gradient so that it neatly frames m_masked (**Figure 38c**).

Gradient used as a mask (m_mask) ——————

Masked content (m_masked) ——————

Figure 38c The movie clip m_mask, on the top layer, frames the content in m_masked, on the bottom layer.

12. Deselect the rectangle on the stage. You can now see m_masked through the white portion of the gradient.

13. Reselect the rectangle and choose Modify > Convert to Symbol to convert it to a movie clip. Name the movie clip *m_mask*.

14. The rectangle (now an instance of m_mask) should still be selected. From the Blending menu in Properties, choose Erase.

The mask disappears temporarily, but that's OK. The Erase blending mode has invisibly "erased" the areas of m_masked that are covered by the more opaque portions of the mask.

15. Click Scene 1 on the breadcrumb trail to return to the main timeline. The instance of m_sandwich should still be on the stage.

16. Select the instance of m_sandwich if it's not already selected. From the Blending menu in Properties, choose Layer.

The content of m_masked is now framed by a soft-edged mask. If you wish, put some sort of background behind it to complete the effect (**Figure 38d**).

Figure 38d A cloud-filled background completes the effect. The Layer blending mode applied to m_sandwich allows the background to show through.

An alternate technique is to lower the alpha of the black in Steps 8 and 9, leaving the alpha of the white at 100%. In this case, you'd use the Alpha blending mode instead of Erase in Step 14.

#39 Using (and Not Using) Scenes

Scenes are a prominent part of the Flash interface. There's a Scene panel; there's an Edit Scene menu (identified by a Hollywood clapper board icon) right above the timeline; and whenever you're in group-editing or symbol-editing mode, you follow the breadcrumb trail back to Scene 1. Naturally, you want to know what scenes are and how to use them.

There's one catch: *Nobody* uses scenes anymore. Even Adobe recommends that you not use them.

The original idea was that scenes would be a convenient way to organize the timeline. If you were working with a long movie, you wouldn't have to scroll through thousands of frames; you could just divide the movie into short, manageable scenes. The default, when you opened a new document in Flash, was Scene 1; you then had the option of adding Scene 2, Scene 3, and so on. When you played the movie's SWF file, Flash would concatenate the scenes into a single movie, in numerical order. (If you wanted to, you could even give the scenes descriptive names and rearrange their order; that's what the Scene panel is for.)

There are, however, several drawbacks to using scenes:

- No matter how efficiently you divide your movie into scenes, they still add up to one very long SWF file. If your movie is posted on the Web, anybody who watches it has to download that large file, even if they don't intend to see the whole movie.

- Scenes are confusing in collaborative environments. If you give someone a FLA file to edit, and it's divided into scenes, that person has no way of getting a bird's-eye view of the structure and organization of your movie. Instead of setting the timeline's cell size to Tiny and seeing most or all of the timeline at once, the person has to go through the movie scene by scene.

- People tend to write their ActionScript scripts as if the current scene is the entire movie, thereby introducing coding errors that are sometimes difficult to debug. In theory, ActionScript works fine with scenes, but keeping track of scene names and numbers adds an unnecessary level of complexity to scripts.

A good alternative to using scenes is to structure your movie as a series of short, individual FLA files. With a line of simple ActionScript, you can instruct each movie to start playing the next one when it ends, so the end result looks the same to the user. But the user gets to download several small SWF files instead of one large one. In fact, you could post individual links to each file in the series, so users need only download the parts of your movie that they want to see.

A collection of FLA files doesn't solve the problem of working in a collaborative environment, where what's in each FLA file is no more apparent than what's in each scene. However, you can have several FLA files open and visible at the same time. With a single FLA file, you can only see one scene at a time.

CHAPTER SIX

Creating Tweened Animation

Thanks to a process called *tweening*, not all animation has to be drawn frame by frame. If you give Flash two keyframes—one showing the way an object looks at the start of a sequence, and the other showing what it looks like at the end—Flash can compare the keyframes, analyze the differences between them, and gradually change one to the other by generating a series of in-between frames.

There are two kinds of tweens: *shape* and *motion*. Both types accomplish similar tasks, but they are suited to different types of objects: Shape tweens are used to animate editable paths; motion tweens are used primarily to animate instances of symbols. You'll be grateful for the amount of time you save when you get into the habit of using tweens.

#40 Creating Shape Tweens

Shape tweening provides an automated way to change an object gradually from one shape to another—a process sometimes known as *morphing*. Shape tweening can also be used to make gradual changes in an object's size, position, orientation, color, and opacity.

These are the basic steps for setting up a shape tween:

1. Draw an object on the stage in an empty keyframe. (Don't group the object or convert it to a symbol. Shape tweens work only with editable paths, primitive shapes, or Drawing Objects.)

2. Decide on a duration for the shape tween, and calculate in which cell of the timeline the last keyframe should fall. (For example, if your frame rate is 15 fps, and you want the tween to take 3 seconds, the last keyframe should be 45 frames after the first keyframe.) Select that cell.

3. Press F6. Flash fills the in-between cells with regular frames, creates a new keyframe in the selected cell, and copies the object from the preceding keyframe into it.

4. With the second keyframe still selected, modify the object. You can reshape it, move it to a different place on the stage, transform it with the Free Transform tool, change its color or opacity, or do any combination of those things.

5. Select the first keyframe again. (This will also work if you select one of the intermediate frames, but selecting the first frame is recommended.)

6. Choose Insert > Shape Tween. The frames between the two keyframes turn green, and an arrow points from the first keyframe to the last (**Figure 40a**). The arrow is your confirmation that you have a working shape tween.

If you see a dotted line instead of an arrow, it means your tween is broken. See #46 for suggestions about how to fix it.

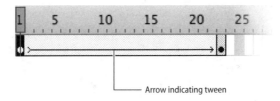

Arrow indicating tween

Figure 40a Choosing Shape Tween from the Insert menu causes the two keyframes to be connected by a right-pointing arrow on a green background.

7. Scrub through or preview the movie. You'll see that in each tweened frame, the object in the first keyframe incrementally takes on the characteristics of the object in the second keyframe (**Figure 40b**).

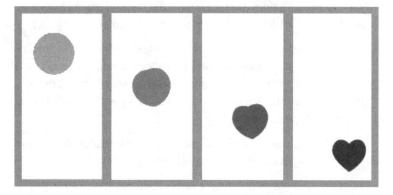

Figure 40b Shape, size, position, orientation, color, and opacity can all be tweened at once.

Shape tweens can be wild or tame (**Figure 40c**). Wild shape tweens are fun to watch because of the interesting patterns they produce; tame shape tweens are better for more realistic types of movement.

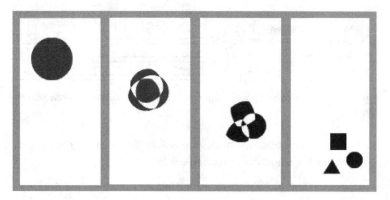

Figure 40c Figure 40b is an example of a tame shape tween; here is an example of a wild one.

(continued on next page)

Tweaking Tweens

Shape tweens are easily adjustable. If the timing doesn't seem right, you can extend or shorten a shape tween by dragging either or both of its keyframes. Flash automatically adjusts the rate of change in the intermediate frames.

If you want to add more nuance to a shape tween—for example, you want an object to shift direction as it moves from one point to another, or you want the rate of change to increase midway through— you can add keyframes within the tween. Select any of the intermediate frames and press F6; then make whatever changes you want in the new keyframe.

If wild shape tweens are what you want, here are some things to try:

- Make the object in the first keyframe and the object in the second keyframe as different as possible. In fact, instead of pressing F6 in Step 3, you can press F7, draw an entirely new object in the second keyframe, and then watch how Flash tweens one into the other.

- Have different numbers of objects in the two keyframes. This sort of tween is especially common with text—for example, morphing the word *no* (two objects) into *yes* (three objects). Keep in mind, though, that if you want to shape-tween text, you first have to break it apart into editable paths (see #20).

If you prefer tame, controlled shape tweens—as most serious animators do—you might consider the following suggestions:

- Tween only one object per layer. Remember that Flash considers the stroke and the fill to be separate objects. If your path has both, move the stroke and the fill to different layers, and tween them separately but simultaneously (**Figure 40d**). Alternatively, you could use a Drawing Object, in which Flash considers the stroke and fill to be part of a single object.

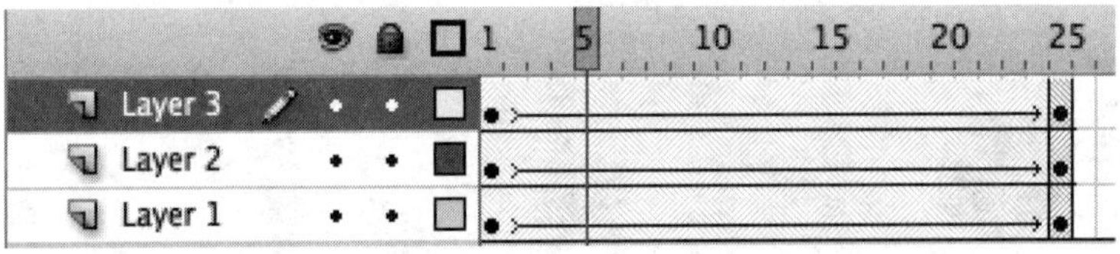

Figure 40d It's fine to have several shape tweens happening simultaneously on different layers.

- Simplify each object as much as possible. The fewer anchor points there are, the smoother the tween will be.

- Use shape hints, which are explained in #41.

#41 Using Shape Hints

Shape tweens are notoriously unpredictable. It may be clear to *you* what the most logical way is to morph one object into another, but that doesn't mean it's apparent to Flash. Even a simple transformation may take place in a way you don't expect (**Figure 41a**).

Figure 41a When a circle morphs into a square, we'd expect the four corners of the square to sprout directly from the circle. Instead, Flash rotates the circle as it becomes a square, making the transition less appealing.

To help with this issue, Flash provides tools called *shape hints.* Shape hints always come in pairs: one to mark a point on a path in the first keyframe of a tween, the other to mark the corresponding point on the path in the second keyframe. You can use shape hints as follows:

1. Select the first keyframe of the tween.

2. Choose Modify > Shape > Add Shape Hint. A red circle with the letter *a* on it appears in the center of the object.

3. Drag the shape hint to the first point you want to mark—in this case, the upper-left edge of the circle. When you release the shape hint, you should see it snap into place (**Figure 41b**).

   If there's no obvious snap, it means you may not have dragged the shape hint fully onto the path. Try dragging it and dropping it again.

Figure 41b Snap the first shape hint to the first object in the tween; then snap the second shape hint to a corresponding point on the second object.

(continued on next page)

4. Select the second keyframe of the tween. An identical red circle with the letter *a* on it is in the center of the object.

5. Drag this second shape hint to the point that corresponds to the point you marked in Step 3—in this case, the upper-left corner of the square. Once again, let it snap into place.

If everything has been done correctly, this shape hint should turn from red to green, and the first shape hint should turn from red to yellow. If the shape hints are not yet yellow and green, repeat the drag-and-snap process until they are.

6. Preview the movie to see whether the shape tween now does what you want. (In many cases—including this one—it won't. Often one pair of shape hints is not enough.) (**Figure 41c**)

Figure 41c Even after we add shape hints, Flash still doesn't get it.

If necessary, repeat the entire process to add a second pair of shape hints (**Figure 41d**). Flash labels the second pair with the letter *b*, the third with the letter *c*, and so on.

Tip
If you add multiple shape hints, be sure to keep the shape hints in order as you work around the perimeter of the object.

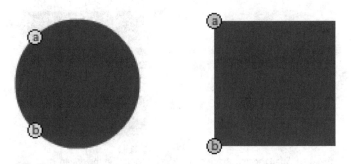

Figure 41d In most cases, multiple shape hints work most effectively when added in a counterclockwise direction form the upper-left corner.

In the example of the circle morphing into the square, using two pairs of shape hints is sufficient (**Figure 41e**). In other cases, more may be needed.

Figure 41e Adding a second pair of shape hints solves the problem.

In general, if five or six pairs of shape hints don't get you the result you want, it's unlikely that adding more shape hints will help. In this case, you might consider deleting the shape tween entirely and trying a new one with simpler paths.

#42 Creating Motion Tweens

Motion tweens can accomplish many of the same things that shape tweens can (see #40). Here are the significant differences:

- Motion tweens work only with text objects and instances of symbols.

- Motion tweens can change an object's position, size, orientation, color, and opacity, but they can't morph one object into another as shape tweens can.

- Unlike a shape tween, which can include multiple objects in a single keyframe, a motion tween works with only one object at a time. If you want to motion-tween several objects simultaneously, each must be tweened separately on a separate layer.

- Motion tweens are more predictable, more reliable, and less processor-intensive than shape tweens. If you have the option of using either a shape tween or a motion tween to achieve the same effect, use the motion tween.

To create a motion tween:

1. Place an instance of a symbol on the stage in an empty keyframe. Make sure that either the object (on the stage) or the keyframe (in the timeline) remains selected.

2. Choose Insert > Motion Tween. In the timeline, a series of frames—beginning with the selected keyframe—turns blue to represent the motion tween.

   The default length of a tween is one second, but you can change that by dragging the last frame of the tween forward or backward.

3. Move the playhead to any frame within the tween. On the stage, change one or more of the object's properties (including position, color, and so on). The corresponding frame in the timeline becomes a *property keyframe*, indicated by a small black diamond (**Figure 42a**).

   Repeat this step as many times as you like.

A Note to Old-Timers

If you've used earlier versions of Flash, you may be startled when you try to set up a motion tween in Flash CS4. Previously, the steps for creating shape tweens and motion tweens were substantially the same. Now, motion tweening requires a whole new way of working: Flash creates a standard-length motion tween from a single keyframe; additional keyframes within a tween appear automatically without your having to press F6; and motion guides no longer require a separate layer. Even the familiar arrow in the timeline is gone.

If the old way worked fine, why did Adobe make such drastic changes? Here are some reasons:

- The old way didn't *really* work fine. Broken motion tweens, which were a frequent and frustrating problem, have been eliminated.

- The new way is simpler: It brings together motion tweens, motion guides, and Timeline Effects into a single, consistent interface.

(continued on next page)

Creating Tweened Animation

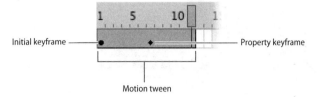

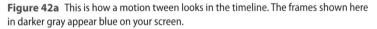

Initial keyframe ——————— ● ———— ◆ —————— Property keyframe

Motion tween

Figure 42a This is how a motion tween looks in the timeline. The frames shown here in darker gray appear blue on your screen.

4. Scrub through or preview the movie to see the motion tween in action.

When you drag a motion-tweened object to a different place on the stage, Flash connects the object's new location to its previous location with a thin, colored line called a *motion path*. The motion path is marked with a series of dots representing the number of frames in which the movement takes place. If you lengthen or shorten a tween by dragging its last frame in the timeline, the number of dots changes accordingly.

By default, a motion-tweened object moves in a straight line. To change the straight motion path to a curve, drag it from the middle with the Selection tool (**Figure 42b**), just as you do with the straight outlines of editable objects (see #6). If you're comfortable working with the Pen tool, you can also reshape the line segment by treating its endpoints as the anchor points of a Bézier curve (see #12).

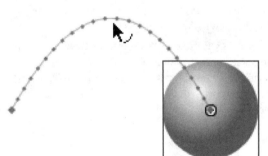

Figure 42b You can change a straight motion path to a curved path by dragging with the Selection tool.

Creating a motion tween causes the layer the motion tween is on to become a *tween layer*. Unlike a regular layer, a tween layer can hold only one object at a time, and only if that object is motion-tweened. It's possible to put several motion-tweened objects on one layer, but only if each tween ends before the next one begins (**Figure 42c**).

- Flash now looks and works more like other motion-oriented applications from Adobe, such as Premiere Pro, After Effects, and Director.

For the sake of flexibility, Flash still allows you to make old-style motion tweens, now called *classic tweens* (see #45). But don't use that as an excuse to avoid learning the new procedures—those *classic tweens* most likely won't be around forever.

118

Back in Black

It's a cinematic tradition to have the first scene of a movie fade up from a black screen, and the last scene fade to black. An easy way to achieve these effects in Flash is to create a graphic symbol of a black rectangle and to place an instance of it in the timeline so it covers everything on the stage. At the beginning of the movie, you can motion-tween the rectangle from full opacity to zero opacity; then do the opposite at the end.

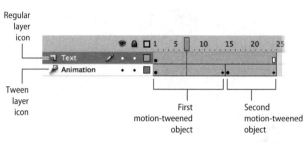

Regular layer icon

Tween layer icon

First motion-tweened object

Second motion-tweened object

Figure 42c A tween layer has a distinctive icon in the timeline. The layer can hold multiple motion-tweened objects, but only one at a time.

Looking Out for Number One

A tween layer can hold only one object at a time. What happens, then, if you have several objects in a single keyframe and attempt to motion-tween them?

- If two or more of the objects are selected, Flash displays a dialog box asking whether you want to convert the selected objects into a symbol. Clicking OK causes those objects to be motion-tweened as a single instance of a new symbol.

- If only one of the objects is selected, and it's an object that can be motion-tweened (such as a group or an instance of a symbol), Flash motion-tweens that object. At the same time, Flash creates a new layer and moves the remaining objects into a new keyframe on that layer.

- If only one of the objects is selected, and it's an object that *can't* be motion-tweened (such an editable shape), Flash displays a dialog box asking whether you want to convert the object into a symbol. Clicking OK causes the selected object to be converted and motion-tweened; the remaining objects are moved into a new keyframe on a new layer.

#43 Setting Motion Tween Properties

Flash allows you to enhance a motion tween in several ways. When you select a motion tween in the timeline by clicking anywhere within it, the following controls appear in Properties:

- **Ease.** By default, a tween moves at a constant speed. The Ease control allows you to vary the speed by choosing a number from –100 to 100. A negative number represents "easing in," in which the tweened object starts moving slowly and gradually speeds up; a positive number represents "easing out," in which the object starts quickly and gradually slows down. The differences in speed are reflected in the spacing of the dots along the motion path: Dots that are closer together represent slower movement; dots that are farther apart represent faster movement (**Figure 43a**).

Ease in   Ease out

Figure 43a The spacing of the dots along a motion path indicates variations in the speed of the tween.

- **Rotation.** The Rotation Count and Additional Rotation controls determine how many times the tweened object rotates between the start and the end of the tween (**Figure 43b**). The default Rotation Count setting is 0—no rotation—but you can set the number of rotations as high as you like.

Tip
Flash needs several frames to animate the rotation of an object. Therefore, it's best to limit the number of rotations to less than one-third of the number of frames in the tween.

(continued on next page)

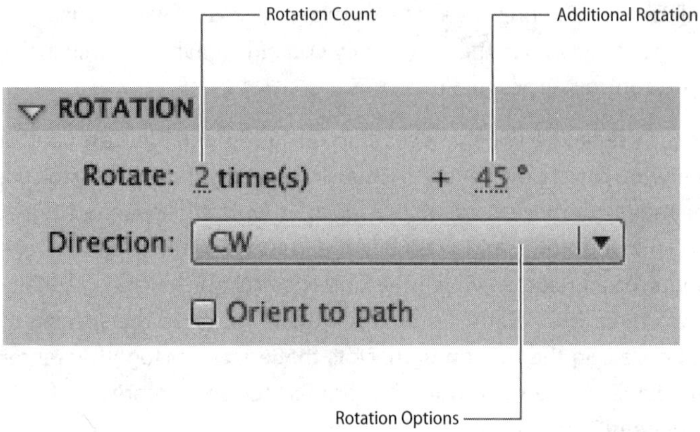

Rotation Count   Additional Rotation

▽ **ROTATION**

Rotate: <u>2</u> time(s)   +   <u>45</u> °

Direction: | CW | ▼ |

☐ Orient to path

Rotation Options

Figure 43b The Rotation controls.

The Additional Rotation control allows you to specify a partial rotation. For example, if you want the tweened object to rotate two-and-a-half times, you can set the Rotation Count to 2 and Additional Rotation to 180 degrees. (A full rotation is 360 degrees.) The direction of the rotation may be set on the Rotation Options menu.

Selecting the Orient to Path option causes the tweened object to "face forward" along the motion path the way a car would follow a road (**Figure 43c**). With this option deselected, the object keeps a constant orientation regardless of the direction of the path.

Oriented to path   Not oriented to path

Figure 43c Left: a motion tween with Orient to Path turned on. Right: the same tween with Orient to Path turned off.

- **Path.** These four controls allow you to change the horizontal position, vertical position, width, and height of the motion path. To keep the width and height in proportion to one another, click the link icon to the left of the width control.

- **Options.** The Sync Graphic Symbols option affects the behavior of graphic symbols that contain animation (see #36). If several symbol instances are tweened sequentially on a single layer (see Figure 42c in #42), selecting this option keeps the instances in step with one another. Let's say you have two graphic symbols, each of which contains 36 frames of animation. If an instance of the first symbol is motion-tweened in the timeline for 24 frames, followed immediately by a tweened instance of the second symbol, selecting Sync Graphic Symbols causes the second instance's internal animation to begin playing from frame 25 rather than from frame 1.

#44 Using the Motion Editor

As you learned in #42, the changes you make to a motion-tweened object's properties are marked by property keyframes. The Motion Editor, a new feature in Flash CS4, allows you to assign property keyframes, not just to an object's position on the stage, but also to the object's scale, skew, color effects, filters, and rate of easing (**Figure 44a**). You can access the Motion Editor by clicking its tab in the Timeline panel.

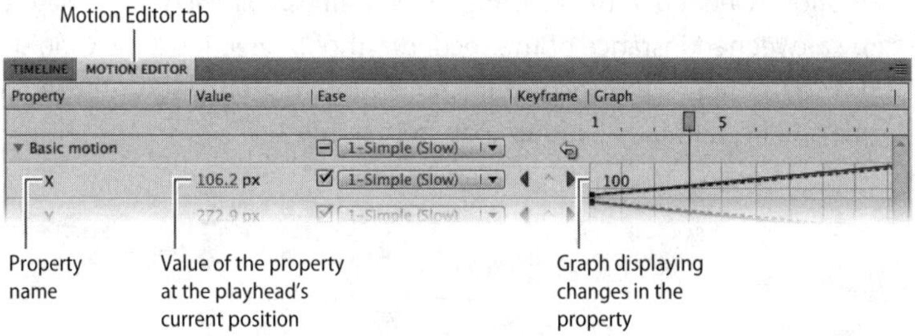

Motion Editor tab

Property name

Value of the property at the playhead's current position

Graph displaying changes in the property

Figure 44a The Motion Editor provides independent controls for each of a motion tween's properties.

Each property in the Motion Editor is accompanied by a graph—essentially a miniature timeline—displaying the changes in that property. You can drag the playhead through the graph and watch the results on the stage, just as you would with the full timeline.

Tip
To enlarge the graph for a particular property, click the property name in the Motion Editor. Only one graph can be enlarged at a time.

A property that remains unchanged is indicated by a horizontal line in the graph. By right-clicking (Windows) or Command-clicking (Mac) anywhere along that line, you reveal a contextual menu containing an Add Keyframe command (**Figure 44b**). Choosing that command inserts a property keyframe at the point where you clicked. Dragging the property keyframe upward increases the setting for that property; dragging it downward decreases it. (If you prefer, you can adjust the setting by typing or selecting a number in the Value column.)

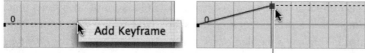

Property keyframe has been dragged upward ⎤

Figure 44b Choosing Add Keyframe from the contextual menu (left) inserts a draggable property keyframe (right).

By default, property keyframes in the graph are connected by straight lines. Changing those lines to curves causes a property's value to accelerate or decelerate—similar to easing in or easing out—instead of increasing or decreasing linearly. To make this change, right-click (Windows) or Command-click (Mac) a property keyframe and choose Smooth Point from the contextual menu (**Figure 44c**). Flash adds direction lines and direction points to the keyframe, allowing you to treat it as the anchor point of a Bézier curve (see #12).

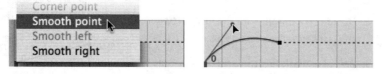

Figure 44c Choosing Smooth Point from the contextual menu (left) adds direction points to a property keyframe (right). Dragging a direction point turns the adjacent line into a curve.

Each property in the Motion Editor can be adjusted independently. Keyframes and settings for one property don't have to correspond to those for any of the other properties; even the use of easing can differ (**Figure 44d**).

Figure 44d The realistic flip of a coin on the stage (left) is made possible by an assortment of property settings in the Motion Editor (right). Dotted lines indicate that easing is in effect.

Easing with Ease

While the Properties panel allows only the choice of easing in or easing out (see #43), the Motion Editor offers many more types of easing, including fun settings such as Spring and Bounce. You can choose as many types as you want from the Add Ease menu (whose icon looks like a plus sign) in the Eases section of the Motion Editor. You can even select Custom and design your own easing style.

All the types of easing you've chosen—including any custom eases—are made available on the menus in the Ease column of the Motion Editor, allowing you to apply them to any property you like.

#45 Working with Classic Tweens

Flash offers an alternative technique for creating motion tweens that's similar to the process for creating shape tweens (see #40). Tweens created in this way are called *classic tweens*, because they are the only type of motion tween supported by prior versions of Flash.

Those of you who use Flash to do character animation—which traditionally is executed initially as a series of keyframes, with the in-between frames added later—may find that classic tweens fit your workflow better than the new-style motion tweens. However, using classic tweens has some significant drawbacks. The Motion Editor doesn't work with classic tweens; a tween's motion path isn't visible or editable on the stage; and the Path controls aren't available in Properties. Most important, classic tweens are more likely than their newer counterparts to have things go wrong. Some common problems are dealt with in #46.

Here are the usual steps for setting up a classic tween:

1. Place an instance of a symbol on the stage in an empty keyframe. (The tween won't work if the keyframe contains more than one object.)

2. Decide on a duration for the motion tween, and select the cell in which the last keyframe should fall.

3. Press F6. Flash fills the in-between cells with regular frames, creates a new keyframe in the selected cell, and copies the object from the preceding keyframe into it.

   Note
   In order for a classic tween to work, the objects in both keyframes must be instances of the same symbol.

4. With the second keyframe still selected, modify the object. You can move it to a different place on the stage, transform it using the Free Transform tool, change its color or opacity with the Style menu in Properties, or do any combination of those things.

5. Select the first keyframe again. (As with shape tweens, the process will work if you select one of the intermediate frames, but selecting the first frame is recommended.)

6. Choose Insert > Classic Tween. The frames between the two keyframes turn blue (not green, as with a shape tween), and an arrow points from the first keyframe to the last.

Creating Tweened Animation

7. Scrub through or preview the movie to see the classic tween in action.

When you tween an object from one location on the stage to another, the tweened object moves in a straight line. Since the Motion Editor doesn't work with classic tweens, the only way to make the object to follow a more interesting path is to use a feature called a *motion guide*.

To create a motion guide:

1. Tween an object from one point to another. It doesn't matter where the object starts and ends; you'll adjust that later.

2. Right-click (Windows) or Control-click (Mac) the layer in the timeline that contains the tweened object, and choose Add Classic Motion Guide from the contextual menu. A new layer appears, with the layer you selected indented beneath it (**Figure 45a**).

The new layer's icon indicates that it's a specialized type of layer called a *guide layer*. The layer containing your tweened object has become a *guided* layer.

Guide layer ——— Guide: Football
Guided layer ——— Football
Goalpost

Figure 45a The timeline looks like this when it contains a guide layer.

3. Select the empty keyframe at the beginning of the guide layer.

4. On the stage, draw the path you'd like the tweened object to follow. You can draw it with any tool, but the Pencil or Pen is recommended.

5. Drag the tweened object to one end of the motion guide and snap it to the guide (**Figure 45b**).

The snapping maneuver is tricky. Try to drag the object by its registration point and drop it a short distance inward from the beginning of the path.

(continued on next page)

Guidance Counselor

The technical requirements for a motion guide are loose: The path can be any length and any shape; it can be open or closed; and it can be drawn with any tool. However, there are some things you can do to make a motion guide more effective and easier to use:

- Make sure the motion guide is a single path with no gaps.

- Simplify the path as much as possible. Use the Smooth or Optimize commands to get rid of sharp corners and unnecessary anchor points.

- Don't allow the path to cross over itself.

- Lock or hide the guide layer when you're working on other parts of the movie. (The motion guide functions even if it's locked or hidden.)

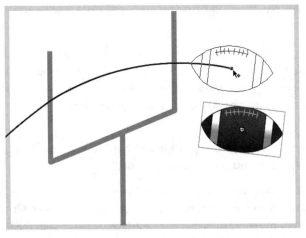

Figure 45b The registration point of a symbol instance is marked with a white circle. Grab the instance by that circle, and drop the circle precisely onto the motion guide.

6. Drag the playhead to the last keyframe of the tween and snap the object to the other end of the motion guide.

7. Scrub through or preview the movie. Instead of traveling in a straight line, the tweened object should follow the motion guide. If it doesn't, try repeating Steps 5 and 6 a few more times.

By default, the tweened object maintains the same orientation no matter where it moves along the path. If you'd prefer that the object vary its orientation, always staying perpendicular to the portion of the path it's on, select Orient to Path in Properties.

#46 Repairing Tweens

Every so often, when you create a shape tween or classic tween, the timeline fails to display the confirming arrow on a green or blue background; it displays a dashed line instead (**Figure 46**). The dashed line indicates that there's something wrong with the tween. Despite notifying you of the problem, Flash won't tell you *why* the tween is broken. Diagnosing and fixing the problem is left to you.

Figure 46 This dashed line indicates that a tween is broken.

Here are some of the most common causes of broken tweens:

- The first or last keyframe of the tween is empty.

- You've tried to shape-tween groups or symbols, or you've tried to make a classic tween with editable paths.

- In a classic tween, the object in the first keyframe and the object in the last keyframe are different.

- You've tried to classic-tween more than one object on a single layer.

The last of these causes is often the most frustrating, because it's not always obvious. At some point, without realizing it, you may have made a stray mark with the Pencil tool or failed to erase a path fully, leaving a tiny, unnoticeable object on the stage. If such an object is hiding out in the first or last keyframe of a classic tween, the tween will fail.

If you suspect that a barely visible object is what's breaking your tween, here's an easy way to solve the problem:

1. Move the playhead to the first keyframe of the tween.

2. On the stage, select the object that's being tweened.

3. Choose Edit > Cut. The tweened object disappears.

4. In the timeline, look at the color of the circle in the keyframe. If it's white, then the object you just cut was the only object in the keyframe. You can skip to Step 7. But if the circle is black, it means that

(continued on next page)

Boulevard of Broken Tweens

Because broken tweens are often difficult to diagnose and repair, many people handle them in an understandable way: they ignore them. In some cases, even though Flash displays a dashed line in the timeline, the tween seems to work anyway, so the animator leaves well enough alone. In other cases, when the tween doesn't work at all, the animator just conveniently forgets that there was a tween there in the first place.

It's never a good idea to leave a broken tween in a FLA file; the dashed line in the timeline may be a sign of more fundamental corruption in the file. If none of the suggestions here are effective, you might try the clean-slate approach: Delete the tweened material and rebuild that portion of the movie from scratch.

the keyframe isn't empty, and that there must be something else occupying the keyframe.

5. Click the keyframe in the timeline. Doing so selects all the objects in the keyframe.

6. Press Delete to clear the unwanted objects out of the keyframe. The circle in the keyframe turns white, indicating that the keyframe is empty.

7. Choose Edit > Paste in Place to return the original tweened object to the stage.

8. Look at the tween in the timeline. If the dashed line has been replaced by an arrow, you've solved the problem. If not, go to the last keyframe of the tween and follow Steps 2 through 7 again.

Creating Tweened Animation

#47 Applying Filters

Filters are a powerful, yet easy way to add special effects to your movie. Flash offers seven filters: Drop Shadow, Blur, Glow, Bevel, Gradient Glow, Gradient Bevel, and Adjust Color. They can be applied to text objects or to instances of movie-clip or button symbols.

The simplest way to apply a filter is to select an appropriate object on the stage, go to the Filters section of the Properties panel, click the Add Filter icon, and choose a filter from the menu that appears (**Figure 47a**). You can then adjust the filter's settings as desired.

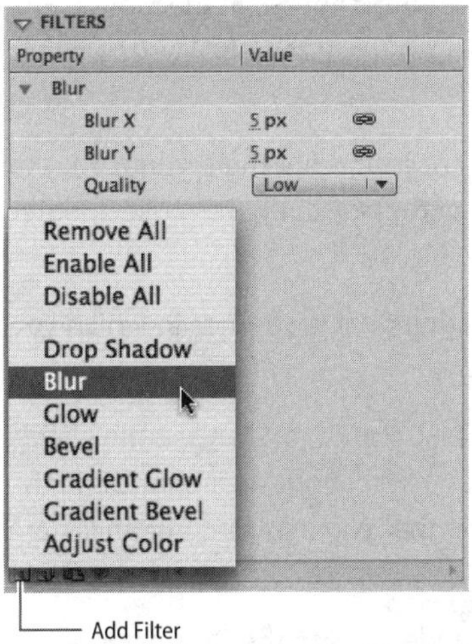

Figure 47a Clicking the Add Filter icon in Properties brings up a menu of filters.

However, to take full advantage of filters, you'll want to apply them to motion-tweened objects in the Motion Editor (see #44). Doing so allows you to change a filter's settings gradually over time (**Figure 47b**).

Figure 47b Flash tweens a filter's settings—in this case, the Glow filter.

(continued on next page)

Filters are a Drag

Although it's tempting to apply filters to objects, keep in mind that filters put heavy demands on the computer that plays back your SWF file. There are several things you can do to keep your filters from dragging down a computer's performance:

- Remove all unnecessary filters and unnecessary tweening of filters. Try to achieve the same effects through standard animation.

- Apply as few filters as possible to any single object.

- Set the quality for all your filters to Low.

- If an object has filters applied to it, keep the object still, or confine its movement to a small area of the stage.

- Whenever possible, avoid applying filters to objects that are rotating or being resized.

Filterpedia

Although each filter has different controls, there are some controls that appear more frequently than others. Here are some definitions and tips:

- **Blur X** and **Blur Y.** Normally, you'll want the amount of blurring to be the same both horizontally and vertically. If not, you can click the lock icon next to the Blur values, allowing each to be set independently.

- **Strength.** Strength is a combination of darkness and opacity. At 100% strength, all filters have some transparency around the edges; if you boost the strength over 100%, the transparency begins to disappear.

- **Quality.** The higher the quality setting, the more demands the filter makes on the computer's processor. In most cases, Low is sufficient.

- **Angle.** Three-dimensional effects such as Drop Shadow and Bevel depend on the illusion of light coming from a particular direction. The

(continued on next page)

To apply a filter in the Motion Editor:

1. Motion-tween a text object or an instance of a button or movie-clip symbol (see #42).

2. In the timeline or the Motion Editor, select the keyframe where you want the filter to begin.

3. In the Filters section of the Motion Editor, click the Add Filter icon (which looks like a plus sign) and choose a filter from the pop-up menu. The chosen filter and its associated controls appear in the Motion Editor, and the motion-tweened object on the stage displays the filter's effects.

4. Use the controls in the Motion Editor to modify the settings for the filter. As you do so, the appearance of the object on the stage updates in real time.

5. Repeat Steps 2 through 5 for any additional keyframes in which you want to change the filter's settings.

Most of the filter names are self-explanatory. (You can see the effects of each filter in **Figure 47c**, and you can learn about their controls in the "Filterpedia" sidebar.) However, the two that you may find unfamiliar are Gradient Glow and Gradient Bevel:

- **Gradient Glow.** This filter is almost identical to the Drop Shadow filter. The only significant difference is that while a drop shadow must be a uniform color, Gradient Glow allows you to make a multicolor shadow. You do this by using a gradient slider similar to the one in the Color panel (see #8).

- **Gradient Bevel.** Like the standard Bevel filter, Gradient Bevel gives an object a three-dimensional appearance by adding a highlight to one edge and a shadow to the opposite edge. The difference between them is that Bevel allows you to choose independent colors for the highlight and shadow, while Gradient Bevel requires both colors to be part of a single gradient.

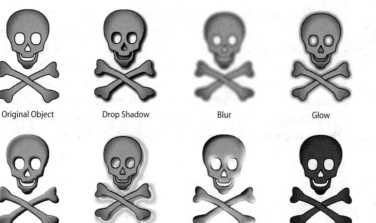

Original Object	Drop Shadow	Blur	Glow
Bevel	Gradient Glow	Gradient Bevel	Adjust Color

Figure 47c Typical effects of the seven filters are illustrated here.

You can add multiple filters to a single object. Each time you add a filter, its controls are added to the Motion Editor. To remove a filter, click the Remove Filter icon (a minus sign to the left of the Add Filter icon) and choose the filter's name from the pop-up menu.

default is for the light to come from the upper left, but you can change this with the Angle control.

- **Knockout.** Turning Knockout on causes the object to become invisible, leaving only the effect. Since Knockout is a toggle—it's either on or off—it can't be tweened.

- **Outer/Inner.** Outer causes the effect to radiate outward from the edge of the object; Inner causes it to radiate inward. For most filters, the Outer option looks better.

#48 Inverse Kinematics

As you've seen throughout this chapter, Flash gives you all the tools you need to make objects move. However, making an object move *in a natural way* is much more of a challenge, especially if that object has a complex internal structure—as do, for example, the bodies of humans and animals.

Experienced animators know that it's easier to animate the movement of an arm or a leg by dividing it into parts. To create a leg, for example, they might create symbols for an upper leg, a lower leg, a foot, and a toe, and then overlap the instances where the joints belong (**Figure 48a**).

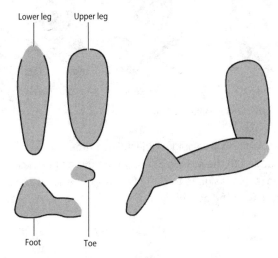

Lower leg   Upper leg

Foot   Toe

Figure 48a On the left, the symbols for parts of the leg; on the right, those symbols assembled into the leg's initial pose.

In previous versions of Flash, animating these instances would be a time-consuming process: In each keyframe, the animator would have to move and rotate each one individually, trying to maintain the illusion that they're all parts of a single leg. This traditional way of animating—maneuvering the upper leg, then repositioning the lower leg in a way that relates naturally to the upper leg, and so on—is known as *forward kinematics*.

A powerful new feature in Flash CS4 allows you to attach these pieces together so that they function mechanically as a single leg, complete with bones and joints. This movable, jointed model is called an *armature*. Once the armature is in place on the stage, you can drag one part of the leg— for example, the knee—and the rest of it will bend at the joints the way a real leg would. This time-saving animation technique is called *inverse kinematics*, or IK for short.

Let's imagine you want to use IK to animate a soccer player's leg kicking a ball. The steps are as follows:

1. As illustrated earlier in Figure 48a, create a symbol for each part of the leg.

2. Insert a keyframe in the timeline at the point where the animation is to begin. In that keyframe, place instances of the symbols on the stage, arranged in the way you want the leg to be posed at the start of the kick.

3. Select the Bone tool in the Tools panel (**Figure 48b**).

Figure 48b The Inverse Kinematics tools: Bone and Bind.

4. Click the upper leg at the point where you want its internal "bone" to begin; drag the mouse to the top of the lower leg, and release at the point where the knee should be.

(continued on next page)

Bone of My Bone

Bones in Flash are arranged in a hierarchical order. The first bone you create in an armature is known as the parent; the next bone is the first bone's *child*. Each successive bone you add is considered to be the child of the preceding bone.

Holding down the Shift key allows you to move a bone and its children without moving its parent. If you delete a bone, its children are deleted as well.

When you select a bone and edit its Rotation, X Translation, and Y Translation properties, you're affecting the properties of the joint that connects that bone with its parent. Since the last bone in the hierarchy has no children, you can't change the properties of its final joint. (For example, in the armature shown in Figure 48c, you can't constrain the rotation of the joint that connects the foot to the toe.) This deficiency will likely be fixed in a future version of Flash.

In a Bind

The IK example on this page uses bones to create an armature from a series of symbol instances. However, some animators prefer an alternative procedure: creating an armature from a single editable shape. For example, you could draw an entire leg with the Pencil tool, then use the Bone tool to draw a series of bones inside the leg. The resulting armature could be manipulated and animated just like a leg constructed from symbol instances.

The only drawback of this technique is that Flash has to guess which parts of the shape should be attached to which bones. The guesses it makes are surprisingly accurate, but occasionally you'll find that an editable shape takes on a deformed appearance when you drag its bones.

To deal with this problem, Flash offers a Bind tool (Figure 48b) that can assign individual anchor points to a particular bone. For example, suppose you want all the anchor points in the knee to be attached to the thigh

(continued on next page)

Flash displays the bone as an inverted triangle, with circles at each end representing the joints (**Figure 48c**). It also creates a specialized *pose layer* in the timeline and moves the two newly connected instances to a keyframe in that layer. (The layer is labeled Armature_1 by default, but you can rename it to whatever you like.)

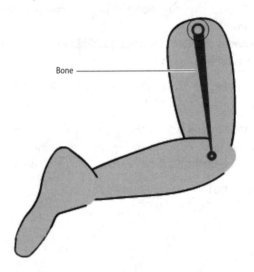

Bone

Figure 48c This is how Flash displays a bone on the stage.

5. Repeat Step 4 twice more: once to add a bone connecting the knee and the ankle, and once to add a bone connecting the ankle and the toe. The newly connected instances join the others in the Armature_1 layer.

6. Click the Selection tool in the Tools panel. Test the armature by dragging it from various points and seeing how it responds. You'll notice that the leg bends at the joints, but not in a realistic way; for example, the knee offers much more freedom of movement than a real knee would.

Creating Tweened Animation

7. With the Selection tool still active, click the bone in the lower leg. In the Joint Rotation section of the Properties panel, select Constrain to limit the knee's range of motion. Flash fills in default values of –45 and 45 degrees, but you can change those values to whatever you like. (In this case, 0 and 90 degrees might be more appropriate.) A small arc superimposed on the joint indicates the range of motion graphically (**Figure 48d**).

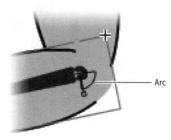

Arc

Figure 48d This arc illustrates the knee joint's range of motion.

8. Repeat Step 7—this time on the foot—to constrain the motion of the ankle joint.

Note

Flash also permits you to enable X Translation and Y Translation, which allow a bone to move away from the bone it's connected to. (Constraining these properties limits the distance the bone can travel.) In this example, however, both properties should remain disabled to keep the leg intact.

9. In the Armature_1 layer of the timeline, click in the frame in which you want the animation of the armature to end. Press F5 to insert a series of frames connecting that frame to the initial keyframe.

10. Right-click (Windows) or Control-click (Mac) the last frame in the series and choose Insert Pose from the contextual menu.

(continued on next page)

bone (where the default is for some of them to be attached to the thigh bone and others to the shin bone). You can click the Bind tool in the Tools panel, click an anchor point in the knee, and then click the thigh bone; then repeat that procedure for the other anchor points in the knee.

It's Alive!

Do you enjoy dragging the parts of an armature and watching the armature bend and flex? You can give your audience the same experience. Make sure that the armature is constructed from movie clip symbols only; make sure also that the armature's layer in the timeline contains only one pose. Then select the entire armature by clicking one of its frames in the timeline, and choose Runtime from the Type menu in the Properties panel. When you create a SWF file from the movie, anyone who views the movie can drag to reshape the armature in whatever way they like.

11. Reshape the armature to pose the leg in the way you want it to look at the end of the kick. Flash tweens the animation, repositioning the leg gradually from its pose in the first keyframe to its pose in the last frame (**Figure 48e**).

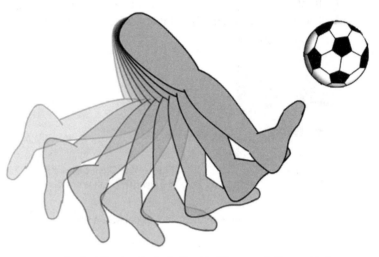

Figure 48e The final IK animation looks like this. (The soccer ball was added on a separate layer and motion-tweened.)

Creating Tweened Animation

CHAPTER SEVEN

Working with Imported Artwork

Flash has a versatile set of drawing tools, but they may not always be enough to meet your needs. Perhaps you're not very good at drawing from scratch, and you find it helpful to bring in outside images and trace them. Perhaps you prefer the tools in Fireworks or Illustrator and want to create your drawings in those programs. Perhaps you want to use bitmap images such as photographs or scanned artwork.

For reasons such as these, Flash lets you import artwork in a variety of vector and bitmap formats. In many cases, you can even modify the artwork in Flash. Thanks to the program's flexible import capabilities, you can be an animator without drawing a single stroke.

#**49** Using Bridge to Connect with Other Applications

Before you can import artwork, you first have to figure out what you want to import. You may need to sort through hundreds of files on your hard drive, preview them in Photoshop or Illustrator, rate their suitability, and gather together the ones you decide to use.

Doing these things becomes easier when you use Bridge, a versatile file manager-viewer called Bridge (**Figure 49**). Bridge isn't part of Flash; it's a separate program that's accessible from any CS4 application by choosing File > Browse in Bridge.

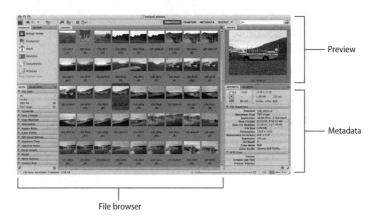

Preview

Metadata

File browser

Figure 49 This is the default Bridge workspace. Like the Flash workspace, it can be reconfigured in different ways for different purposes.

Bridge is the glue that ties Creative Suite together. Instead of trying to describe everything Bridge can do, we'll just look at the simplest features—the ones you can use right away with no learning curve:

• You can navigate to any folder on your computer or network and instantly see thumbnails of nearly all the visual content—not just bitmap images and vector drawings, but even video files and PDFs.

• You can select any one of the thumbnails and see what's inside it without opening the file. A Preview panel at the upper-right corner of the Bridge window lets you preview artwork and even watch movies and animation. (The viewer doesn't support FLA files, but it can preview SWF files.)

- A Metadata panel below the Preview panel gives you information about the selected file, including its name, type, creation date, and size. Depending on the type of file and where it came from, there may be other information as well, such as who took a photo and what kind of camera it was taken with.

- If you find a file that you want to import into Flash, you can drag it from the Bridge window directly onto the Flash stage. The appropriate Import dialog box appears, just as if you had chosen File > Import from the menu (see #50).

Creative Suite includes another "meta-application" besides Bridge: Version Cue, a workflow manager designed for multi-user environments. It ensures, for example, that if one person is editing a FLA file, nobody else can edit the same file at the same time. Setting up and maintaining a Version Cue server is usually the job of computer professionals, which puts it outside the scope of this book.

When you begin to import files, you'll see that membership in the Creative Suite gives Flash another benefit: integration with Illustrator, Photoshop and Fireworks that makes it possible to move artwork from one program to another with minimal loss of information or functionality. (Import options for those programs are covered in #50 through #52.) Adobe has enhanced this integration with each new release, moving closer to the goal of making Flash, Photoshop, Bridge, and the other members of the suite work together as if they're all parts of a single program.

#50 Importing from Adobe Illustrator

Although the drawing tools in Flash are easy for beginners to learn, many experienced artists and designers prefer to create their vector drawings in Illustrator. The usual ways to bring Illustrator artwork into Flash are to copy and paste it directly from Illustrator, or to save it in Adobe Illustrator (AI) format and import it into Flash.

Let's look at the copy-and-paste technique first. You can select individual objects or entire layers from an Illustrator document and choose Edit > Copy to copy the selection to the computer's clipboard; then switch to Flash and choose Edit > Paste in Place or Edit > Paste in Center. A dialog box appears with the following options:

- **Paste as Bitmap.** This option causes all the copied material to be pasted into Flash as a single bitmap image. This is the simplest option; it places only one object on the stage and one item in the library. However, pasting as a bitmap means losing all the advantages of vector objects—for example, you can no longer reshape paths or select individual anchor points.

- **Paste Using AI File Importer Preferences.** This option preserves most of the attributes of the copied artwork. Editable paths and text remain editable; Illustrator symbols become Flash symbols; masks remain masks. You can go to Edit > Preferences (Windows) or Flash > Preferences (Mac) and select AI File Importer to determine how Flash handles specific types of objects—for example, whether text objects are imported as editable text or vector paths.

The remaining two options are available only if you've chosen Paste Using AI File Importer Preferences.

- **Apply Recommended Import Settings to Resolve Incompatibilities.** This option determines how Flash handles objects with attributes that it doesn't support (such as Illustrator's Distort & Transform or 3D effects). If you choose this option, Flash converts these objects as simply as possible to bitmaps or groups of drawing objects. If you don't choose this option, Flash maintains the editability of the imported objects by converting them to complex, multi-layered symbols. Either way, the objects maintain the same appearance that they had in Illustrator (**Figure 50a**).

Figure 50a On the left, a simple path in Illustrator with the 3D effect applied. In the center, the same path pasted into Flash using the Apply Recommended Import Settings option; it's been converted to a bitmap. On the right, the path pasted without using that option; it's become a group of subgroups nested within more subgroups.

- **Maintain Layers.** If the artwork you're pasting has multiple layers, choosing this option preserves those layers in Flash. The drawback is that Flash does this by ignoring the layers and keyframes already in the timeline: No matter what keyframe is selected at the time you paste, Flash creates new layers and pastes the artwork into frame 1. If you don't choose this option, your pasted artwork comes in on a single layer, but you can paste it into any keyframe on any existing layer.

The other technique is to save your Illustrator artwork as an AI file and import the file into Flash. This technique gives you more control than you get with copying and pasting.

In Flash, choose File > Import > Import to Stage and navigate to the AI file that you want to import. When you click OK (Windows) or Import (Mac), a large Import to Stage dialog box appears.

The left pane shows a hierarchical list of every layer and sublayer in the AI file. Each is accompanied by a check box that indicates whether it will be imported to Flash. All the check boxes are initially selected, but you can deselect them for layers or sublayers that you want to exclude.

When you click any item in the left pane, the right pane offers a list of possible import options for that item. Each has an option already selected; if you don't want to look at every item, you can accept those default choices. In most cases, the items you'll want to look at are those that have a warning icon (an exclamation mark in a yellow triangle) to their right. The icon indicates that the layer or sublayer contains features that Flash doesn't support (**Figure 50b**). To see a list of those problem items, click the Incompatibility Report button below the left pane.

(continued on next page)

Group Therapy

To say that Flash "preserves the editability" of imported objects is not just a figure of speech. Vector paths that were created in Illustrator can be edited and modified in Flash, even with tools (such as the Ink Bottle) that don't exist in Illustrator. Similarly, text that was created in Illustrator can be edited with the Text tool in Flash, and Illustrator symbols can be stored and edited in the library just like Flash symbols.

You may occasionally try to edit an imported path or text object and find that it can't be done. In those cases, the problem usually is that Flash grouped the object in the process of importing it. Imported objects often contain nested groups, and you may have to choose Modify > Ungroup several times— or go several levels deep in group-editing mode— before you can do your editing. Once you've unpacked the editable objects, there's no need to regroup them unless you want to.

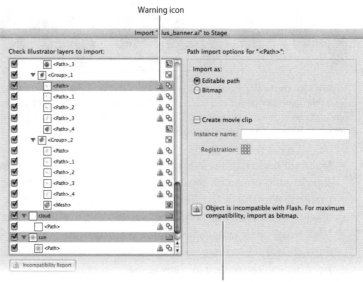

Warning icon

Import "lus_banner.ai" to Stage

Check Illustrator layers to import:

Path import options for "<Path>":

Import as:
- ● Editable path
- ○ Bitmap

☐ Create movie clip

Instance name:

Registration:

⚠ Object is incompatible with Flash. For maximum compatibility, import as bitmap.

⚠ Incompatibility Report

Recommended import option

Figure 50b This is the upper portion of the Import to Stage dialog box. An incompatible item is selected in the left pane; the right pane shows the recommended import option.

The bottom area of the dialog box provides a series of options:

- **Convert Layers To.** This menu offers three choices. Two of them, Flash Layers and Single Flash Layer, do the same things as Maintain Layers in the Paste dialog box. The third choice, Keyframes, converts Illustrator layers to a series of keyframes in a Flash layer.

Tip
If you don't like the drawing tools in Flash, you can do frame-by-frame animation in Illustrator. Draw each frame on a separate layer, then import the AI file to Flash by selecting Keyframes in the Convert Layers To menu. In Flash, you can refine the animation and add tweens.

- **Place Objects at Original Position.** This option causes the location of the imported artwork to have the same relationship to the Flash stage as it had to the Illustrator artboard. (It's similar to choosing Edit > Paste in Place as opposed to Edit > Paste in Center.)

- **Set Stage Size to Same Size as Illustrator Artboard.** This option is self-explanatory.

- **Import Unused Symbols.** Use this option to put all of the symbols from the Illustrator Symbols panel into the Flash library, regardless of whether they've been used on Illustrator's artboard.

- **Import As a Single Bitmap Image.** This option is the same as the Paste As Bitmap option in the Paste dialog box.

Directly below Import to Stage in the Edit > Import submenu is the Import into Library option. It does the same things as Import to Stage, except that it doesn't place the imported artwork on the stage or in the timeline. Instead, it creates a symbol in the library with the same name as the AI file, and puts the imported artwork inside it.

Tip
Another way to import AI files (or any files) is to drag them directly onto the Flash stage from a folder or your computer's desktop. The Import to Stage dialog box appears just as if you had chosen File > Import > Import to Stage.

#51 Importing from Adobe Photoshop

Flash is fundamentally a vector-based program that includes no tools for creating bitmap images. Although Flash can import bitmaps, it has very limited capacity to edit them. When you import a PSD file from Photoshop, however, Flash can identify some of the *non*-bitmap elements of the file and keep them editable. Although the default settings are to import Photoshop files as simple bitmaps, it offers options that let you preserve the editability of layer styles, text, and vector paths (**Figure 51a**). To set those options, choose Edit > Preferences (Windows) or Flash > Preferences (Mac) and click the PSD File Importer category.

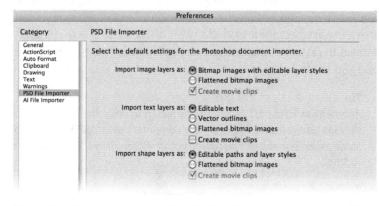

Figure 51a If you want to preserve the editability of the non-bitmap parts of a PSD file, use these preference settings instead of the defaults.

These import capabilities are not quite as comprehensive as they seem. When Flash refers to *layer styles,* it really means *blending modes.* Real Photoshop layer styles (such as Drop Shadow and Outer Glow) are still flattened into bitmaps when imported to Flash. Even text and vector paths—which normally remain editable after import—are rasterized in Flash if layer styles have been applied to them in Photoshop.

On the positive side, Flash recognizes and preserves Photoshop layers and layer groups. It also preserves transparency in PSD files (**Figure 51b**).

Flash is Not Your Mother

Flash can do a lot with imported artwork—scale it, change its color mode, merge layers, and so on—but those are tasks that Flash shouldn't have to do. You should take responsibility for preparing your files *before* you import them into Flash.

- **Color Mode.** Flash uses the RGB color mode exclusively. If you import a CMYK, grayscale, or indexed-color file, Flash silently converts it to RGB. For the best results, however, you should convert the files to RGB yourself. Flash does a satisfactory job of conversion, but Photoshop and Illustrator do it better. Those programs also give you a chance to make any necessary tweaks to the color.

- **Scaling.** Flash will let you import huge bitmaps and scale them down on the stage, but there's no good reason to do that. By importing more pixels than will be seen in your movie, you make the FLA file unwieldy, bloat the

(continued on next page)

Figure 51b Anything that appears against a gray-and-white checkerboard in Photoshop (left) will have a transparent background when imported into Flash (right).

The procedure for importing PSD files is basically the same as that for importing AI files (see #50). When you choose File > Import > Import to Stage and navigate to a PSD file, Flash opens an Import to Stage dialog box with a list of layers, allowing you to choose an import option for each layer. (These individual import options can override the ones you set in Preferences.)

One significant difference from importing AI files is the ability to merge layers when importing PSD files. In the Import to Stage dialog box, you can select multiple layers by clicking the first layer and Control-clicking (Windows) or Command-clicking (Mac) additional layers. When two or more layers have been selected, a Merge Layers button becomes available below the left pane. Clicking that button causes the selected layers to become dimmed and a specialized layer labeled *Merged Bitmap* to take their place. If you change your mind, you can select the Merged Bitmap layer and click the Merge Layers button (which is now labeled Separate).

It's possible to copy and paste from Photoshop directly into Flash, but with severe limitations. Copying and pasting works only with bitmaps, not with vector paths or text. Flash doesn't recognize transparency, layers, blending modes, or other non-bitmap elements when you copy and paste.

SWF file unnecessarily, and slow down the performance of your movie. Scaling the bitmaps before you import them will also make them look better, because Photoshop does a better job of resizing than Flash does.

- **Layers.** Unless you plan to do round-trip editing in Fireworks, there's no need to have Flash flatten your bitmaps. Do it yourself in Photoshop. If you want to preserve layers instead of flattening your artwork, reduce your number of layers to the smallest number possible by merging them strategically in Photoshop or Illustrator.

#52 Importing from Adobe Fireworks

The Thing about PNG

PNG (which stands for Portable Network Graphics and is usually pronounced *ping*) was originally intended to replace GIF and JPEG as the standard file formats for the Web. Although that goal was never realized, PNG became popular among artists and designers for its robustness, flexibility, and small file size. Instead of creating a new, proprietary format, the developers of Fireworks adopted PNG as the program's native format.

Although other programs can also save to the PNG format, most don't take full advantage of its features. A PNG file created by Fireworks may contain bitmaps, vectors, editable text, layer information, and so on. A PNG file created by most other programs—including Photoshop—is often just a flattened bitmap.

Because they're both former Macromedia products, Flash has a much closer relationship with Fireworks than it has with Illustrator or Photoshop. In many ways, Flash and Fireworks behave as if they're a single program.

Unlike Photoshop and Illustrator files, Fireworks files can contain multiple frames (for animation) or multiple pages (for Web publishing). Both of these features are preserved in Flash. In fact, copying and pasting from Fireworks to Flash preserves nearly all attributes of the pasted artwork; so does importing a Fireworks PNG file into Flash. In either case, an Import Fireworks Document dialog box appears, containing these options:

- **Import As a Single Flattened Bitmap.** Any aspects of the artwork that would otherwise have been editable in Flash, such as layers, text, and vector paths, are reduced to pixels. If the file contains multiple frames or pages, only the first is imported. Choosing this option causes the others in the dialog box to become unavailable.

- **Import [Page #].** This option allows you to choose which page of a multipage file you want to import. You can choose a single page or all pages. If you import all pages, each page comes in as a separate movie clip.

- **Into.** This option lets you specify whether the imported artwork will be placed in the currently selected keyframe or whether Flash will create new layers for it. This option is similar to the Maintain Layers option in the Paste AI to Stage dialog box (see #50).

- **Objects** and **Text.** Each of these options provides two choices. Import As Bitmaps to Maintain Appearance has the same effect as Import As a Single Flattened Bitmap (above), except that layers from the Fireworks file are preserved. Keep All Paths [or Text] Editable preserves full editability.

If you want to edit imported AI or PSD files, you have to go back to the original application (Illustrator or Photoshop), edit the artwork there, and then re-import it to Flash. With Fireworks PNG files, that's not always necessary. Here's the easiest method for round-trip editing between Flash and Fireworks:

1. Import a Fireworks PNG file to Flash by choosing File > Import > Import to Stage (or by dragging the PNG file icon onto the stage).

2. In the Import to Stage dialog box, choose Import as a Single Flattened Bitmap.

   This option makes the artwork uneditable in Flash, but that's OK—you'll be doing your editing in Fireworks.

3. When you're ready to edit the Fireworks artwork, select it on the stage. An Edit button appears in the Properties panel (**Figure 52a**).

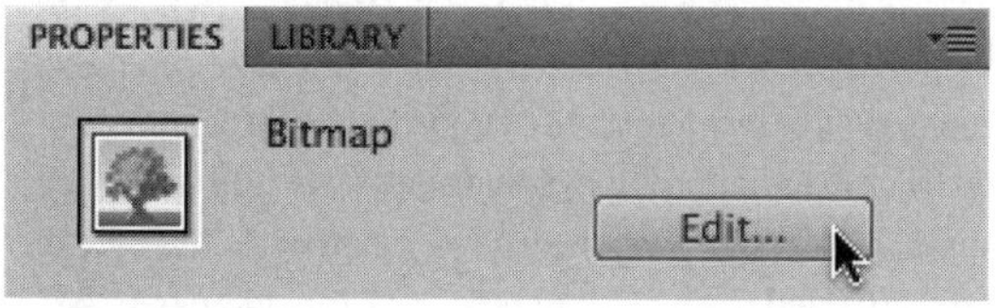

Figure 52a When you select a Fireworks bitmap on the stage, this button appears in Properties.

4. Click the Edit button. Fireworks launches, if it's not already running. The PNG file corresponding to the imported bitmap opens in Fireworks. (See the sidebar "Side Trip" for more information about this step.)

   Near the top of the Fireworks editing window, you'll see an Editing from Flash icon and a Done button (**Figure 52b**).

Figure 52b This bar appears in the Fireworks editing window when round-trip editing from Flash is in process.

(continued on next page)

When you've selected a Fireworks bitmap on the stage, you'll sometimes see that the Edit button in Properties is dimmed. This means that Flash has lost track of the original PNG file from which you imported the artwork. To fix the problem, you'll have to take a slight detour from the round-trip editing process:

1. Check Properties for the name of the selected bitmap; then locate that bitmap in the library.

2. Double-click the Bitmap icon (a tiny tree) to the left of the bitmap's name. A Bitmap Properties dialog box opens.

3. In the dialog box, click the Import button. An Import Bitmap window opens.

4. Navigate to the appropriate PNG file and click OK (Windows) or Open (Mac).

5. Click OK to close the Bitmap Properties dialog box. The bitmap on the stage remains selected, and the Edit button should now be available in the Properties panel.

5. Modify the artwork in any way you want; then click the Done button.

Flash comes back to the foreground. Your revised version of the bitmap artwork has replaced the previous version on the stage. Behind the scenes, Fireworks automatically saves the revised PNG file.

Keeping the Fire in Fireworks

Before the Adobe-Macromedia merger, Macromedia was at a distinct disadvantage in image editing: Adobe had Illustrator and Photoshop; Macromedia had only Freehand and Fireworks. Freehand, a once-popular vector drawing program, was phased out not long after Macromedia acquired it. Fireworks could easily have suffered the same fate: Although it has a useful mix of vector- and bitmap-oriented features, it's not as powerful in either of those areas as Illustrator and Photoshop are.

Macromedia kept Fireworks alive by integrating it tightly with Flash and Dreamweaver. A single click in either program could send an image to Fireworks for editing; another click could bring the edited image back. The ease of this round-trip editing feature led many designers to use Fireworks when they would otherwise have used one of the Adobe programs.

When Flash and Dreamweaver became part of the Adobe Creative Suite, it seemed unlikely that Fireworks would survive. Why would anyone use Fireworks when they could just as conveniently use Photoshop or Illustrator? To many people's surprise, Fireworks has remained in the suite. Perhaps this is because Flash still can't do round-trip editing with Photoshop and Illustrator. (If so, when that limitation is overcome, Fireworks might indeed disappear.) But it's also possible that Adobe intends to give Fireworks a more prominent role, making it as indispensable for web-related image formats as Illustrator is for vectors and Photoshop is for bitmaps. Adobe has already moved in that direction, giving Fireworks new features—such as the ability to store multiple pages in a single file—that Photoshop and Illustrator lack.

#53 Importing from Other Sources

Although the Import feature in Flash is geared primarily for Illustrator, Photoshop, and Fireworks, Flash can import files in several other formats, including:

- **DXF.** This vector file format is used by AutoCAD and other computer-aided drawing applications. Flash imports DXF files that fit a narrow set of criteria: They must be coded in ASCII rather than binary; they must be 2D rather than 3D, and they must use the AutoCAD 10 file format. Once imported into Flash, DXF files are fully editable.

- **FH7 through FH11.** Although Adobe has stopped developing and marketing FreeHand (a former competitor of Illustrator), it still includes special support for FH files in Flash. When you import an FH file, Flash opens a FreeHand Import dialog box (**Figure 53**). All of the FreeHand features are preserved when the file is imported.

Figure 53 Although the options in the FreeHand Import dialog box are worded slightly differently, they function almost identically to those in the dialog boxes for AI and Fireworks imports.

- **BMP, GIF, JPEG, PNG.** Flash imports these common bitmap file formats, but without offering any import options. (The Import to Stage dialog box doesn't appear, and the PSD and AI File Importer preferences don't apply.) The file comes into Flash as a flattened bitmap with no layers, editable text, transparency, or other special features.

- **TIFF, TGA.** Flash doesn't import files in these formats directly, but if QuickTime 4 or later is installed on your computer (as it is on all Macs and many PCs), Flash will use it as a translator for these and a few more obscure formats. You don't have to do anything special; Flash handles the QuickTime translation behind the scenes.

cccccc

cccccccc

#54 Setting Bitmap Properties

Bringing a bitmap into Flash is easy, but using the bitmap effectively is more difficult. Unlike vector drawings, bitmaps suffer a loss in quality every time they're scaled or rotated. In addition, bitmap files tend to contain more information than equivalent vector-based files, which makes them less suitable for animation. Adding bitmaps to a movie can significantly increase the size of the SWF file and put a heavy load on the computer's processor.

You can minimize these problems by fine-tuning each bitmap's properties. Select a bitmap in the library and either double-click its icon or click the Properties icon at the bottom of the Library panel (see #29). Either way, the Bitmap Properties dialog box appears (**Figure 54a**).

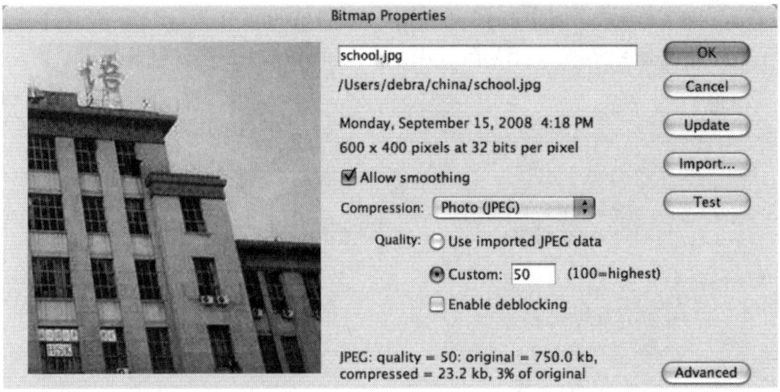

Figure 54a The Bitmap Properties dialog box is where you change the smoothing setting and compression options for each imported bitmap. (If the bitmap is in a format other than JPEG, the contents of the dialog box will look slightly different than what's shown here.)

If the bitmap looks rough or ragged when it's been resized or rotated on the stage, you can select the Allow Smoothing check box. Nearly every bitmap—except, perhaps, for very small ones—looks better with smoothing applied. The trade-off is that animating a smoothed bitmap requires more work from the processor than animating an unsmoothed bitmap, so it's possible that the playback performance of your movie will suffer.

An unwieldy bitmap file size can be dealt with by applying compression to the bitmap. Flash lets you choose between two types: *lossless compression* and *photo compression* (often referred to as *JPEG compression*). Lossless compression squeezes the file's information into a smaller space with no loss in quality. It's effective on bitmaps that have large areas of flat color, such as diagrams or cartoons. For images that have many colors or gradients, such as paintings or photographs, JPEG compression is more effective. It shrinks the file size by deleting nonessential information from the file.

JPEG compression is the type you'll probably use most frequently. JPEG offers varying degrees of image quality, on a scale from 0 to 100. As image quality increases, so does file size. Your challenge is to find the ideal quality setting for each bitmap: the point on the scale at which the file size is as small as it can be without a significant sacrifice of image quality. There's no right or wrong quality level; it's entirely a matter of judgment.

Here's how you set the JPEG compression level:

1. In the Bitmap Properties dialog box, choose Photo (JPEG) from the Compression menu.

2. If you're satisfied with the default level of compression, skip to Step 6. In most cases, however, you can compress the image further with no significant loss of quality. To do so, click the Custom radio button.

3. Type a number into the Quality field, replacing the default value of 50. (Some people like to start with a high quality setting and work downward; others like to start with a low quality setting and work upward.) Click the Test button to try out the setting.

4. Look at the preview pane on the left side of the dialog box to see what effect the quality setting has on the bitmap. If you see blocky or muddy areas, the quality is too low (**Figure 54b**).

Figure 54b An optimal level of JPEG compression (left) may include some minor flaws, such as a bit of fuzziness around sharp edges. If you see obvious blockiness or muddiness (right), the compression level is too high.

(continued on next page)

Update Your Image

If you import a bitmap file into Flash and later make changes in the original file, you can double-click the image in the library and click the Update button in the Bitmap Properties dialog box. Doing so replaces the old version of the bitmap with the new one—not only in the library, but in every instance of that bitmap that's already on the stage.

If you click the Update button and Flash can't find the file you're trying to update—for example, if the name of the file has changed, or if it's in a different location than when you originally imported it—an Import dialog box appears, allowing you to navigate to the updated file. (Clicking Import instead of Update takes you to that same dialog box; you can use it if you want to replace the previously imported bitmap with a different image.)

When you begin to work with audio in the next chapter, note that the Update and Import buttons are available in the Sound Properties dialog box as well (see #62).

Look also at the text at the bottom of the dialog box. It shows you the original file size, the compressed file size, and their relationship expressed as a percentage. In most cases, if the compressed file size is more than 5 percent of the original, the quality is too high.

5. Repeat Steps 3 and 4 as many times as necessary to find the best balance of quality and file size.

6. Click OK to close the Bitmap Properties dialog box.

#**55** Breaking Apart Bitmaps

Flash treats bitmaps much like it does symbols. Once a bitmap is in the library, you can drag as many instances as you like to the stage, and you can motion-tween those instances just as you would instances of symbols.

In some cases, you may want to convert bitmaps to actual symbols. For example, if you want to apply a blending mode to the bitmap, you have to turn it into a movie clip first.

In other cases, however, you may want to do the opposite—make a bitmap behave more like an editable path than like a symbol. To do this, select the bitmap on the stage and choose Edit > Break Apart.

Breaking apart a bitmap allows you to do two things to it that you couldn't do otherwise: You can select portions of the bitmap, and you can turn the bitmap into a fill for a path.

- **Selecting.** If you've used Photoshop or similar programs, you know that you can use a variety of tools to select different portions of a bitmap. The same is possible in Flash, albeit on a more primitive level. You can use the Selection tool to select rectangular areas (**Figure 55a**), or the Lasso tool to select irregular areas.

Figure 55a Left: drawing a marquee with the Selection tool to select a rectangular portion of a broken-apart bitmap. (Note that the marquee must start outside the bitmap.) Right: Flash highlights the selected area with a dot screen.

Flash even has an equivalent to Photoshop's Magic Wand tool. If you select the Lasso tool and look at the options area at the bottom of the Tools panel, you'll see a Magic Wand icon. Directly below it is the Magic Wand Settings icon, which opens a dialog box in which you can set the wand's tolerance. The Magic Wand allows you to select contiguous areas of similar color with a single click (**Figure 55b**). For more about the Magic Wand, see the sidebar "Abracadabra."

Abracadabra

The Magic Wand is one of the most timesaving tools you can use with bitmaps. You can select an entire irregularly shaped area by clicking the Magic Wand inside it, provided that all the pixels in that area are approximately the same color.

You can control the sensitivity of the Magic Wand by clicking the Magic Wand Settings icon and entering a value in the Threshold field. The higher the Threshold setting, the more tolerant the Magic Wand is. For example, with a Threshold setting of 0, the Magic Wand selects only pixels that are exactly the same color as the pixel you click. With a Threshold setting of 36, the Magic Wand accepts pixels that aren't quite the same color, as long as they're not more than 36 shades away from the color of the first pixel. With a Threshold setting of 200 (the maximum), clicking the Magic Wand anywhere in the bitmap selects nearly every pixel.

Figure 55b Clicking a black pixel with the Magic Wand causes that and all contiguous black pixels to be selected.

Once you've selected a portion of a bitmap, you can move, transform, delete, or change the color of the selected area.

- **Converting to a fill.** If you click a broken-apart bitmap with the Eyedropper tool, a tiny thumbnail of the bitmap appears in the Fill Color control. Any path you create at that point will be filled not with a color or a gradient, but with an instance of the bitmap (**Figure 55c**).

Figure 55c The Paintbrush tool, which can make only fills, is being used here to "paint" a new instance of the bitmap.

#56 Autotracing Bitmaps

Given the drawbacks of bitmaps in Flash—large file sizes, poor scalability, and limited editability—it might seem like a good idea to convert your bitmap images to vectors. Doing this, however, is not as straightforward as it sounds. In real life, there are no outlines: Photographs typically contain soft-edged shapes, blurriness, noise, and subtle gradations of color.

Originally, the only way to "vectorize" a bitmap image was to trace it by hand, figuring out where each new outline should go. Since then, some programs have automated the process: The software guesses where the edges are by looking for boundaries between differently colored groups of pixels; then it draws paths along those edges. This process is generally known as *autotracing*.

The autotracing feature built into Flash is good, but it's far from perfect. A bitmap image—especially a photograph—that's been converted to vectors never looks like the original image, but more like an Andy Warhol silkscreen (**Figure 56**). Still, in some cases, that may be the look you want.

Figure 56 The original photograph (left) is autotraced with a low color threshold (center) and a high color threshold (right).

To convert a bitmap to a vector drawing, select it on the stage and choose Modify > Bitmap > Trace Bitmap. A Trace Bitmap dialog box appears, containing four settings for you to specify.

- **Color Threshold.** This should be a number between 1 and 500. A low number produces an image with lots of color variation and a large file size; a high number produces an image with fewer colors, a posterized appearance, and a smaller file size.

- **Minimum Area**. This number should be between 1 and 1000. This is the number of pixels that Flash looks at to determine the average color of an area. A low number produces a more detailed image with a large file size; a high number produces a "blobbier" image with a smaller file size.

(continued on next page)

- **Curve Fit.** This setting determines how Flash will draw outlines. The tightest fit (Pixels) results in a very precise, detailed image, but the file size may be greater than that of the original bitmap. The loosest fit (Very Smooth) yields an image that looks like it was drawn in a moving car, but its file size is much smaller.

- **Corner Threshold.** This setting determines the degree to which jagged outlines will be smoothed. Choosing the Many Corners option produces a sharper image with a larger file size; choosing Few Corners produces a softer image with a smaller file size.

As with compression, there's no hard-and-fast formula for determining the proper settings. Every image is different, and you have to experiment with different combinations of settings to see what works best in each case.

This process of trial and error has become much easier now that a Preview button has been added to the Trace Bitmap dialog box. Each time you change the settings, you can click Preview to see what the autotraced image will look like on the stage.

CHAPTER EIGHT

Working with Sound

Animation and sound go together like pie and ice cream. No matter how appealing your animation is, it will engage your audience even more if you back it up with appropriate music and add some well-chosen sound effects.

Flash can't create or record sound, and its sound-editing ability is minimal. If you want to add music or other sounds to a Flash movie, you either have to record it yourself or use prerecorded sounds from CDs or the Web. Either way, you'll almost always want to use a sound-editing program to adjust the length, volume, and quality of the sound. The cost of sound-editing software ranges from free (Audacity, an open-source program downloadable from sourceforge.net) to thousands of dollars (ProTools, the choice of most audio professionals). A good intermediate choice is Adobe Soundbooth, a member of the Creative Suite that can export files compatible with ActionScript.

Once you've imported your sound files, Flash takes care of the rest. You can play multiple audio tracks at once, synchronize sound to animation in a variety of ways, and even apply effects such as fades and pans. Best of all, you can do these things using the techniques you're already familiar with: inserting keyframes, setting compression levels, and using Properties to modify instances.

#57 Importing Audio Files

To import a sound file, choose File > Import > Import to Library, navigate to the file you want to import, and click Open (Windows) or Import to Library (Mac). There are no options and no dialog boxes; the file appears immediately in the library. If you select the filename in the library, you see a visual representation of the sound—called a *waveform*—in the viewing pane (**Figure 57**). To hear the sound, click the Play button above the waveform.

> **Note**
> *Choosing Import to Stage instead of Import to Library makes no difference. Either way, the audio file is imported to the library. (Since a sound isn't visible, it can't appear on the stage.)*

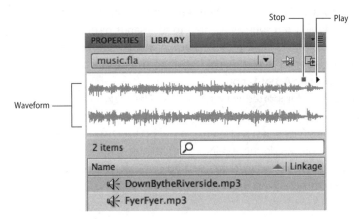

Figure 57 Because this is a stereo sound file, two parallel waveforms display in the library's viewing pane. For a mono sound, only one waveform would appear.

On its own, Flash can import only three audio file formats: WAV (Windows only), AIFF (Mac only), and MP3 (both platforms). If your computer has QuickTime installed, Flash can import WAV and AIFF on both platforms, along with a few other specialized formats such as Sun AU.

Of the audio formats that Flash imports, only MP3 is a compressed format: It uses both lossless and "lossy" compression (see #54) to squeeze high-quality audio into a relatively small file. If a particular sound is available in a variety of formats, it's generally recommended that you choose to import one of the uncompressed formats (such as WAV or AIFF) and let Flash compress them in a way that's optimized for Flash Player.

Copyright: This is Serious

Whenever you import assets that were created outside of Flash—drawings, photographs, sound, or video—you have to pay attention to copyright laws. The basic rule is simple: unless the imported item is something you created yourself, you *can't* use it in your Flash movie. The recording industry and Hollywood movie studios have become especially vigilant about stopping misuse of their material, even to the point of suing individuals like you for thousands of dollars.

There are plenty of myths about copyright: that it's okay to use copyrighted work if you're not making any money from it, or if you use less than ten seconds of it, or if you make minor changes in it. None of these are true. Legally, the only way you can include someone else's work in your Flash movie is if you have written permission from the creator of that work (or, for example, the company to whom the creator has sold the rights). The copyright

(continued on next page)

Although Flash always compresses sounds when it generates a SWF file (see #62), you can reduce the movie's file size even more by starting out with the smallest possible sound files. Here are suggestions for using your sound-editing software to prepare files for import to Flash:

- Convert stereo sounds to mono. (Because it contains two audio channels, a stereo file is twice the size of an equivalent mono file.)

- Downsample your sounds to the lowest acceptable sampling rate. Music and speech usually don't sound good at rates below 22 kHz, but sound effects can often be brought down to 11 kHz with adequate quality.

- Save your sounds at a lower bit rate. You'll probably want a 16-bit file for most music, but 8 bits is usually sufficient for speech and sound effects.

- Edit out unnecessary portions of your sound files. If you're experienced at sound editing, you may be able to extract part of an instrumental track and edit it so it loops seamlessly. Doing so gives you a drastically smaller file than you'd have if you imported the whole track, and most members of your audience won't notice. At the very least, trim off the couple of seconds of silence that come at the beginning and end of many music tracks.

owner can require that you do something in exchange for that permission, such as pay a fee.

If you don't want to deal with copyright owners directly, there are more convenient solutions. All over the Web, you'll find stock-photo or stock-music sites that streamline the permissions process by letting you download material (and giving you the necessary license to use that material) in exchange for paying a fee online. Some of these sites even let you use the material at no charge if it's for personal or educational use. There are online communities such as flashkit.com, where Flash users share their own animation and music loops with other users. Finally, you can purchase "buy-out CDs," for which the purchase price includes permission to reuse the CD's music or video files. You may not be able to use your favorite pop song in your movie, but at least you can go to sleep at night without fear of being summoned to court in the morning.

#58 Comparing Event Sounds with Streaming Sounds

Flash divides sounds into two categories: *event sounds* and *streaming sounds*. The difference isn't inherent in the sounds themselves; you can use any sound file either as an event sound or a streaming sound. The difference is in how the Flash Player handles the sounds when it plays a SWF file.

When you open a Flash movie in a Web browser, the Flash Player *streams* the movie—that is, it downloads just enough of the SWF file to begin playing it, and it continues to download the file while the movie plays. All the elements of the movie—paths, bitmaps, text, sounds, video, and so on—download in the order they appear in the timeline.

Because sounds tend to have large file sizes, they're sometimes not fully downloaded by the time the playhead reaches them in the timeline. Event sounds and streaming sounds behave differently in this situation.

If an event sound is still downloading at the time it's needed in the movie, the movie pauses to let the download continue and then resumes when the sound file has downloaded completely. If a streaming sound isn't fully downloaded, it begins to play and continues to download behind the scenes, just as the full SWF file does. Therefore, a general rule is that short, fast-downloading sound files work better as event sounds, while longer sound files work better as streaming sounds.

An exception to that rule applies to looping sounds. Any sound that's intended to loop—that is, to play multiple times in a row—should be designated an event sound regardless of how long or short it is. That's because no matter how many times it plays in a movie, an event sound only has to download once. If you were to loop a streaming sound, the sound would have to download anew each time it repeats, seriously wasting bandwidth.

A final difference lies in the way the sounds behave in the timeline. An event sound works like a movie clip: Once it begins to play, it continues until it's explicitly stopped, even if the SWF file ends in the meantime. A streaming sound works more like a graphic symbol: it plays in synchronization with the timeline. When the SWF file ends, a streaming sound ends too.

Because they're in frame-by-frame lockstep with the timeline, streaming sounds are suitable for situations where exact synchronization between animation and sound is important—for example, in scenes with lip-synced dialog, or when the animated action has to match the precise beat of a music track.

This chart sums up the criteria for deciding whether a sound file should be treated as an event sound or a streaming sound:

Event Sound	Streaming Sound
Short sound file	Long sound file
Suitable for looping	Unsuitable for looping
Independent of timeline	Synchronized with timeline

Some of these criteria may contradict each other. For example, if a sound file is short but intended to loop, should it be an event sound or a streaming sound? How about if it needs to loop, but also to be in sync with the timeline?

There's no right answer in situations like these. Test the movie both ways and see which way it performs better. You can easily switch a sound from event to streaming and back again with no impact on the rest of the movie.

#59 Putting Sounds in the Timeline

Once you've imported a sound file to the library, follow these steps to put it in your movie:

1. Create a new layer for the sound in the timeline. (Although this isn't strictly necessary—technically, a sound can share a layer with animation—putting each sound on its own layer is preferable.)

2. Insert a keyframe where you want the sound to begin.

3. With the new keyframe selected, do one of the following:

   • Choose the name of the sound file from the Sound menu in Properties (**Figure 59a**).

   or

   • Drag an instance of the sound file from the library onto the stage. (The sound obviously can't be seen on the stage, but it does appear in the timeline.)

Figure 59a The Sound menu lists all the sound files that are in the library. Choose one to place that sound in the selected keyframe.

In either case, the sound's waveform appears in the layer, beginning in the designated keyframe (**Figure 59b**).

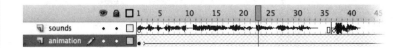

Figure 59b This timeline shows sounds beginning at frames 1 and 37. (It's fine to have two sounds on the same layer, as long as they're sequential.)

Note
When you attach a sound to a blank keyframe, the circle in the keyframe remains white. A black circle indicates the presence of objects on the stage, not the presence of sound.

4. With the keyframe still selected, choose either Event (to make the sound an event sound) or Stream (to make it a streaming sound) from the Sync menu in Properties.

5. If you want to add an effect to the sound, such as a fade or a pan, choose the effect you want from the Effect menu (just above the Sync menu).

6. If you want the sound to repeat a fixed number of times, choose Repeat from the menu to the right of the Sync menu; then enter the desired number of repeats in the next field to the right. (The default setting, Repeat 1, just plays the sound once.) If you want the sound to loop endlessly, choose Loop instead of Repeat.

   Looping and repeating should not be applied to streaming sounds (see #58).

7. If you want the sound to end at a particular frame, select that frame in the timeline and choose Insert > Timeline > Blank Keyframe (or press F7).

   That's sufficient to end a streaming sound, but an event sound requires an extra step: With the new blank keyframe still selected, choose Stop from the Sync menu in Properties. Doing so explicitly stops the sound, which—since it's independent of the timeline—would otherwise continue to play regardless of how many frames are assigned to it.

#60 Managing Looping Sounds

As you'll remember from #35, the default behavior of a SWF file is to loop. If you have a looping sound within a looping SWF file, the result can be chaotic.

Consider, for example, the timeline shown in **Figure 60**. Assume that the waveform represents a 15-frame-long event sound that's set to loop. Here's what happens when you play the movie's SWF file:

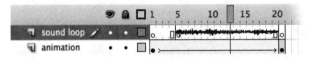

Figure 60 The sound that begins in frame 6 is a looping event sound that's 15 frames long.

1. At frame 1, the animation begins.

2. At frame 6, the sound begins. Because it's an event sound and there-fore independent of the timeline, it will loop continuously unless something stops it.

3. At frame 21, the sound repeats.

4. At frame 22, the animation ends. The movie loops back and plays again from frame 1.

5. At frame 6, the sound begins. However, the sound that began at frame 21 during the first run of the movie is still playing. There are now *two* instances of the sound playing at the same time.

From here on, every time the movie repeats, a new instance of the sound is added to the others that are already looping, with their start times staggered by seven frames. The result is an endless (and often unbearable) stack of sound upon sound.

The way to avoid this problem is to use a special type of event sound called a *start* sound. Before it begins to play, a start sound verifies whether any other instances of the same sound are already playing. If so, it stays silent.

To convert a sound to a start sound, select the keyframe in which the sound begins and choose Start from the Sync menu in Properties.

For this example, let's imagine that the sound beginning in frame 6 is now a start sound. When we play the movie, Steps 1 through 4 are the same as before. However, in Step 5, the start sound detects that another instance is already playing, and so it doesn't play. The result is a single looping sound rather than a cacophony.

Repetitive Stress

One of the best ways to save space in a SWF file is to use music loops instead of long pieces of music. Many beginning Flash developers are reluctant to do this, because they're afraid that repeating the same few bars of music will be boring. Keep in mind, however, that:

- Most music includes lots of repetition anyway.
- Your audience is paying more attention to the animation than to the music.
- Allowing the Flash Player to download smaller sound files will improve your movie's performance.

If you check out professionally made, media-rich Flash Web sites—promotional sites for Hollywood movies, for example—you'll find that the background music is always looped. If it's good enough for the experts, it's good enough for you.

#61 Synchronizing Sound to Animation

By default, the Flash Player plays every frame of a SWF file, no matter how long it takes. Because some frames take longer to download or make extra demands on the computer's processor, Flash movies often don't play at a steady rate.

The speed variations in a movie's playback are usually too subtle to notice. The addition of sound, however, adds an extra challenge. Sound—and music in particular—demands a fixed, steady playback speed. Speedups, slowdowns, and gaps are unacceptable. For this reason, one of the Flash Player's top priorities is to make sure that sound plays back smoothly and without interruption, regardless of what's happening on the stage.

This policy has different consequences for event sounds than for streaming sounds. While an event sound plays back at a steady rate, the visual portion of the movie continues to speed up and slow down according to the demands of each frame. As a result, an event sound and the rest of the timeline align only at one point: the keyframe in which the sound begins to play. After that, the sound and the action may drift apart fairly quickly.

For this reason, event sounds are best used in situations where extended synchronization isn't needed. In the case of a car collision, for example, it's important that the sound of the crash start at the same moment as the impact shown on the stage, but after that, it doesn't matter how precisely the sounds of buckling metal and shattering glass match the animation.

When playing back streaming sounds, however, the Flash Player uses a different strategy. A streaming sound is locked to the timeline frame by frame, so that, for example, a character's speech and mouth movements can match continuously. (It wouldn't be acceptable for the character's mouth to be ending one sentence while the voice has gone on to the next.) Since sound playback takes priority, Flash skips frames of animation wherever necessary to keep the sound and the action in sync. The price for precise synchronization is occasional jumps in the animation.

Because of these differences, syncing with event sounds and with streaming sounds demand different strategies on your part. When you're working with event sounds, the best approach is to do the animation first and add the sound later. You can scrub through the movie and see exactly where a rock hits the water, then insert a keyframe at that point to trigger the sound of the splash.

When you're working with streaming sounds, it's often preferable to create the *soundtrack* first and then create animation to match it. For example, if you want a character's dance movements to match the rhythm of a piece of music, put the music in the timeline first. By looking at the waveform, you can see where each beat of the music falls (**Figure 61**). You can then pace the animation so that the keyframes for each movement coincide with the musical beats.

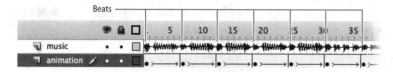

Figure 61 Once you find the steady rhythm in the waveform for a piece of music, you can insert keyframes in another layer to match the animation to the beat.

#62 Setting Sound Properties

As with bitmaps (see #55), Flash allows you to set compression levels and other properties for each sound file you import. There's no need to do this for every sound file, however; Flash pays attention to an individual sound file's properties only if it's used as an event sound. (Streaming sounds are compressed at a uniform rate, using either the settings of the highest-quality streaming sound in the movie or the global sound settings in Publish Settings. See #76 for more explanation.)

To open the Sound Properties dialog box, select a sound file in the library and either double-click its icon or click the Properties icon at the bottom of the Library panel (**Figure 62a**).

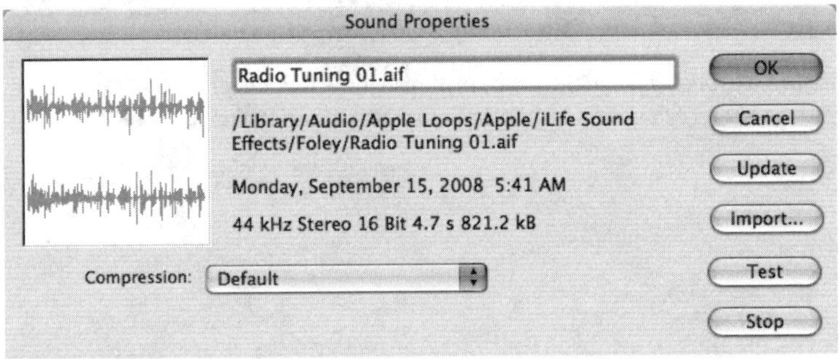

Figure 62a Most of the elements in the Sound Properties dialog box are similar to those in the Bitmap Properties dialog box.

The first option in the dialog box, Device Sound, applies only to mobile devices using the Flash Lite player (a stripped-down version of the standard Flash Player). If you're creating Flash movies to be viewed on traditional computers, you can ignore this field.

The second option, Compression, is more important. This menu determines how Flash will compress the sound for inclusion in the movie's SWF file. The menu choices are:

- **Default.** This choice tells Flash to apply the global compression settings in Publish Settings. (If the sound file is used only as a streaming sound, Flash will do that anyway.) Since event sounds should be as small as possible for quick download, you'll usually want to apply more than the default amount of compression to them.

- **ADPCM.** This is an old-style form of compression that's included mainly for compatibility with early versions of the Flash Player. It's sometimes effective for very short sounds, but in most other cases, MP3 compression yields better results.

- **MP3.** Whether you're compressing sound effects, music, or speech, MP3 will almost always give you the highest quality with the lowest file size. If you choose MP3 compression for a file that's already in MP3 format, a check box labeled Use Imported MP3 Quality appears above the menu (**Figure 62b**). Deselecting the check box allows Flash to recompress the file, which may result in reduced sound quality.

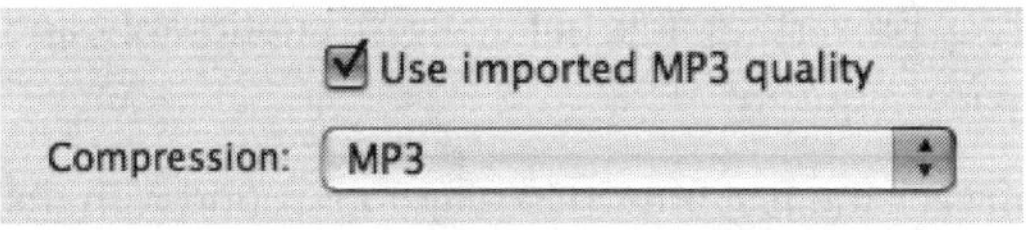

Figure 62b This check box appears only if MP3 is selected on the Compression menu, and only for a sound file that's already in MP3 format.

- **Raw.** *Raw* is another word for "no compression at all." If you're creating a movie where file size isn't important—such as an animated cartoon that will be distributed on a DVD—uncompressed sound will give you the best quality. However, if you're creating movies for the Web, Raw isn't a practical option.

- **Speech.** Like ADPCM, this is an old form of compression that's usually inferior to MP3. Use it only for movies that need to be compatible with Flash Player version 3 or earlier.

Choosing any of these menu items causes additional settings to display at the bottom of the dialog box. Since MP3 is the most common choice, we'll look at those settings, but the explanations here can be applied to other forms of compression as well.

- **Preprocessing.** The Convert Stereo to Mono check box is selected by default, but it can be deselected for bit rates of 20 kpbs (kilobits per second) or more. Use stereo sound only when necessary; as mentioned in #58, it can double the size of the SWF file.

- **Bit rate.** This setting is different from the bit-rate setting in most sound-editing programs, which determines how much information is used to describe each sound sample. In Flash, *bit rate* refers to how many kilobits (1000 bits) of sound information the Flash Player has to process each second. Higher bit rates yield higher sound quality, but they also yield larger SWF files and possibly reduced performance. The default, 16 kbps, is the lowest bit rate that's usually acceptable for music.

- **Quality.** A setting of Fast reduces processing time at the expense of sound quality, Best does the opposite, and Medium compromises between the two. In most cases, the Quality setting doesn't matter very much: The difference in processing time generally isn't noticeable, and neither is the difference in quality.

At any time, you can click the Test button to play your sound with the current compression settings. The text at the bottom of the dialog box will tell you the predicted file size and the degree of compression. As with bitmaps, you have to use trial and error to find the best trade-off between file size and quality.

#63 Editing Sounds

It's highly recommended that you edit your sound files in a real sound-editing program before you import them to Flash. However, Flash does offer some elementary tools for modifying sounds. To get to them, select a keyframe that contains a sound in the timeline; then click the Edit Sound Envelope icon (which looks like a pencil) in the Sound section of the Properties panel.

Note
There's no way to edit a sound file globally in Flash; you can edit only instances of sounds in the timeline. Editing one instance has no effect on the others.

An Edit Envelope dialog box appears, revealing the sound-editing controls (**Figure 63a**). The dialog box is accurately labeled Edit Envelope rather than Edit Sound because you can't change the content of the sound file; all you can do is change the size and shape of the metaphorical container that holds the sound.

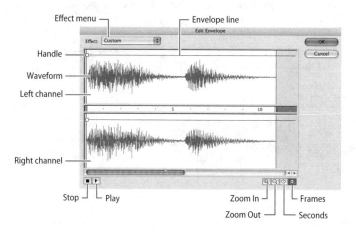

Figure 63a The Edit Envelope dialog box offers the basic controls that you'd find in any sound-editing program.

The dialog box displays the sound's waveform in two panes: The upper pane represents the computer's left sound channel; the lower pane represents the right channel. If the sound is stereo, the waveforms in the two panes are different; if it's mono, they're the same.

A time scale runs between the two panes. By clicking either of the two icons at the lower right corner of the dialog box, you can control whether the scale displays seconds or frames. To trim unwanted material at the beginning or end of the sound, slide the Time In and Time Out markers along the scale.

Tip

The portions of the sound that you cut out with the Time In and Time Out markers will be excluded from the SWF file. Trimming your sounds down to what's absolutely necessary is one of the best ways to reduce a movie's file size.

The horizontal black line above each waveform is called an *envelope line*; it controls the volume of the sound. You can reduce the overall volume by using the handles to drag each envelope line downward. To adjust the volume differently for different parts of the waveform, click anywhere along either of the envelope lines to create new handles (**Figure 63b**). Adding a handle to one line automatically adds a corresponding handle to the other.

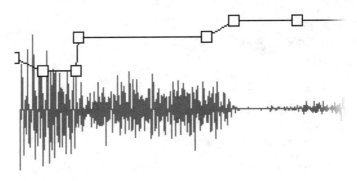

Figure 63b You can smooth out a sound by reducing the volume of the louder portions and boosting the volume of the softer portions.

Some commonly used envelope patterns, such as fading in and fading out, can be chosen from the Effects menu. (It's identical to the Effects menu in the Properties panel.) Choosing an effect causes the handles and envelope lines to jump to the appropriate positions—but any manual editing that you've done will be wiped out in the process. Going in the other direction is fine; you can use an effect as a starting point and then tweak it manually.

#64 Adding Sounds to Buttons

Users expect some sort of feedback when they click a button, which was discussed in #27. The feedback can be visual (a change in color, for example), but the addition of a confirming click or a beep is especially satisfying to most users.

To attach a sound to a button:

1. Import an appropriate sound file to the library. (The most effective button sounds are less than half a second in length and have no empty space at the beginning of the sound file.)

2. Double-click a button symbol in the library or on the stage to place it in editing mode. You'll see the familiar four-frame timeline (**Figure 64**).

3. Click the Insert Layer icon to add a new layer to the timeline.

4. Select the Down cell of the new layer and press F6 or F7 to insert a keyframe.

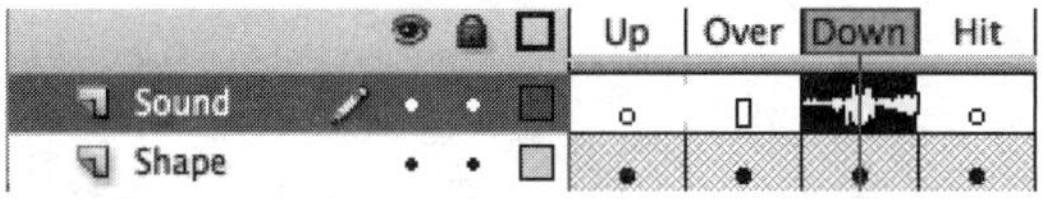

Figure 64 To make a button beep or click, attach an event sound to a keyframe in the Down cell.

5. Drag an instance of the button sound to the stage, or select its name from the Sound menu in Properties.

6. Choose Event from the Sync menu. (A button sound should always be an event sound.)

7. Click Scene 1 in the breadcrumb trail to exit symbol-editing mode.

8. Choose Control > Enable Simple Buttons and test the button.

Although it's technically possible to attach a sound to the Over state as well, it's best to avoid doing so (except perhaps as part of a game). Users generally find it annoying to have a button make noise when they roll over it.

Don't Try This at Home

It's not clear why anyone would want to do these things, but:

- Attaching a sound to a button's Up keyframe causes the sound to play when the user rolls the pointer *out* of the button.

- Attaching a sound to a button's Hit keyframe causes the sound to play when the user releases (not depresses) the mouse button.

CHAPTER NINE

Working with Video

The rapid growth in high-speed access to the Internet has made video one of the most popular features in Flash. Unlike other forms of video whose players vary between platforms, Flash video works identically on any computer that has a recent version of the Flash Player. And because Flash video can be controlled by ActionScript, any developer can easily create a custom video player with its own unique style and functionality. It's no wonder that popular video sites such as MSN Video and YouTube use Flash Video as their delivery format.

Digital video is a huge topic, and using it to its full potential requires more technical information than this book can offer. By reading this chapter, however, you'll learn the basics of getting video into your Flash movie and making it playable on the Web.

#65 Getting Familiar with Digital Video

To work effectively with video in Flash, it's helpful to know a few things about digital video in general.

Fundamentally, all digital video is a succession of bitmap images, each visible for a fraction of a second (**Figure 65**). As with animation, the slight changes from one frame of video to the next give the illusion of motion. Because displaying so many bitmaps so quickly requires a powerful processor and a fast hard drive, it's only recently that most home computers have become capable of playing full-screen, full-motion video.

Figure 65 Each frame of digital video is a separate bitmap.

Companies such as Apple and Microsoft pioneered techniques for storing and playing back digital video in formats such as QuickTime and Windows Media. Web sites often must make their video content available in a variety of formats, since there's no way to predict which type of player (or players) a user might have.

A further complication for users is *compression*. To be downloadable and playable by the average computer, digital video must be squeezed into as small a file as possible. Software developers offer dozens of compression schemes, each of which is embodied in a file called a compressor/decompressor—a *codec* for short. If a video file is created using a certain codec, it can be played only on a computer that has that codec. For example, if someone sends you a QuickTime file that was compressed with the DivX codec, your QuickTime Player won't play it unless DivX is installed on your computer.

Adobe has been able to bypass these obstacles because of the popularity of the Flash Player, which is installed on nearly all Macs and PCs (not to mention many Linux and Solaris computers). Adobe's proprietary video format, Flash Video (FLV), can be played by recent versions of the Flash Player with no need for additional software. As a result, FLV has become the closest thing to a universal Web video format.

Unlike QuickTime, which offers a choice of about 20 codecs, FLV uses only two: Sorenson Spark (the latest version of which requires Flash Player 7 or later) and On2 VP6 (which requires Flash Player 8 or later). In addition,

Adobe recently introduced a new video format called *F4V*—a variation of Flash Video using the open-standard H.264 codec—which requires Flash Player 9.2 or later.

Note

The Flash Player can play an FLV file only if the file is embedded in or linked to a SWF file. To play an FLV file directly, you need the Adobe Media Player (bundled with CS4 software) or a third-party application such as VideoLAN's VLC media player.

To use a video file in your Flash movie, you must convert it to a format that Flash can use. Flash CS4 will accept any video file that's been compressed with the H.264 codec, even if it's in a non-Adobe format such as QuickTime. Nearly every up-to-date video-conversion program—including free ones such as MPEG Streamclip (from Squared 5) or Any Video Converter Free Version (from AnvSoft)—can do H.264 compression; so can Apple's popular QuickTime Pro.

Most Flash users prefer to convert their video files to Adobe's FLV format, which is compatible with earlier versions of the Flash Player. You can do so with the Adobe Media Encoder, a standalone program that's installed on your hard drive when you install Flash (see #72).

Compression Digression

To make video files small and more easily playable, most codecs use both *image compression* and *temporal compression*. You're already familiar with image compression; we applied it to imported photos in #54. When you consider what a difference it made to apply JPEG compression to a single bitmap, imagine how much disk space you can save by applying similar compression to each of the thousands of bitmaps in a typical video file.

Image compression works by throwing away non-essential information without changing the overall appearance of a bitmap. Temporal compression uses a different principle: Although each frame in a video file is slightly different from the others, some elements remain the same. For example, in a talking-head interview, the subject's lip movements and facial expressions change from frame to frame, but the background stays still. By limiting the information stored in each frame to what has changed since the previous frame, temporal compression eliminates a tremendous amount of redundancy.

#66 Importing Video Files

As with audio files, it's best to edit your video files before importing them into Flash. Nearly every computer these days comes with a simple video-editing program (such as Apple's iMovie or Microsoft's Windows Movie Maker). You may prefer a higher-end program such as Adobe Premiere Pro, which—unlike some other video-editing software—can export files in FLV format.

You're already familiar with the import dialog boxes that Flash uses with certain types of vector and bitmap files. Because video is so much more complex, Flash gives you not just a dialog box, but a whole *series* of dialog boxes—collectively known as the Video Import wizard—that guide you through the process of importing a video file.

Tip
*If the video file that you want to import is on your computer's hard drive, move it into the folder that contains your FLA file. Do this **before** you begin to import the video.*

To begin the import process, choose File > Import > Import Video. (It's OK to choose Import to Stage or Import to Library instead; if you select a video file to import, Flash recognizes it and launches the Video Import wizard.)

The first screen of the Video Import wizard asks you to locate the file you want to import. If the file is on your hard drive:

1. Click the On Your Computer radio button.

2. Click the Browse button.

3. Navigate to the video file you want to import and click Open.

4. Choose a deployment method (see #67).

5. Click Next (Windows) or Continue (Mac). If the video file you've chosen is in a format that Flash can import (see #65), a new dialog box—either Embedding or Skinning, depending on the deployment method—appears.

6. If the file can't be imported, Flash displays an alert box advising you to launch the Adobe Media Encoder. Click OK to dismiss the alert box; click the Launch Adobe Media Encoder button, and convert the file (see #72). Then repeat Step 5.

If the file is online:

1. Click the Already deployed to a Web server, Flash Video Streaming Service, or Flash Media Server radio button.

2. Type the URL of the file, including the protocol (for example, `http://`).

3. Click Next (Windows) or Continue (Mac). The Skinning dialog box appears (see #70).

Unlike the On My Computer option, the Already Deployed. . . option doesn't verify the format of the video file you've selected. Even if the video file is incompatible, Flash lets you proceed through the rest of the Video Import wizard without telling you that anything is wrong. The first sign of trouble you'll see is when you test the movie in Flash (see #35): Flash displays an alert box beginning with the phrase "Netstream.Play" (**Figure 66**). If you see this dialog box, you'll have to delete the incompatible video file and import another.

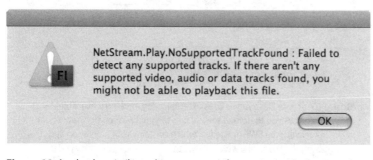

Figure 66 An alert box similar to this one appears if you test a movie that uses an online video file with an incompatible format. The warning will vary depending on the file format, but it always begins with the phrase "Netstream.Play."

Getting Ex-stream-ly Precise

Flash treats a video file on a Web server the way it treats a streaming audio file (see #58): It downloads just enough of the file to begin playing the video, and then downloads the rest of the file while the already downloaded portion continues to play. Although this process is known informally as streaming, it's more properly referred to as a *progressive download*.

Technically speaking, *streaming* requires two-way communication between the server and the client computer, which can't be handled by an ordinary Web server. True streaming of Flash video requires the Flash Media Server, which monitors the speed of the Internet connection and adjusts the stream's data rate accordingly; it also responds to navigation commands such as fast forward, rewind, and seek. Large organizations often have their own Flash Media Server, while individuals and smaller organizations who want to stream Flash video usually have accounts with a hosted streaming service.

#67 Choosing a Deployment Method

When you import a video file from your own computer (see #66), the Video Import wizard offers you three different ways to incorporate that video into your Flash movie:

- **Load External Video with Playback Component.** This is the most common choice. Your video remains in a separate file; when you publish your movie, Flash links the video file to the SWF file. You must upload both files to your Web server (**Figure 67**).

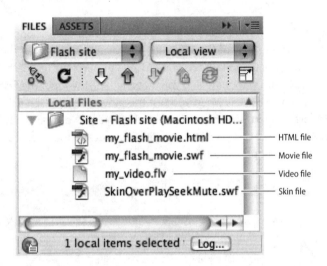

Figure 67 If your Flash movie uses external video, making it available on the Web requires you to upload several files to your Web server (shown here in Dreamweaver): the SWF movie file, which contains your animation and ActionScript; the HTML file, which allows the movie file to be displayed in a Web browser (see #75); the video file; and—if you want the user to be able to control the video with an onscreen video player—a skin file (see #69).

- **Embed FLV in SWF and Play in Timeline.** This option is a legacy from older versions of Flash, in which video was treated like a bitmap or sound—stored in the library, dragged to the timeline, and played from inside the SWF file. Embedded video is used much less often now that streaming and progressive download are available, but it's still a convenient way to handle short video clips (see #68).

- **Import as Mobile Device Video Bundled in SWF.** Choose this if your video file is intended to be played on a mobile device (such as a cell phone) using the Flash Lite player, which is outside the scope of this book. Unless you've deliberately set Flash Lite as your target format in Publish Settings (see #74), the Video Import wizard won't let you select this option.

When you've made your choice, click Next (Windows) or Continue (Mac).

If you've chosen Embed FLV in SWF and Play in Timeline, the Video Import wizard takes you to the Embedding dialog box, which is covered in #68. If you've chosen any of the other options, you can skip to #69, which deals with the Skinning dialog box.

Casting Light on Flash Lite

If you're wondering why there's so little information for beginners about using Flash Lite, it's because creating Flash movies for mobile devices isn't an activity suited to beginners. Flash can be used to create games, utilities, and other applications for devices such as cell phones, but doing so requires familiarity with programming techniques in general and ActionScript programming in particular. Most serious books on ActionScript include the information you'd need to adapt your scripts to the Flash Lite environment.

#68 Choosing Embedding Options

Adobe discourages the embedding of video in Flash movies, and for good reasons: Embedded video bloats the SWF file, has to be downloaded in its entirety before it can be played, and frequently has audio synchronization problems. It also demands a lot of memory, and if the user's computer doesn't have enough, the Flash Player may crash. To minimize these problems, Adobe recommends that embedded video be limited to clips that are less than 10 seconds long and have no audio tracks.

However, there are also some good reasons to embed video. Embedded video is easy to work with: Each frame of video corresponds to a frame in the timeline (**Figure 68**), allowing you to synchronize events in your movie to the action in the video without using ActionScript (see #69). You don't have to remember to upload multiple files to your Web server, because the video and its playback controls are contained in a single SWF file.

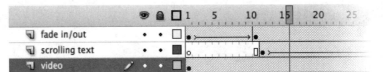

Figure 68 When you put your video in the timeline, you can synchronize animation to it just as you would with a streaming sound (see #62). Unlike streaming sounds, however, embedded video doesn't stream; it has to be fully downloaded before it can play.

To embed a video file, choose Embed FLV in SWF and Play in Timeline in the first screen of the Video Import wizard (see #67). The Embedding dialog box appears, offering these options:

- **Symbol Type.** If you choose Embedded Video, your imported video is stored in the library simply as a video file. If you prefer, you can import the video as a movie clip or graphic symbol. Importing it as a movie clip allows the video to play independently of the main timeline (see #28). There's no real advantage to importing it as a graphic symbol.

- **Place Instance on Stage.** This option—selected by default—causes Flash to put the imported video both on the stage (with a single keyframe in the timeline) and in the library. Otherwise, the video is imported only into the library.

- **Expand Timeline if Needed.** This option is available only if Place Instance on Stage is selected. It causes Flash to insert enough frames in the timeline to play the entire video.

- **Include Audio.** As of this writing, this option doesn't do anything. Flash imports the entire file, including the audio track, regardless of whether the Include Audio check box is selected.

After you've made your choices, click Next (Windows) or Continue (Mac) to go to the Finish Video Import screen, which summarizes the choices you've made. Click Finish to exit the Video Import wizard.

#69 Choosing a Skin for the Video Player

The FLVPlayback component—known informally as the video player—is what displays your video on the stage (**Figure 69a**). Normally, to use the user-interface components that come with Flash, you have to write ActionScript (see Chapter 12). In this case, however, no scripting is required; all you have to do is choose a skin for the player.

Figure 69a One example of the many skins that you can apply to the FLVPlayback component.

"Skin" is a somewhat misleading term. Applying a skin to an object usually means changing only its outward appearance; its functionality remains the same. In this case, however, your choice of skin determines what the player is able to do.

From a menu on the Video Import wizard's Skinning screen, you can choose from 34 different skins. (As you can see from the SWF file extensions, each skin is itself a Flash movie.) The skins vary in size, in types of video controls, and in where they're positioned in relation to the video (**Figure 69b**).

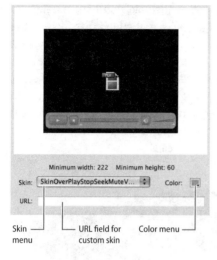

Minimum width: 222   Minimum height: 60

Skin: SkinOverPlayStopSeekMuteV... Color:

URL:

Skin — URL field for   Color menu —
menu   custom skin

Figure 69b Flash names each skin according to what it does. The selected skin—shown in use in Figure 69a—is called *SkinOverPlayStopSeekMuteVol.swf*, indicating that the control bar is superimposed over the video rather than placed beneath it, and that the player has Play, Stop, Seek, Mute, and Volume controls.

To the right of the Skin menu is a standard Flash color menu from which you can choose a skin color. A preview window lets you see the skin and use its controls, but your video doesn't appear there, and the controls don't have any effect.

Some advanced Flash users design their own skins instead of using the ones supplied by Flash. (Designing a custom skin is not a trivial task; it's something you should not try until you're very familiar with Flash and ActionScript.) To use a custom skin, enter the URL of its SWF file in the field below the menus.

If you don't want your movie's audience to interact with the video, you can choose None from the Skin menu, allowing the video to appear on the stage as a plain rectangle with no controls.

When you've selected a skin, click Next (Windows) or Continue (Mac). You're taken to a text screen that summarizes your choices. Click Finish to exit the Video Import wizard.

If you've chosen a skin for the video player, the skin's SWF file will be created when you test or publish the movie. This file must be uploaded to your Web server along with the movie's other files (see #67).

#**70** Using a Video Clip in Your Movie

After you've imported and encoded a video file, you'll find a new item in the library: the video file itself (if you've embedded the video) or the FLVPlayback component (if you've chosen one of the other deployment methods). You can drag multiple instances of these items to the stage or embed them in symbols; you can use the Free Transform tool to scale, rotate, or skew those instances (**Figure 70a**); you can even motion-tween instances. (Actually, motion-tweening the FLVPlayback component doesn't work, but if you embed the component in a movie clip, you can motion-tween an instance of the movie clip.)

Figure 70a A video instance can play normally even if it's been scaled, rotated, or skewed.

In all these cases, however, the rule you learned in childhood applies: Just because you *can* do something doesn't mean you *should* do it. Watching video—not to mention starting and stopping it—is difficult when the video is rotated or skewed, or is moving around the stage. More important are the technical limitations: Playing back video in a Flash movie already puts a big load on the computer's processor; playing back video that's been transformed or animated can challenge even a powerful computer. Out of courtesy to your audience and their hardware, it's best just to put the video somewhere on the stage and leave it there.

If you must animate or transform a video instance, you can reduce its demand on the user's computer by keeping the video's frame rate low and its dimensions small. Scaling down the video on the stage doesn't help; you have to reduce its dimensions *before* you import it, using the Adobe Media Encoder (see #73) or a video-editing or file-conversion program.

If you haven't embedded your video, you can change some characteristics of the video player by using a panel called the *Component Inspector*. For example, the default behavior of the FLVPlayback component is to start playing the video as soon as an instance of the player appears on the stage. In some cases, however, you may want the video to remain paused until the user clicks Play. To make that change, select the video player on the stage and choose Window > Component Inspector. On the Parameters tab of the Component Inspector (**Figure 70b**), change the value of the autoPlay parameter from "true" to "false." (Do this only if your video player has a skin with a Play button; otherwise, there's no way for the user to start the video.)

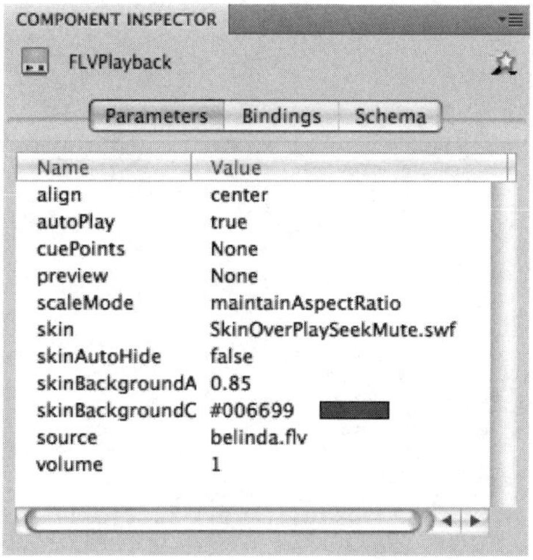

Figure 70b The Component Inspector displays parameters and values for a selected instance of any component—in this case, the FLVPlayback component.

Some of the parameters in the Component Inspector call for technical expertise, but others are easy to change. For example, use the skin parameter to change the player's skin, use the skinBackgroundColor parameter or skinBackgroundAlpha parameter to change the color or opacity of the skin, and use the volume parameter to set the initial volume of the video's audio track. (To do this, enter a number between 0 and 1, where 0 represents silence and 1 represents full volume.) If you move the FLV file that's linked to the player, use the source parameter to tell Flash where to find it.

#71 Updating Video Files

Flash has no tools for editing video. If you've imported a video file and then decide to change it, you'll have to open the file in an external video-editing program. The process for getting the re-edited file back into Flash depends on how it was originally deployed (see #67).

If the video was deployed as a linked external file:

1. Open the video file in the video-editing program of your choice. (If the video file is in FLV format, you may have to work with the original file from which the FLV file was made. Most video-editing programs can't open FLV files.)

2. Edit the video file and save it with a new name.

3. If necessary, use the Adobe Media Encoder (see #72) to convert the file to FLV or F4V format.

4. Move or copy the file to the folder where the earlier version of the video file resides.

5. Select the instance of the video file on the Flash stage.

6. Edit the source parameter in the Component Inspector to replace the original filename with the new one.

7. Remove the earlier version of the video file from the folder.

If the file was imported as embedded video:

1. Make a backup copy of the original video file and store it in a safe place.

2. Open the original video file (not the backup) in the video-editing program of your choice.

3. Edit the file and save it with the same filename to the same folder. (In other words, overwrite the original video file.)

(continued on next page)

4. In the library, double-click the icon next to the embedded video file to open the Video Properties dialog box (**Figure 71**).

5. Click the Update button in the dialog box. Flash replaces the embedded video with the new version.

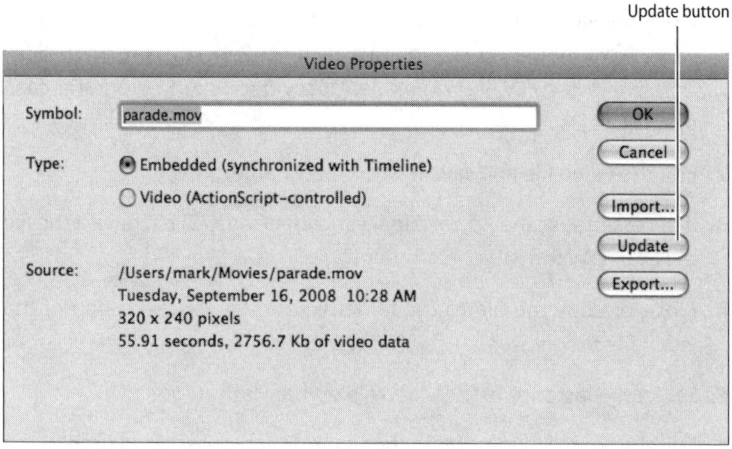

Update button

Figure 71 The Update button in the Video Properties dialog box replaces embedded video with a new version, so long as the new version has the same filename as the old one.

#72 Using the Adobe Media Encoder

The Adobe Media Encoder is a separate application that's included with version CS4 of the Creative Suite. Unlike its predecessor, the Flash Video Encoder, this new program can import and export many kinds of media in a variety of file formats used by Soundbooth, Premiere Pro, and other CS4 programs. For Flash users, its main purpose is to convert video files to the FLV and F4V formats preferred by Flash.

To use it:

1. Locate the Adobe Media Encoder application on your hard drive and double-click its icon to launch the program. Alternatively, click the Launch Adobe Media Encoder button in the Video Import wizard (see #66).

2. Drag one or more video files into the program's list pane (**Figure 72**), or click the Add button to navigate to the files that you want to convert.

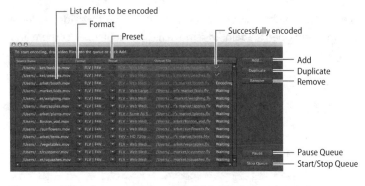

Figure 72 This is the upper portion of the Adobe Media Encoder window.

3. If you wish, drag files up and down within the list pane to change their order in the queue.

4. For each filename, click the arrow in the Format column to choose the file format that you want it to be converted to. You'll generally want to stay with the default option, FLV/F4V.

(continued on next page)

5. For each filename, click the arrow in the Preset column to choose the encoding options for the file (see #73).

Tip
You can select multiple files by clicking the first one and then Control-clicking (Windows) or Command-clicking (Mac) additional ones. Changing the Format or Preset setting for one of the selected files makes the same change for all of them.

6. Click Start Queue. The Adobe Media Encoder converts the files one by one, giving you constant progress reports in the lower portion of the window. By default, each newly converted file is placed in the same folder as the original.

When the batch is complete, all the files in the list will have green check marks next to them.

7. Files on the list don't disappear, even when you quit the Adobe Media Encoder and open it again. To remove files manually, select them and click Remove.

#73 Setting Encoding Options

To convert video files in a way that best suits your needs, the Adobe Media Encoder needs input from you: for example, which codec you want to use, how much compression you want to apply, and at what frame rate you want the video to play. Applying these settings when the video is converted is known as *encoding* the video.

The easiest way to specify encoding options is to use the Preset menu (see #72). Each item on the menu is a collection of video and audio settings designed to fit a particular audience. For example, if your Web site is aimed at frugal families, many of whom have old computers and dialup connections, you might choose the FLV–Web Modem preset. If your Web site is directed at corporate executives, you might go for one of the F4V–Web Large presets.

Many of the presets are optimized for particular kinds of source video, including NTSC or PAL (usually output by camcorders) and 720p or 1080p (usually found on DVDs). If you're not sure what kind of video you're converting from, it's safest to use one of the Same as Source presets found at the top of the menu.

If none of the presets fits your needs, and you have some technical knowledge of video and audio, you can modify settings individually to create your own custom presets. To do so:

1. From the Preset menu next to one of the files in the queue, choose the existing preset that's closest to what you want.

2. Open the Preset menu again and choose Edit Export Settings. An Export Settings dialog box appears, displaying the individual settings for the preset you chose.

3. Change the settings in any way you like. Most of the settings are organized into seven tabbed groups. Here are some of the controls that you'll find on each tab:

   - **Source.** Scale the video, crop it, set its in and out points, and set cue points that can trigger ActionScript commands at selected moments in the video.

   - **Output.** Decide how the scale and crop settings are interpreted— for example, a widescreen video can be letterboxed or "squished" to fit in a standard-size video window.

(continued on next page)

Seven is Heaven; Eight is Great; but Nine's Less Benign

The version numbers included in the Preset menu—Flash 7, 8, and 9—refer to the oldest Flash Player version compatible with each preset. Surprisingly, according to Adobe's statistics, the number of people who have Flash Player 9 is only about 2 percent less than the number who have Flash Player 7, so you won't lose much of your audience by using a preset geared to version 9.

The important difference is technical: if you're targeting version 7, you have to use an older codec, Sorensen Spark; if you're targeting version 8, you can use a newer codec, On2 VP6; if you're targeting version 9, you can use the state-of-the-art H.264 codec. The more recent the codec, the better the ratio of quality to file size. However, newer codecs require significantly more processing power; H.264, in particular, is a demanding codec that can lead to stuttering and pausing when video is played back on older computers.

- **Filters.** Blur the video horizontally, vertically, or both.
- **Format.** Choose whether the converted video will be in FLV or F4V format.
- **Video.** Choose between the Sorensen Spark, On2 VP6, or H.264 codecs; set the frame rate and bit rate.

Tip

If your video was created with a transparent background (as is possible in Adobe After Effects), use the On2 VP6 codec and select Encode Alpha Channel to preserve the transparency.

- **Audio.** Choose an audio codec; choose between mono and stereo.
- **Others.** Enter FTP information that lets you upload encoded files to a remote server.

4. If you wish, click the Save icon in the Export Settings pane to save your custom preset for future use (**Figure 73**); otherwise, click OK to apply the current settings to the selected file in the queue.

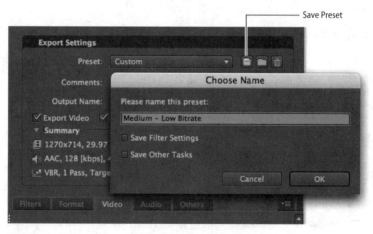

Figure 73 Clicking the Save button opens a dialog box in which you can name your preset and append it to the Preset menu.

CHAPTER TEN

Publishing and Exporting

The process of converting a Flash movie into a format suitable for public consumption is called *publishing*. Effective publishing requires that you know as much as possible about the audience who will be viewing your movie: What kind of computers are they likely to have? How fast are their connections to the Internet? What versions of Flash Player can you expect them to have installed? The answers to questions like these help you choose the most appropriate output options for a movie. Those options—called *Publish Settings*—are stored in the movie's FLA file.

In addition to publishing movies in SWF and other distribution formats, Flash has the capacity to convert Flash movies—or single frames of Flash movies—into a variety of file types through a process called *exporting*. Although Flash offers more export formats than publishing formats, export settings are not saved in the FLA file.

The emphasis of this chapter will be on publishing for the Web, although we'll also look briefly at distribution media such as QuickTime movies and desktop computer applications.

#74 Choosing a Publishing Format

The first step in publishing a movie is deciding how you plan to distribute it. Will the movie be posted on the Web, burned to a DVD, emailed, displayed continuously on a public kiosk, or presented to your audience in some other way? Each distribution method requires a suitable file format.

To select the distribution formats for your movie, choose File > Publish Settings. In the Publish Settings dialog box, click the Formats tab (if it's not selected already). You can choose one or more of the following formats:

- **Flash (.swf)** and **HTML (.html).** Both of these options are selected by default, because most Flash movies are published for the Web. See #75 for an explanation of how SWF and HTML files work together on a Web site.

- **GIF image (.gif).** Before Flash, most animation on the Web was in GIF format. Unlike SWF files, GIF files don't require a plug-in; any Web browser can play an animated GIF file. The drawbacks are that the GIF format doesn't work very well with photos or gradients (**Figure 74a**); it doesn't support sound; and its file sizes are often impractically large because each frame is a separate bitmap. Nevertheless, the GIF format is still used occasionally for short, simple animations.

Flash allows an entire movie to be saved as an animated GIF file, or a single frame to be saved as a static GIF file.

| Original | Banded | Dithered |

Figure 74a A GIF file supports only 256 colors. If an object contains more colors than that, it will appear banded when converted to GIF format. You can avoid banding by choosing one of the Dither options, which allow Flash to simulate missing colors by interspersing dots of available colors.

- **JPEG image (.jpg)** and **PNG image (.png).** For information on these single-image bitmap formats, see #80.

- **Windows projector (.exe)** and **Macintosh projector.** These are Flash movies in the form of standalone, executable files. For more information, see #82.

Each format has options that you can set by clicking the appropriate tab at the top of the Publish Settings dialog box (**Figure 74b**). The only options covered in this book are those for the SWF and HTML files; you can learn about the others from the Help panel.

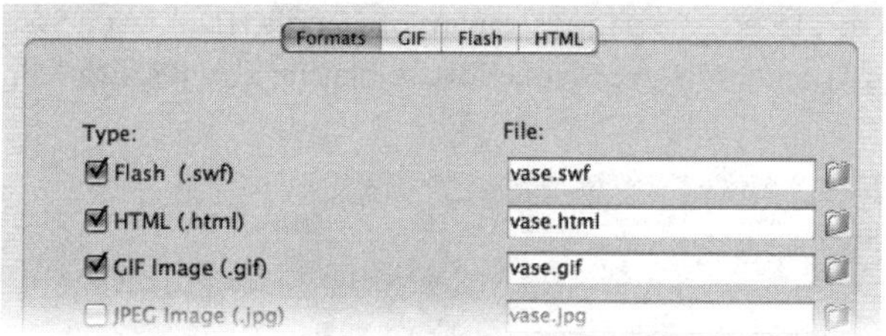

Figure 74b The leftmost tab in Publish Settings is always Formats. The remaining tabs vary according to which file formats you've selected.

By default, published files are saved in the same folder as the FLA file they're generated from. To specify a different name or location for a file, use the File field to the right of each format in Publish Settings.

#75 Linking SWF Files to HTML Files

Standard Web pages are coded HTML (Hypertext Markup Language). HTML language consists of plain text; in fact, you can create a Web page from scratch in a text-editing program. Non-text elements, such as graphics, video, and Flash movies, aren't part of the HTML file; they're uploaded separately to the Web server. The HTML code includes pointers to those external files that tell the browser where and how to display them on the page.

When you publish a SWF file, Flash creates an HTML file containing the code needed to display the Flash movie in a browser. The exact content of this file depends on the HTML options you choose in Publish Settings (see #77). Even with the default settings, the code isn't trivial: Although a still image can be placed on a page by means of a single HTML tag, a SWF movie requires a paragraph's worth of HTML to play reliably (**Figure 75**).

Figure 75 This HTML file illustrates the complexity of the code needed to display a Flash movie in comparison to the code required for a still image.

The Web page created by the Flash HTML file is a bare-bones affair: All it does is show your movie against a solid-color background. If you want other content to appear on the Web page, you have three options:

- Add more HTML code to the file that Flash created, either by hand or by using the Web-page editing program of your choice.

- Copy the necessary code from the Flash HTML file and paste it into another Web page that has the content you want. (This option requires some familiarity with HTML.)

- If you have Dreamweaver, use it to create your Web page. When you import the SWF file, Dreamweaver automatically inserts the HTML code to play it, making the Flash HTML file unnecessary.

Cut Out the Middleman?

When you include a Flash movie in a Web page, you need an HTML file for the page and a SWF file for the movie. But what if your movie *is* the Web page? Why not skip the HTML file, use an address such as www.myDomain.com/myFlashMovie.swf, and let the SWF file open directly in the user's browser?

Here's why not. Without an HTML file:

- You have no control over how the movie is displayed in the browser, such as what its dimensions are, how it scales, and where it appears in the browser window.

- You lose the opportunity to do Flash detection (see #79).

- Your site is much less likely to be indexed or listed by search engines.

#76 Adjusting the Flash Publish Settings

If you've chosen Flash and HTML as your file formats in Publish Settings, you'll see a tab for each file type at the top of the dialog box. Clicking the tabs allows you to set options for both files: The HTML options will be covered in #77; the Flash options are covered here. In both cases, we'll look only at the most significant options; you can read about the others in the Help panel.

- **Player.** Each time the Flash Player is updated, the new version may take months or years to catch on. Therefore, to make your movie available to the largest possible audience, you may want to publish a SWF file that's compatible with earlier versions of the player.

  The catch is that earlier versions of the player don't support the features in later versions of Flash. For example, if your movie uses 3D translation, which was introduced in Flash CS4 (also known as Flash 10), the 3D effect will disappear if your publish your movie in Flash 9 format.

  Once you've decided which version of the Flash Player you want to use—a process often referred to as *targeting*—choose that version from the Player menu. Thereafter, if you add a feature to your movie that isn't supported in the targeted version, Flash will give you a warning (**Figure 76**).

Figure 76 An alert box appears if you try to use a feature that isn't supported by the version of Flash Player that you've targeted.

(continued on next page)

Playing the Numbers

Which came first: Flash MX or Flash CS3? Unlike Flash Player, for reasons known only to a handful of marketing executives, Flash releases have rarely been designated by consecutive numbers. To help with your publishing decisions, here's a list pairing each recent version of the Flash Player with its corresponding version of Flash.

- Player 10: Flash CS4
- Player 9: Flash CS3
- Player 8: Flash 8
- Player 7: Flash MX 2004
- Player 6: Flash MX

To find out what percent of Web users have each version of the player, consult the Flash Player Version Penetration statistics on Adobe's website: http://www.adobe.com/products/player_census/flashplayer/version_penetration.html

- **Script.** Like targeting earlier versions of Flash Player, targeting earlier versions of ActionScript may make your movie available to a larger audience. The Script menu lets you choose from ActionScript 1.0, 2.0, or 3.0 (see #83). Early versions of Flash Player may not support higher levels of ActionScript. ActionScript 3.0, the latest version, will work only in Flash Player 9 or later.

- **JPEG Quality.** This slider sets the default quality level for images compressed with JPEG compression. It doesn't override the individual settings that you made under Bitmap Properties (see #54).

- **Audio Stream.** When you publish a SWF file, Flash combines all of the movie's streaming sounds into a single audio stream. By default, it applies the compression settings of the highest-quality streaming sound to the entire stream. If you want Flash to use different settings, you can specify them here and select the Override Sound Settings option (described below).

- **Audio Event.** These settings apply to event sounds for which you didn't specify individual compression settings in Sound Properties (see #62).

- **Override Sound Settings.** Selecting this option causes the Audio Stream and Audio Event settings to apply to all sounds in the movie, regardless of whether you set their compression rates individually.

#**77** Adjusting the HTML Settings

Most of the settings that affect your Flash movie's appearance are contained not in the SWF file, but in the HTML file to which the SWF file is linked (see #75). Some of these settings—particularly those involving dimensions, alignment, and scale—interact in unintuitive ways.

The HTML settings are:

- **Template.** This menu allows you to choose the underlying HTML code that Flash will modify according to your settings. The default template, Flash Only, displays your Flash movie on an empty Web page as described in #75. Most of the other templates offer minor variations for special situations. The Detect Flash Version option is treated separately in #79.

- **Dimensions.** This menu allows you to specify the dimensions of the rectangular frame in which your movie is displayed in the Web browser window. (Although Flash refers to it as a window, we'll call it a *frame* to distinguish it from the browser window.) The default choice is Match Movie, which means that the frame will be the same size as your movie. The other choices are Pixels, which allows you to specify exact dimensions for the frame, and Percent, which allows you to specify the frame size as a percentage of the size of the browser window, so it resizes along with the browser window.

  Note that these settings apply to the *frame*, not to the movie itself. Keeping that distinction in mind will make the alignment and scale settings easier to understand.

- **Playback.** These options control the behavior of your movie rather than its appearance. For example, the Loop option is selected by default, and you can deselect it if you want the movie to play once and stop. However, the Loop and Paused at Start options are controlled much more reliably by ActionScript than by HTML. (One obvious reason is that ActionScript commands continue to work if the SWF file is separated from the HTML file.) The Display Menu option determines whether the user can right-click the movie to see a contextual menu, but the menu doesn't allow the user to do much besides zoom in and out.

- **Quality.** These settings control the trade-off between processor load and image quality. The higher settings improve the appearance of bitmaps—particularly those that rotate or resize—but they make

(continued on next page)

greater demands on the user's computer processor. The default choice, High, is suitable in most situations, but the most appropriate setting will depend on the content of your movie and on the computers likely to be used by your target audience.

- **Window Mode.** Choosing Transparent Windowless from this menu causes the background of the stage to become transparent, allowing other content on the HTML page (such as a background pattern) to show through. Because this feature doesn't work reliably in all browsers, most Flash developers stay with the default choice, Window, which leaves the movie's background opaque.

- **HTML Alignment.** This menu determines how the frame in which the movie appears is positioned relative to the user's browser window.

- **Scale.** This menu works with the Dimensions options described earlier. It controls how the movie adapts to frame dimensions that are different from the size of the original movie (**Figure 77**). Show All and No Border both assure that the movie always maintains its original aspect ratio (ratio of width to height). If the aspect ratio of the frame is different from that of the movie, Show All adapts by using letterbox-type borders, while No Border crops part of the movie. In contrast, the Exact Fit setting causes the movie to adopt the aspect ratio of the frame, even if this distorts the image. The No Scale setting is similar to No Border, but it keeps the movie from scaling even if the size of the frame changes dynamically.

Show All   No Border   Exact Fit

Figure 77 The Scale settings determine how a movie adapts to a frame whose dimensions are different from those of the movie.

- **Flash Alignment.** This setting comes into play if the dimensions of the frame are smaller than those of the movie, and Scale is set to No Border or No Scale, causing the movie to be cropped. Flash Alignment determines which area of the movie remains visible. (For example, in the No Border illustration in Figure 77, Flash Alignment is set to Top Left.)

#78 Previewing and Publishing a Movie

Once you've adjusted the Publish Settings as needed, you can publish your movie by clicking the Publish button at the bottom of the Publish Settings dialog box. Alternatively, you can click OK to store the settings in the FLA file, and then publish the movie later by choosing File > Publish.

Flash has a Publish Preview feature, but its name is misleading: It might more accurately be called Publish *Post*view. That's because there's no way to see what your published movie is going to look like without actually publishing it. When you choose File > Publish Preview and pick a file type (**Figure 78**), Flash responds in the same way as it would to File > Publish—that is, it publishes the movie—but then it goes one step further: It opens the published file in a suitable application so you can look at it. If you've published an HTML file, Flash loads it into your default browser; if you've published a PNG file, Flash opens it in Fireworks (or your computer's default image-editing program). If you don't like what you see, you can modify the movie or the Publish Settings and publish it again; the new files will overwrite the old ones.

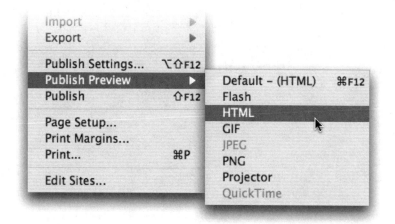

Figure 78 The choices available in the Publish Preview submenu depend on which file formats you've selected in Publish Settings.

(continued on next page)

204

Good Riddance

If you've used the two most recent versions of Flash, you're probably accustomed to seeing a mysterious JavaScript file called AC_RunActiveContent.js. Flash would generate this file whenever you published a movie that included ActionScript, and you'd have to upload the file to your web server along with the HTML and SWF files. (If you forgot to upload it, browsers would display an error message when they tried to play the movie.) The file was a workaround to deal with tightened security in Internet Explorer and other Web browsers.

Since that time, Microsoft has found more elegant ways to protect users against malicious software, and other browser makers have followed suit. As a result, *AC_RunActiveContent.js* is not required for movies published in Flash CS4, and Flash no longer generates the file. (The file still *is* required for movies that were published in earlier versions of Flash. If you want to delete AC_RunActiveContent.js from your web server, you'll need to reopen the old FLA file in Flash CS4 and re-publish the movie.)

By default, published files are saved to the same folder as the original FLA file. Assuming you've published your movie for the Web, you'll end up with at least two new files: SWF and HTML. In addition, if your movie includes imported video, another file may appear in the folder: a SWF file containing the skin you selected for the video player (see #69). All of these files—except, of course, the FLA file—have to be uploaded to your Web server for the movie to work properly (see #67).

CHAPTER TEN   Publishing and Exporting

#**79** Using Flash Detection

Ever since Flash came into being, its developers have grappled with the problem of how to handle users who don't have the latest version of Flash Player, or who don't have Flash Player at all. What happens when they visit a Web site with Flash content?

Early versions of Flash left this problem to the individual user; later versions experimented with various ways to detect the existence and version number of Flash Player. Because of the many differences among browsers, platforms, and users' preference settings, no form of Flash detection turned out to be foolproof. The latest implementation of Flash detection in CS4 *still* isn't foolproof—for example, it works only with Player 4 and newer—but it's much more reliable than earlier attempts.

To implement Flash detection:

1. In Publish Settings, select SWF and HTML as the file formats.

2. Click the Flash tab and choose the version of Flash Player that you targeted (see #76).

3. Click the HTML tab and choose a template.

4. Directly below the Template menu, select the Detect Flash Version check box.

5. In the Version field below, enter the version of the Flash Player that you're targeting. (The minor revision numbers are optional.)

   Note
   If your FLA file uses ActionScript 3.0, Flash won't allow you to target versions of the Flash Player earlier than 9.0.

6. Publish the movie. Flash creates a SWF file and an HTML file as usual.

7. Open the HTML file in a text editor or web-page editing program, and scroll down to the line that says `var alternateContent = 'Alternate HTML content should be placed here.'` (**Figure 79a**)

(continued on next page)

Biological Flash Detection

If you find the Flash detection technique described here to be inelegant and unwieldy, consider a low-tech option that's worked well for years: *Let the user take care of it.* Many Web sites start with an entrance page alerting the user that "This site requires version such-and-such of the Flash Player." Below, there's one link to download the Flash Player and another link to enter the site. Most of the time, the user can figure out what to do.

```
52        'allowFullScreen','false',
53        'movie', 'myMovie',
54        'salign', ''
55    ); //end AC code
56  } else {  // flash is too old or we can't detect the plugin
57      var alternateContent = 'Alternate HTML content should be placed here.'
58        + 'This content requires the Adobe Flash Player.'
59        + '<a href=http://www.macromedia.com/go/getflash/>Get Flash</a>';
60      document.write(alternateContent);  // insert non-flash content
61    }
62  }
63  // -->
64  </script>
65  <noscript>
66      // Provide alternate content for browsers that do not support scripting
67      // or for those that have scripting disabled.
68      Alternate HTML content should be placed here. This content requires the Adobe
Flash Player.
69      <a href="http://www.macromedia.com/go/getflash/">Get Flash</a>
70  </noscript>
71  </body>
72  </html>
```

Figure 79a The alternate content is highlighted in this view of the published HTML code.

There are three lines of text, each enclosed in single quotation marks and joined to the others by a plus sign. These lines of text are what will be seen by a user who has the wrong version of Flash Player (or doesn't have it at all). By default, the text provides a link for downloading the latest version of Flash Player, but you can substitute whatever content you want. (You can even add more lines if you're careful to follow the same syntax.)

8. Scroll down further, until you get to the line that says // Provide alternate content for browsers that do not support scripting.

   Below that comment, there's another copy of the alternate content that you saw in Step 7 (although not in quotation marks this time). This text is what will be seen by a user whose browser has JavaScript turned off.

   As before, you can leave the alternate content as it is or replace it with your own.

9. Save the file and upload it to your Web server along with the SWF file and any other necessary files.

   Your setup of Flash detection is complete. Except in rare cases, users who visit your Web page with the appropriate version of Flash Player will see your movie; others will see the alternate content (**Figure 79b**).

Publishing and Exporting

Figure 79b By default, users who have the wrong Flash Player version see this text in the browser window, but you can substitute your own content.

#**80** Exporting Still Images

Standard Web browsers can display images in the JPEG, GIF, and PNG formats, but unlike GIFs, JPEG and PNG files can't contain animation. If you save your movie as JPEG or PNG, the resulting file will contain only the frame at which the playhead is positioned at the time you export.

Although Flash offers the choice of exporting or publishing, single frames often look better when exported than when published. For example, publishing GIF or PNG files with transparent backgrounds doesn't work properly, but exporting the same images is problem-free.

The ability to export a single frame is handy if you want to include portions of your animation in printed material (this book, for example). Also, it allows you to substitute a still image for an animation in Web browsers that don't have the Flash plug-in (see #79).

Each file format has different strengths and weaknesses:

- **GIF.** As noted in #74, GIF has trouble with continuous-tone images; it's better suited to technical or cartoon-style drawings that have sharp edges and areas of flat color. Unlike JPEG, however, GIF supports transparency: If you select the Transparent option, the background color of the stage drops out.

- **JPEG.** As you saw in #54, JPEG compression can store full-color images in amazingly small files. Apart from that, however, the JPEG file format doesn't have much going for it: it doesn't hold color very accurately, and anything more than moderate compression introduces obvious artifacts.

- **PNG.** PNG is a robust, multipurpose format that combines the best aspects of all the others: it supports full color, masking, and transparency, and it's capable of very good compression. Unfortunately, support for PNG's features is still spotty: Flash, for example, doesn't implement compression in PNG files, and some browsers still don't support PNG transparency.

Although the JPEG and PNG file formats don't support multiple frames as GIF does, it is possible to export a Flash movie as an *image sequence*, in which all the movie's frames are saved as a series of serially numbered files in the bitmap format of your choice. (**Figure 80**). You'll find this option below File > Export > Export Movie (not, as you might guess, below Export Image). Image sequences are especially useful when you want to enhance each frame individually in Photoshop and then reassemble the movie. Many video editing programs, including Adobe Premiere Pro, recognize image sequences and import them as continuous video clips.

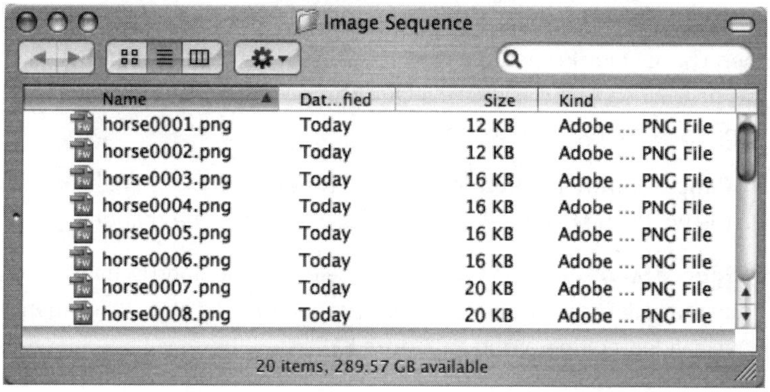

Figure 80 When you export an image sequence, each frame is saved to an individual file.

#81 Exporting a QuickTime Movie

If your Flash movie consists solely of animation, with no ActionScript or interactivity, you can export it in QuickTime format. The resulting file can be viewed in the QuickTime Player, burned to a DVD, or imported into a video-editing program such as Adobe Premiere Pro.

To export a QuickTime movie, choose File > Export > Export Movie; then choose QuickTime from the Format menu in the Export Movie dialog box. When you click Save, a QuickTime Export Settings dialog box appears. The basic settings are:

- **Render Width** and **Render Height.** These dimensions are locked to the width and height of the Flash stage; they can't be changed.

- **Ignore Stage Color.** If this option is selected, the stage is made transparent, allowing the animation to be superimposed on other elements in a video-editing program (**Figure 81**).

Figure 81 When the stage is made transparent, characters in Flash can be composited with live video.

- **Stop Exporting.** To export a QuickTime file, Flash essentially plays your movie in real time and records what it sees. As you learned in #31, Flash rarely plays back animation at a steady frame rate; therefore the exact duration of a movie can't be predicted. You can choose to have Flash export the entire movie regardless of its playback time, or to cut the movie short after a certain number of hours, minutes, and seconds.

- **Store Temp Data.** To keep playback smooth, Flash *buffers* the animation, moving data in and out of temporary storage areas. Buffering in memory provides the best results, but only if the movie is short enough to fit in your computer's available RAM. There's no harm in trying the In Memory option; if the movie stalls because of insufficient RAM, you can try exporting again with On Disk selected.

- **QuickTime Settings.** If you're experienced with digital video, you can click this button to access advanced settings such as audio and video codecs, data rates, and so on.

TV Guidance

For best results, animation for video has to meet strict technical requirements. There are many different video formats, each of which requires different frame rates, stage dimensions, and action-safe zones. Make sure you know what your project's specifications are before you start to animate.

#82 Creating a Standalone Application

The publishing formats we've looked at in this chapter have one important thing in common: They all require some sort of player. Viewing a SWF file requires the Flash Player; viewing a QuickTime file requires the QuickTime Player; even viewing animated GIF files requires a graphics program or a Web browser. In some cases, however, you may want to create a Flash movie that acts like a freestanding computer program—that is, an *application*. This is particularly desirable if the movie uses ActionScript to interact with the user.

Flash offers two ways to create applications—one older, one newer. The old way is to create a *projector*—a hybrid file that combines a SWF file with the playback mechanism of Flash Player. Regardless of whether a computer has Flash Player installed, double-clicking a projector causes the embedded movie to play.

To create a projector, select Windows Projector or Macintosh Projector on the Formats tab in the Publish Settings dialog box. (A Windows projector won't work on a Mac, nor vice versa.) No extra tabs appear, and there are no options for you to set. When you publish the movie, the projector file appears in the same folder as the FLA file.

Because most computers these days already have Flash Player installed, projectors aren't needed very often. Their large file size (at least 2 MB for Windows, and nearly 10 MB for Mac) makes them unsuitable for use on the Web. They're most often used for distributing Flash movies on CD-ROM or DVD-ROM, or for kiosk applications in which a movie runs directly off a computer's hard drive.

Projectors have long been used by amateur software developers as a tool for creating standalone applications: The developer creates the user interface in Flash, adds programming in ActionScript, and then outputs the result as a projector. Double-clicking the projector icon initiates whatever the projector has been programmed to do, even if that has nothing to do with animation (**Figure 82a**).

Figure 82a This desktop clock/timer was built in Flash, programmed in ActionScript, and published as a projector.

Adobe's recent introduction of a technology called *AIR* has made this use of projectors essentially obsolete. AIR, which stands for Adobe Integrated Runtime, is a more sophisticated way of turning Flash movies into applications.

Unlike a projector, an AIR application is cross-platform: It can run on any computer that has the AIR Runtime software installed. *Your* computer already has AIR Runtime; it was installed when you installed Flash. Users who don't have it can download it free from Adobe's website. It's available for both Windows and Macintosh, and a Linux version is being developed.

Here are the basic steps for creating an AIR application:

1. Choose File > New, and then select Flash File (Adobe AIR) from the New Document dialog box; or open an existing FLA file and choose Adobe Air 1.1 from the Player menu in Publish Settings (see #76). Click OK.

2. Add content to the movie as usual, and test it by choosing Control > Test Movie.

3. Make sure Flash (.swf) is selected on the Formats tab in Publish Settings (see #74).

4. Publish the movie. A Digital Signature dialog box appears, with the Sign the AIR File with a Digital Certificate radio button selected by default.

(continued on next page)

5. Click Create. A Create Self-Signed Digital Certificate dialog box appears. (The certificate you're creating will identify you to anyone who installs your AIR application; if they don't have reason to trust you, they can choose not to proceed with the installation.)

6. Fill in the text fields with whatever information is appropriate; then type in a password and confirm it.

7. Click the Browse button at the bottom of the dialog box, navigate to a folder on your hard drive where you want to keep the certificate, and click Choose.

8. Click OK to close the Create Self-Signed Digital Certificate dialog box. An alert box appears, telling you that a certificate has been created. Click OK to close the alert box.

Note
After you've completed Steps 5 through 8, you can reuse the certificate as many times as you like. When you create future AIR applications, you can go directly from Step 4 to Step 9.

9. Enter your password (the one you created in Step 6) in the Password field of the Digital Signature dialog box, and click OK. An alert box appears, informing you that an AIRI file—a temporary installation file—has been created. Click OK to close the alert box.

   Flash has now added three files to the folder in which the FLA file resides. If the name of the FLA file is MyMovie.fla, the new files would be MyMovie.swf (a normal SWF file), MyMovie-app.xml (a data file with information about the movie), and MyMovie.airi (the temporary installation file).

10. Choose File > AIR Settings. An Application & Installer Settings dialog box appears.

11. Change any of the settings in the dialog box (see Help for explanations), or just keep the defaults.

12. At the bottom of the dialog box, click Publish AIR File.

13. As you did in Step 9, enter your password in the Password field of the Digital Signature dialog box, and click OK. An alert box appears, telling you that an AIR file has been created. Click OK to close the alert box.

Flash has added another file to the folder in which the FLA file resides. This file, which has the file extension .air, is the installation file for your application.

When a user double-clicks the AIR file, a dialog box asks whether he or she is willing to install your application. If the user agrees, the application is installed in the standard folder (Program Files on Windows, Applications on Mac) and launches automatically (**Figure 82b**).

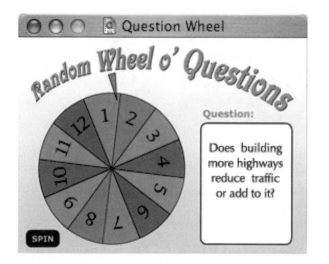

Figure 82b An AIR application looks and runs like any other program on your computer.

CHAPTER ELEVEN

Using Basic ActionScript

Using Flash can be like visiting a restaurant in a foreign country. To request one of the restaurant's standard meals, you can point to what you want on the menu. But to get something prepared a special way, you have to talk to the waiter—and to do that, you have to speak the waiter's language.

The language that Flash understands is ActionScript. If you can "speak" in ActionScript, you can get Flash to do almost anything you want.

Like any other language, ActionScript requires serious study and practice. You can't learn it from a chapter in a book—especially a book like this, which is focused on tasks rather than fundamental principles. All that can be provided here is a taste of how ActionScript works and what its capabilities are. To learn underlying principles and more techniques, try a more in-depth book such as *Flash CS4 Professional Advanced for Windows and Macintosh: Visual QuickPro Guide* by Russell Chun (Peachpit Press).

In the meantime, you can learn a few phrases to use in a pinch—the Flash equivalent of being able to say "Diet Coke, no ice" in a way that the waiter will understand.

#83 Choosing an Appropriate ActionScript Version

The original version of ActionScript, now known as ActionScript 1.0, was designed to be as easy as possible for beginners to learn and use. It had a set of intuitive commands and a simple syntax that made it possible to add *interactivity* to Flash movies—the ability of viewers to start, stop, skip around in, and otherwise affect the movies they were watching.

At the time ActionScript 1.0 was released, no one envisioned that Flash would become a professional-level tool for building complex interfaces and Web applications. Nevertheless, as more serious programmers began to use Flash, they began to develop sophisticated kinds of interactivity—such as allowing users to input data or interact with server-side software—that pushed against ActionScript's limitations. The Flash development team responded with a revised and extended scripting language, ActionScript 2.0, which gave experienced programmers many of the tools they needed while remaining accessible to nonprogrammers.

The current version, ActionScript 3.0, created a stir when it was released a couple of years ago. Unlike its predecessors, it's an industrial-strength, object-oriented programming language (see #87) that has much in common with widely used languages such as C++ and Java.

On the positive side, ActionScript 3.0 makes Flash a viable development tool for sophisticated applications, both on the Web and—with the help of Adobe AIR (see #82)—on the desktop. On the negative side, it puts ActionScript further out of beginners' reach. Unless you're familiar with the principles and techniques of object-oriented programming—or are willing to learn them—you won't be able to do much with ActionScript 3.0.

Fortunately, Flash CS4 continues to support earlier versions of Action-Script (**Figure 83**). When you create a new document, the first decision Flash requires you to make is whether you want to use ActionScript 2.0 or 3.0. (Choosing 2.0 allows the use of 1.0 as well.) The choice you make determines which versions of Flash Player you can target in Publish Settings (see #76) and which commands are available to you in the Actions panel (see #84).

If you're a newcomer to ActionScript, you have two options.

The first is to start with 1.0 and work your way gradually toward 3.0. A drawback of this approach is that it instills bad programming habits that you'll have to unlearn when you begin scripting in 3.0. Another drawback is that it limits the things you can do with Flash—for example, the 3D and Inverse Kinematics tools work only in ActionScript 3.0 FLA files.

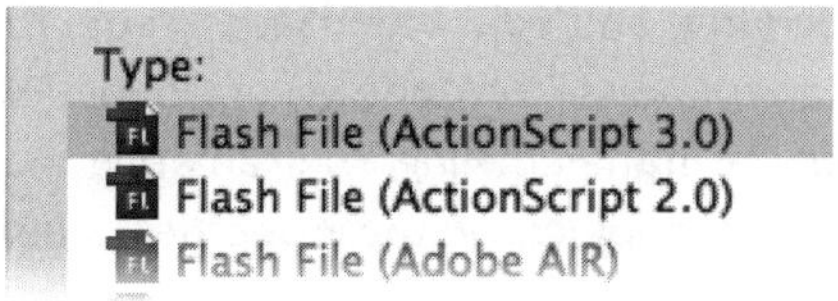

Type:

🗋 **Flash File (ActionScript 3.0)**

🗋 Flash File (ActionScript 2.0)

🗋 Flash File (Adobe AIR)

Figure 83 There's no such thing as a generic FLA file. When you choose File > New, you're required to choose between an ActionScript 2.0 file and an ActionScript 3.0 file. Once you've made that decision, you can't change your FLA file from one type to the other.

The second option is to start working with 3.0 right away. Although the learning curve is steeper and the scripting process is slower, the skills you acquire will be up to date.

This chapter is geared to the second option; it focuses entirely on ActionScript 3.0. Although you can't learn how to program in a span of 25-or-so pages, you can learn enough fundamentals and see enough simple examples to get you started.

Scripting vs. Programming

You often hear the words *script* and *program* used interchangeably to describe coded instructions to a computer. What's the difference?

As you know, a computer's processor can respond only to instructions in binary code—a string of 0's and 1's, often referred to as *machine language*. Instructions written in more complex languages have to be translated into machine language before a computer can use them.

That translation can occur in either of two ways. The more common way is to use a program called a *compiler*, which analyzes the set of written instructions (*source code*) and converts them to machine language (*compiled code*). The other way is to let a program called a *runtime environment* convert the instructions to machine language on the fly, while the instructions are being executed. For example, the Flash Player and AIR (see #82) both provide runtime environments for ActionScript.

Technically speaking, languages whose code is meant to be compiled—such as C++ and Java—are programming languages, while those whose code requires a runtime environment—such as ActionScript and JavaScript—are scripting languages. However, from the code writer's point of view, there's no fundamental difference between them; writing instructions in either type of language requires the same skills and techniques.

Double Play

ActionScript 3.0 is a complete rewrite of ActionScript. Not only are its structure and syntax significantly different from those of ActionScript 1.0 and 2.0, but its technical underpinnings have changed so radically that it's no longer compatible with its predecessors. The only reason Flash Player 10 can handle versions of ActionScript prior to 3.0 is that it contains two separate players: one to execute the current version and one to execute the earlier versions.

For now, the continued existence of that virtual "second player" allows veteran Flash developers to keep using ActionScript 2.0 without having to learn the new techniques. It's likely, however, that some future version of Flash will strip out that older code and support only ActionScript 3.0 and later.

#84 Using the Actions Panel

The Actions panel is where you write and edit ActionScript code. To open it, choose Window > Actions or press F9 (Windows) or Option-F9 (Mac). If you've selected a keyframe in the timeline, you can open the Actions panel by clicking the ActionScript icon in the Properties panel (**Figure 84a**).

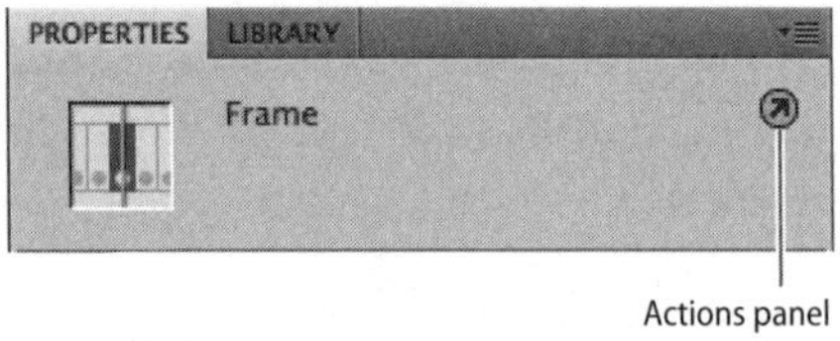

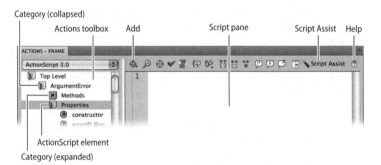

Figure 84a This icon appears in the Properties panel when you've selected a keyframe or a symbol instance to which a script can be attached. Click the icon to open the Actions panel.

By default, the Actions panel has three panes, although it can acquire a fourth pane if you turn on Script Assist (see #85). The top-left pane is the Actions toolbox, which contains a categorized list of ActionScript elements, including commands, functions, classes, methods, properties, and other items (**Figure 84b**). The right pane is the Script pane, where you write and edit your scripts. Double-clicking an ActionScript element in the toolbox causes it to appear in the Script pane, accompanied by any necessary punctuation.

Figure 84b In the Actions panel, categories are indicated by an open or closed book icon; ActionScript elements are indicated by a round ActionScript icon.

Many beginners prefer to look up the ActionScript elements they need in the toolbox and double-click them to let Flash "write" a script in the Script pane, often with the aid of Script Assist. If you're not sure what an item means or how it's used, you can select it and click the Help icon for an explanation. (If you prefer, you can choose ActionScript elements from menus and submenus by clicking the Add icon, but you can't use Help in that case.)

Tip
Another way to add an element to your script is to drag it directly from the toolbox into the Script pane.

Once you have enough experience with ActionScript, you may choose to type your code directly into the Script pane—a much faster technique, but one that can more easily lead to mistakes.

If your FLA file contains more than one script, the bottom-left pane—called the *Script Navigator*—helps you find the one you're looking for. Double-clicking a script in the Script Navigator "pins" the script, keeping it visible in the Actions panel even if you select something else on the stage or in the timeline.

#85 Using Script Assist

Most ActionScript commands require additional information for Flash to carry them out. For example, if you use the command gotoAndStop (which moves the playhead to a specified frame and pauses it there), Flash has to know which frame you want to move to and which timeline that frame is in. These extra pieces of information are called *parameters*.

If you're not experienced with ActionScript, you probably don't know what parameters a particular command requires and how they need to be coded. Clicking the Script Assist button (Figure 84b) opens a new pane in the Actions panel that helps answer these questions.

Script Assist does two things: If you select an ActionScript element in the toolbox, the Script Assist pane displays a brief description of that element (**Figure 85**). If you bring that element into the Script pane (by double-clicking or dragging it), Script Assist adds a field or menu for each parameter that the command requires. As you fill in each parameter, Script Assist adds it to the script with the proper syntax.

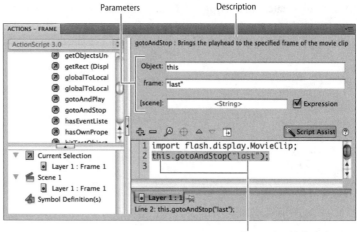

Figure 85 The Script Assist pane defines the selected ActionScript element and provides a convenient way to specify parameters.

For clarity of presentation, the coding examples you'll see in this chapter assume that Script Assist is turned off. When you begin to do your own coding from scratch, however, you may find it helpful to keep the Script Assist pane open.

Thanks but No Thanks

Since ActionScript 3.0 is more difficult to learn than earlier versions were, you'd think that beginners would want all the help they could get. Regrettably, many users have reported that Script Assist mode is much less helpful for ActionScript 3.0 than it was for earlier versions.

ActionScript 1.0 and 2.0 were somewhat intuitive; users could browse through the Actions toolbox and find the commands they needed to carry out simple tasks, then use Script Assist to help them work those commands into usable code. ActionScript 3.0, by contrast, is plainly *not* intuitive. Most new users find that the easiest way to get the code they want is to look for model scripts (such as those in this book) and adapt those samples to their own needs. In such situations, it's usually easier and less time-consuming to type the code directly into the Actions panel than to navigate through Script Assist.

#86 Writing a Simple Frame Script

In ActionScript 3.0, every script must be attached to a keyframe in the timeline. When you play a movie, and the playhead arrives at a keyframe that has an attached script, Flash executes the instructions in that script.

For a very simple example, suppose you have a movie that's 20 frames long. When the playhead leaves frame 20, its default behavior is to snap back to frame 1, causing the movie to loop. In this case, however, you don't want the movie to loop—you want it to play once and stop.

You can accomplish this with a script:

1. Insert a keyframe in frame 20.

2. With that keyframe still selected, make sure that the script type on the upper-left corner of the Actions panel is Actions – Frame (**Figure 86a**). If it's anything other than that, the keyframe isn't selected. Go back and reselect it.

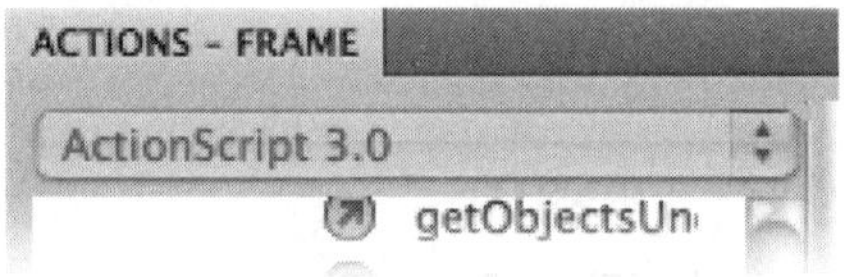

Figure 86a Before you create a script, make sure that the tab at the top of the Actions panel says Actions – Frame.

3. In the Script pane, type the following:

```
stop();
```

Keep all the letters lowercase, and be sure to include the parentheses and the semicolon. (For an explanation of the odd punctuation, see the sidebar "Syntax, Part 1.")

Note
When you write a script in the Actions panel, you don't have to press Enter or click an OK button to make the script "stick." A script becomes active the moment it's entered in the Script pane.

4. Preview or test the movie. When the playhead reaches frame 20, it executes the script; as a result, the movie stops.

You can tell that a keyframe has a script attached to it by the letter *a* that appears in the timeline (**Figure 86b**). Technically, you can attach a script to any keyframe. In practice, however, it's highly recommended that you add a new layer and put all your scripts in that layer. (Most people call the layer *Actions* or *Scripts*, and they put it at the top of the timeline so that it can be seen easily.)

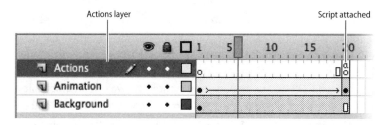

Figure 86b Scripts (indicated by the letter *a*) should be placed in a layer of their own.

Besides `stop`, the command used most frequently in simple scripts is `gotoAndPlay`. For example, imagine 20-frame animation in which a match lights a candle and exits in frame 15, leaving the candle flame flickering. You'd want the candle-lighting portion of the animation to play once, but you'd want the candle to go on flickering indefinitely. In this case, you could attach a script to frame 20 that tells the playhead to jump to frame 16. The technique is illustrated in **Figure 86c**.

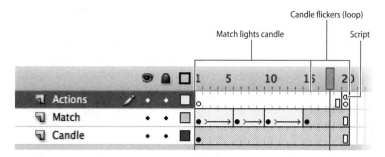

Figure 86c Every time the playhead reaches frame 20, a script causes the playhead to go to frame 16.

Syntax, Part 1

Every ActionScript command or function is followed by a set of parentheses intended to hold parameters. For example, in `gotoAndPlay(16)`, the parameter is the frame number 16. Some commands, such as `stop()`, don't require any parameters, but the parentheses must be there anyway.

Many scripts have multiple commands that are executed in sequence. We tell Flash where each command ends by putting a semicolon after it. Even in a script that comprises only one command, the semicolon must be there:

```
stop();
```

#87 Exploring the Basics of Object-Oriented Programming

Computer programming is sometimes described as feeding a computer a series of instructions. That description was more accurate in the early days of computing, when programmers used line-oriented languages such as FORTRAN and COBOL. Programs in those languages essentially told the computer "First you do this, next you do this. . . ." Even now, the simple scripts we looked at in #86 work in much the same way: They give Flash linear instructions such as "When the playhead gets to frame 20, send it to frame 16."

Starting in the 1980s, a more sophisticated programming model, called *object-oriented programming* (OOP), became common. The basic idea behind OOP was to manage a computer the way we manage large organizations. For example, the president of a company doesn't sequentially dictate every action that takes place in the company; instead, he or she delegates responsibilities to top-level staff, who delegate some of their responsibilities to lower-level staff, and so on. As a result, a variety of actions can take place at the same time, each independent of the others.

Similarly, imagine a Flash movie with a collection of buttons on the stage. Because they're buttons, they all have a common purpose: to respond to a user's mouse movements and clicks. Among them, one group of buttons may look and work a certain way because they're all instances of a particular symbol; another group may look and work another way because they're instances of a different symbol. There are further differences within each group: Each button has its own instructions about what to do when a user clicks it or rolls over it. Each button does its job individually, independent of what the other buttons are doing.

The elementary scripts we'll be working with won't come close to demonstrating the power and flexibility of this sort of programming model. Nevertheless, there are some OOP-related terms and ideas that you need to be familiar with for the rest of this chapter to make sense.

- **Class.** A class is a group whose members have something fundamental in common. As noted earlier, all buttons in Flash have broadly shared characteristics; therefore, ActionScript provides a Button class. (Class names always begin with a capital letter.) Other examples include the MovieClip, Sound, and Math classes.

- **Object.** An object is a member of a class. However, the word is often used loosely—for example, a movie-clip symbol is an object, but so is an instance of that symbol. In practice, anything that you can place in the timeline or control by means of ActionScript can be thought of as an object.

- **Property.** A property is a characteristic of an object—for example, its size, position, or opacity. An object's properties depend on what class it belongs to. A sound, for example, has volume and duration among its properties, but not height or visibility.

- **Method.** A method is an activity that an object is capable of carrying out. As with properties, an object's methods depend on the class that the object belongs to. For example, a movie clip's methods include playing and stopping; a text string's methods include splitting into substrings.

- **Instance Name.** ActionScript can "talk" to instances of movie-clip and button symbols, but only if you assign each instance an *instance name* by which ActionScript can distinguish it from other objects in the movie. To do so, select the instance on the stage and type a name in the Instance Name field in the Properties panel (**Figure 87**). The name can be whatever you like, but it must begin with a lowercase letter and contain only letters and numbers, with no spaces or punctuation. It's recommended—though not required—that you give movie-clip instance names the suffix *_mc*, and button instance names the suffix *_btn* (see #91).

Figure 87 Select an instance and type the name of your choice in the Instance Name field in the Properties panel. Only instances of buttons and movie clips can be given instance names.

#88 Writing a Simple Event-Handling Script

Some commands—such as stop and gotoAndPlay—are carried out automatically when Flash encounters them in a script (see #86). Others are executed only in response to an *event*—something that happens on the stage, in the timeline, or elsewhere in the Flash environment.

In ActionScript 3.0, responding to events is the responsibility of an object called an *event listener*. Each event listener is assigned a particular event to "listen" for—for example, the pressing of a key on the keyboard. If and when that event takes place, the event listener carries out a predefined set of instructions. The event listener and its instructions are usually defined in a script in frame 1 of the timeline.

Let's look at an example. In #27, you created a button symbol that displayed a rollover effect, but didn't do anything else. To make practical use of an instance of that symbol, you have to create an event listener for it. (For easier reading, we'll refer to an instance of a button symbol simply as a *button*.)

Let's say you've placed a button on the stage. You want to use it as a pause button, so that when the user clicks it, the movie stops. Here's a way to do that:

1. Select the button on the stage.

2. In the blank field at the top of the Properties panel, type an instance name (see #87). For this example, we'll name the instance *pause_btn*.

3. Create a Script layer in the timeline and select the keyframe in cell 1.

4. In the Actions panel, click the Insert Target Path icon (**Figure 88**). A dialog box appears, listing all of the objects that have instance names.

5. Select pause_btn and click OK. The Script pane displays this.happy_ btn followed by a flashing cursor.

Note
If you prefer, you could just type the instance name. The advantage of using the Target Path icon is that you can choose the name from a list instead of having to remember it.

Insert Target Path

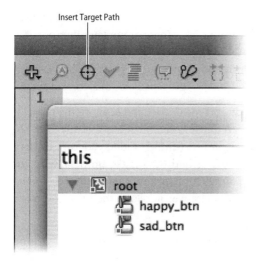

Figure 88 Clicking the Insert Target Path icon opens a dialog box that lists all of the objects with instance names.

6. Press the Period key. A list appears, containing all the possible Action-Script elements that might follow the instance name.

7. From the list, double-click addEventListener. The Script pane now displays `this.happy_btn.addEventListener(`

8. Complete the line of code as follows, paying special attention to the case of the characters:

`this.happy_btn.addEventListener(MouseEvent.CLICK, movie-Pause);`

(continued on next page)

Syntax, Part 2

ActionScript uses braces—often known as *curly braces*, to distinguish them more clearly from parentheses and brackets—to identify commands that will be executed if a condition is met or a function is called. It's technically okay to put the braces and their contents on a single line, for example:

```
function
moviePause(event:
MouseEvent){stop();}
```

Among programmers, however, the convention is to insert a line break after the first brace and before the last, and to indent the commands between the braces. Flash ignores line breaks, tabs, and extra spaces when it interprets ActionScript.

The MouseEvent object causes the button to "listen" for a mouse-related event, in this case a click. (There are many other possible mouse events, such as DOUBLE_CLICK and ROLL_OVER. To see them, go to the Actions toolbox and choose flash.events > MouseEvent > Properties.)

The word *moviePause* doesn't mean anything at all; it's the name of a user-defined *function*. A function can be thought of as an Action-Script command that you invent. (It's like writing your own dictionary—you can make up words and then make up definitions for them.) We used moviePause for this example, but a function's name can be whatever you like, so long as it follows the rules governing instance names (see #87).

9. Press Enter (Windows) or Return (Mac) to start a new line. Type the following lines of code:

```
function moviePause(event:MouseEvent){
        stop();
}
```

This code creates a function called *moviePause*, whose definition—stop();—resides within the curly braces. Once the function has been defined, it can be *called* (executed) at any time.

The phrase in parentheses (event:MouseEvent) isn't strictly part of the function. It's an example of *data typing*, which is used in Action-Script 3.0 to make coding errors easier to detect. In this case, it tells Flash that the only type of event that will be allowed to trigger this function is a mouse event.

10. Preview or test the movie.

When you click the pause button on the stage, the event listener "hears" the click of the mouse button; in response, it calls the movie-Pause function, causing the movie to stop.

To allow the user to resume the movie, you can create a play button: Follow the same steps, but create a different function name (for example, movieResume) in Steps 8 and 9, and replace stop(); with play(); in Step 9.

#89 Organizing the Timeline for Interactivity

When you play an audio CD, you can listen to it all the way through from beginning to end, or you can jump from one track to another. The Flash timeline can work the same way. The techniques we've worked with so far involve playing the timeline continuously from beginning to end, but it's also possible to divide it into discrete segments and let the user decide which segments to play.

For example, imagine a Flash movie that shows a neutral face and two buttons, one labeled Happy and one labeled Sad. If the user clicks the Happy button, you want the corners of the mouth to turn upward; if the user clicks the Sad button, you want them to turn downward (**Figure 89a**).

Figure 89a The static frame at the beginning of the movie is shown on the left. In the center, you see the result of clicking the Happy button; on the right, the result of clicking the Sad button.

You can accomplish this by dividing the timeline into three segments. The first segment displays the neutral face; since it's not animated, it only has to be one frame long. The second segment animates the transition from neutral to happy; the third segment animates the transition from neutral to sad (**Figure 89b**).

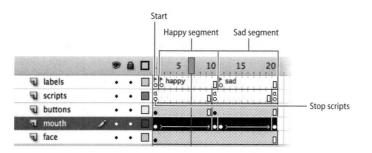

Figure 89b The timeline has been divided into three segments, each of which begins with a frame label and ends with a stop script.

To make this arrangement work, you need to add stop scripts to various frames (see #86): one in frame 1, to keep the playhead paused at the beginning of the movie until the user clicks a button; one in frame 11, to stop the playhead from moving into the "sad" segment when it comes to the end of the "happy" segment; and one in the final frame, to prevent the playhead from snapping back to frame 1.

You also need to write event-handling code for the buttons. As noted in #88, event listeners are usually defined in a script in frame 1. Since frame 1 already contains a script, you'll need to add more code to the existing script. Select the script's keyframe in the timeline and add the following lines of code after the stop command in the Actions panel:

```
this.happy_btn.addEventListener(MouseEvent.CLICK, goSmile);
this.sad_btn.addEventListener(MouseEvent.CLICK, goFrown);
function goSmile(event:MouseEvent) {
        gotoAndPlay(2);
}
function goFrown(event:MouseEvent) {
        gotoAndPlay(12);
}
```

(Note that goSmile and goFrown are made-up function names; you can replace them with whatever names you like.)

There's still one problem with this arrangement: If you decide to move any of the keyframes to lengthen or shorten the animation, you'll have to go back and change the frame numbers in the scripts. If you forget to do this, or if you change the numbers incorrectly, the movie won't work.

The solution to this problem is to use *frame labels* to mark the beginning of each segment. To add a label to a frame, insert a keyframe (if there's not one there already), select the keyframe, and type a label into the Frame Label field in the Properties panel (**Figure 89c**). The label appears in the timeline, marked by a red flag.

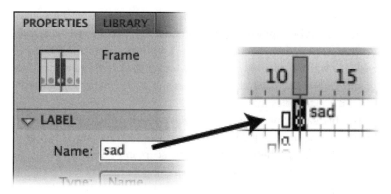

Figure 89c Entering a frame label in the Properties panel (left) makes the label appear in the timeline (right).

You can now change the frame numbers in the scripts to frame labels, as in:

```
function goSmile(event:MouseEvent) {
        gotoAndPlay("happy");
}
function goFrown(event:MouseEvent) {
        gotoAndPlay("sad");
}
```

The frame labels have to be in quotation marks, or Flash won't recognize them. Also, note that ActionScript is case-sensitive, so you can't use "Happy" as the parameter if the frame label is "happy."

Like scripts, frame labels are best placed in a layer of their own at the top of the timeline. If you need to move a keyframe of animation, you can select the frame label at the same time and move them in tandem.

#90 Controlling Movie Clips from a Script

Although the movie we created in #89 is technically "legal," most programmers wouldn't be happy with it. The ActionScript code is scattered among various scripts—a long script in frame 1 and short scripts in frames 11 and 20—with no easy way to know which instructions are where. Programmers prefer to have all their code in one place, where they can easily revise it and troubleshoot it.

For this reason, many professional Flash developers strive to limit their movies to one frame. All the animation is stored inside movie-clip symbols, which can be controlled by a single script in the main timeline. (As you learned in #28, one of the distinguishing features of movie clips is that they respond to ActionScript commands.)

To see how this might be done, let's work with the same example that is used in #89: a movie in which the Happy button causes a face to smile and the Sad button causes it to frown. Here are the steps you might follow:

1. Create two movie-clip symbols—one containing animation of the neutral-to-happy face, the other containing the animation of the neutral-to-sad face. (For this example, we'll name the symbols *m_happy* and *m_sad*, although you can use whatever names you like.) Be sure to put a stop script at the end of each movie clip's animation (**Figure 90a**).

Figure 90a On the left, the internal timeline and animation of the movie clip m_happy; on the right, the same elements of the movie clip m_sad.

2. In frame 1 of the movie's main timeline, recreate the layout shown in Figure 89a: the neutral face and two buttons. In this case, however, use an instance of m_happy for the face.

3. Select the instance of m_happy and give it an instance name—for example, happy_mc.

4. Stack an instance of m_sad on top of the instance of m_happy. Make sure both are positioned in exactly the same place on the stage.

5. Select the instance of m_sad and give it an instance name—for example, sad_mc.

6. Create a layer called *Script*. The timeline should now resemble the one in **Figure 90b**.

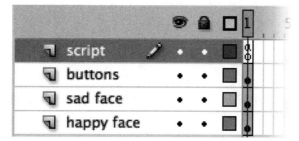

Figure 90b The movie's timeline is only one frame long.

7. Select the keyframe in the Script layer.

8. In the Actions panel, click the Insert Target Path icon (see #88). A dialog box appears, listing all of the objects with instance names.

9. Select happy_mc and click OK. The Script pane displays this.happy_mc followed by a flashing cursor.

Note
Be sure to select happy_mc (the movie clip), not happy_btn (the button).

10. Press the Period key. A list appears, containing all the possible Action-Script elements that might follow the instance name.

11. From the list, double-click *stop*. The Script pane now displays this.happy_mc.stop(

12. Type the closing parenthesis and semicolon: this.happy_mc.stop();

(continued on next page)

#90: Controlling Movie Clips from a Script

Syntax, Part 3

A line of code such as this.happy_mc.stop(); illustrates ActionScript's use of *dot syntax* to communicate with movie-clip instances. The "dot" refers to the period that separates the instance name from the command that follows it. As you saw in Steps 15 and 16, you can use dot syntax to control a movie clip's properties (such as visibility) or methods (such as playing or stopping).

You've seen that when you type an instance name followed by a period in the Actions panel, Flash presents you with a list of all the properties and methods that could conceivably follow the "dot." This list is a real time-saver, but it only appears if the instance name has an _mc suffix (for movie clips) or a _btn suffix (for buttons).

You've just used ActionScript to issue a command to a movie-clip instance. Specifically, you've told the instance called *happy_mc* not to play its internal animation, thus ensuring that the face on the stage will keep its neutral expression.

13. Repeat Steps 8 through 12 for sad_mc.

14. In the Actions panel, create event listeners and functions for the two buttons as you did in #89.

15. Modify the goSmile function as follows:

```
function goSmile(event:MouseEvent) {
    this.sad_mc.visible=false;
    this.happy_mc.play();
}
```

Note

If you wish, you can use the Insert Target Path icon for this step, as you did for Steps 9 through 12.

Once again, you've used ActionScript to communicate with a movie clip—or, in this case, two movie clips. You've told sad_mc to become invisible, so it won't block happy_mc. Then you've told happy_mc to play its internal animation.

16. Modify the goFrown function as follows:

```
function goFrown(event:MouseEvent) {
    this.sad_mc.visible=true;
    this.sad_mc.play();
}
```

This function makes sad_mc visible and causes it to play its internal animation.

17. Test the movie. It should work identically to the movie in #89.

#91 Converting Animation to ActionScript

One of the trickier aspects of using ActionScript is coding an object's movement on the stage. A series of motion tweens that takes a few minutes to create in the timeline could take hours to recreate in ActionScript.

Why would you *want* to animate in ActionScript rather than in the timeline? Usually, it's because you want to be able to vary the animation while the movie is playing—for example, by giving the user controls that allow the movement to be sped up, slowed down, or even redirected. If the animation is coded as a function in ActionScript, you can change any aspect of the animation by feeding new parameters to the function.

Flash has the ability to convert timeline animation to ActionScript code. It works with motion tweens only —not with shape tweens or frame-by-frame animation—and it converts to ActionScript 3.0 only. To use it:

1. Motion-tween an object on the stage. The animation can be as elaborate as you want: It can contain any number of intermediate keyframes, and you can adjust any of its properties in the Motion Editor (see #44).

2. Choose a movie-clip symbol to which you want to copy the animation, and drag an instance to the stage. (Graphic and button symbols won't work.)

3. Give the new object an instance name (see #87).

4. In the timeline, select all the frames of the original object's motion tween (**Figure 91**).

Figure 91 The animation you copy can have as many keyframes as you want, as long as they are confined to one layer.

5. Choose Edit > Timeline > Copy Motion as ActionScript 3.0. A dialog box appears, asking for the instance name of the object to which you want to apply the animation.

6. Type in the instance name from Step 3 and click OK.

(continued on next page)

7. If there's not already an Actions layer in the timeline, create one; then select the keyframe in frame 1.

8. Open the Actions panel (if it's not already open) and click in the Script pane.

9. Choose Edit > Paste. The ActionScript code representing the animation appears in the pane.

10. Test the movie and compare the coded motion of the second object to the timeline animation of the first object. They should look the same.

Try changing some parameters in the ActionScript code; then test the movie again. The coded animation will look different; the timeline animation will stay the same.

If you wish, you can remove the original object from the timeline.

#92 Using External AS Files

The scripts we've worked with so far have all been embedded in the FLA file. You have the option, however, of keeping your scripts in external files. External files are useful for editing scripts without having to open them in Flash, storing scripts that are too long to fit conveniently into the Actions panel, or sharing one script among several movies.

An external script file is a plain text file. You can create one in any text-editing program, as long as you save it with a filename that has an AS extension. Another option is to use the Script window built into Flash. Like the Actions panel, it contains an Actions toolbox and other tools to help you write and edit your script (**Figure 92**). When you save a script in the Script window, the resulting file is automatically given the AS extension.

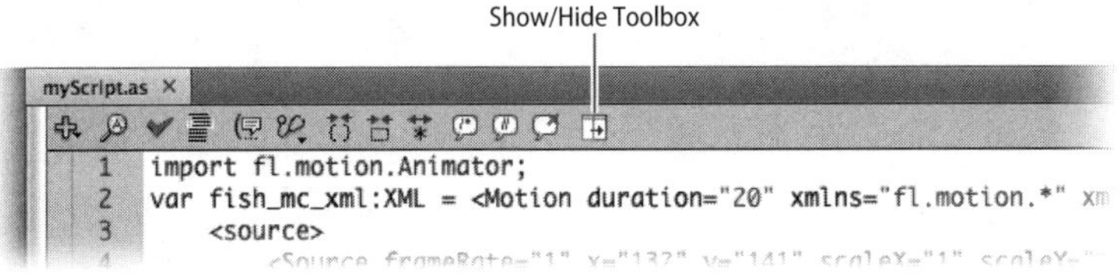

Show/Hide Toolbox

```
1  import fl.motion.Animator;
2  var fish_mc_xml:XML = <Motion duration="20" xmlns="fl.motion.*" xm
3      <source>
```

Figure 92 The Script window initially appears with the Actions toolbox hidden. To access the toolbox, click the Show/Hide Toolbox icon.

The Script window is often overlooked because it's not on the Window menu (or, for that matter, any other menu). To get to it, choose File > New to open the New File dialog box; then choose ActionScript File from the list of file types. To edit an existing AS file in the Script window, choose File > Open and navigate to the file, or double-click the file outside of Flash.

An AS file won't be executed unless you associate it with a specific FLA file:

1. Put the AS file and the FLA file in the same folder.

2. Add a script, or edit the existing script, in frame 1 of the FLA file's timeline. Add the command `include "filename.as"` (keeping the quotation marks, but replacing *filename* with the actual name of the file).

3. Test or publish the movie. Flash incorporates the contents of the AS file into the SWF file.

Because the AS file is needed only when you *create* the SWF file—not when you play it—there's no need to upload AS files to a Web server. Remember, however, that if you make any changes to the AS file, they won't take effect until you generate a new SWF file.

Note

Some types of ActionScript code, such as definitions of classes, are required to be in external files. To associate those with a FLA file, you use the `import` *command rather than* `include`.

#93 Formatting and Validating a Script

As was noted in #88, Flash ignores tabs, line breaks, and extra spaces when it interprets ActionScript. An entire script could be written on one long line, and Flash wouldn't know the difference: To make sense of a script, it pays attention only to punctuation such as parentheses, braces, and semicolons.

Nevertheless, it's important to format a script neatly and consistently, so that people who edit your script can know at a glance what's going on. Flash does some formatting on the fly when you type in the Actions panel or Script window, but it doesn't do really thorough formatting until you click the Auto Format icon (**Figure 93a**).

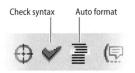

Check syntax   Auto format

Figure 93a These icons appear in the Actions panel only if Script Assist is turned off.

To format your script, Flash has to *understand* the script: It has to know which words are commands, which are variables, which are properties, and so on. Assuming your spelling, syntax, and punctuation are correct, Flash has no trouble figuring out what's what. If you've made even a single error, however, Flash loses its bearings. As a result, when you click Auto Format, you'll often see an alert telling you that formatting was unsuccessful (**Figure 93b**).

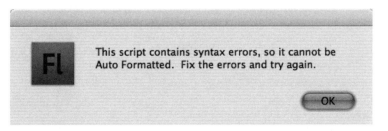

Fl   This script contains syntax errors, so it cannot be Auto Formatted. Fix the errors and try again.

OK

Figure 93b This alert appears if errors in your script prevent Flash from formatting it.

(continued on next page)

Finding a mistake can be difficult when there's only one incorrect character among thousands. Flash makes the task easier by giving you some guidance: A panel called Compiler Errors appears and lists the errors that Flash found (**Figure 93c**).

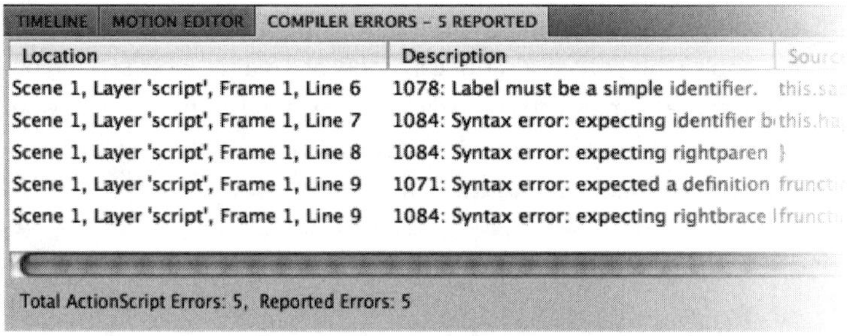

TIMELINE	MOTION EDITOR	COMPILER ERRORS – 5 REPORTED	
Location		Description	Sourc
Scene 1, Layer 'script', Frame 1, Line 6		1078: Label must be a simple identifier.	this.sa
Scene 1, Layer 'script', Frame 1, Line 7		1084: Syntax error: expecting identifier b	this.ha
Scene 1, Layer 'script', Frame 1, Line 8		1084: Syntax error: expecting rightparen	}
Scene 1, Layer 'script', Frame 1, Line 9		1071: Syntax error: expected a definition	frunct
Scene 1, Layer 'script', Frame 1, Line 9		1084: Syntax error: expecting rightbrace	lfrunct

Total ActionScript Errors: 5, Reported Errors: 5

Figure 93c The Compiler Errors panel describes the problems Flash found in your script.

Note
Clicking the Check Syntax icon finds and identifies the same errors that clicking Auto Format does, but without attempting to format your script.

#94 Testing an Interactive Movie

The Check Syntax and Auto Format features find errors in the *structure* of your script, but they don't find errors in the *content*. Suppose you have the following script in frame 1:

```
this.myButton_btn.addEventListener(MouseEvent.CLICK,
disappear);
function disappear(event:MouseEvent) {
        this.myInstance_mc.visible=false;
}
```

When the user clicks the button called *myButton_btn*, this script is supposed to cause a movie-clip instance called *myInstance_mc* to become invisible. In the Actions panel, the script checks out with no errors; the vocabulary and syntax are fine.

But imagine that when you test the movie, it doesn't work. No matter how many times you click the button, myInstance_mc remains visible on the stage. What do you do now?

The first step is to figure out where the problems might be. Perhaps the button isn't receiving your mouse clicks. Perhaps the script isn't communicating properly with the button. Perhaps there's something wrong with myInstance_mc.

The next step is to test each of these possibilities. In a situation like this, the *trace* command is indispensable. Its job is to send you status reports from inside a movie.

For example, you might modify your function as follows:

```
function disappear(event:MouseEvent) {
        trace ("The button has been clicked");
}
```

The trace command always communicates through the Output panel. In this case, when you test the movie and click the button, the Output panel pops open and displays the message "The button has been clicked." This tells you that the button is indeed receiving your mouse clicks and that the script is working.

The trace command can send two types of messages. The first type, shown in this example, is what's called a *string*—a collection of characters that ActionScript doesn't understand, but you do. A string is surrounded by quotation marks. When the trace command is executed, it simply repeats what's between the quotation marks—in this case, "The button has been clicked."

The other type of message the trace command can send is a *value*. For instance, you might modify your function to look like this:

```
function disappear(event:MouseEvent) {
        trace (myInstance_mc.visible);
}
```

In this example, myInstance_mc.visible—which *isn't* in quotation marks—is an expression ActionScript does understand. If myInstance_mc is visible on the stage, the expression should have a value of "true." If not, the value should be "false."

Let's say you test the movie and click the button. On the stage, myInstance_mc remains visible, as it has all along. In that case, you'd expect the Output panel to display true—but instead, it says:

```
TypeError: Error #1010: A term is undefined and has no
properties.
```

Well, that's strange. An instance has to be either visible or invisible— how can it be undefined and have no properties?

One possible answer is that the instance called *myInstance_mc* doesn't exist. But that seems unlikely; after all, you can see it on the stage.

On the other hand, is the object you're seeing on the stage really myInstance_mc? If you double-check, you might discover that the object's instance name doesn't match what's in the script. For example, if you accidentally named the instance myIntance_mc, then there *is* no object called *myInstance_mc*.

The bottom line is that there's no straightforward procedure for troubleshooting an interactive movie. Troubleshooting is an exercise in creative thinking: You have to be part plumber, part Sherlock Holmes, and part gunslinger with the trace command in your holster.

#95 Using the Debugger

Using the Debugger for the simple scripts we're using in this book is like using a sledgehammer to swat flies. For tracking down errors in a beginner's ActionScript file, the trace command (see #94) is usually all you need.

Most of the Debugger's features become useful with scripts that contain variables, nested functions, and if-else statements, all of which are beyond the scope of this book. There is, however, a feature that can come in handy for scripts of any size: the ability to set breakpoints.

A *breakpoint* is a pause that you insert between lines of ActionScript code. When you play a movie in the Debugger, the script stops executing at each breakpoint and continues only when you want it to. By seeing how your script executes step by step, you can often find out where the problems are.

You can add breakpoints to a script in the Actions panel by clicking in the margin to the left of any line of code. Clicking once turns a breakpoint on (identified by a red dot); clicking again turns the breakpoint off (**Figure 95a**). Breakpoints are saved with the FLA file, but they don't have any effect unless the movie is played in the Debugger.

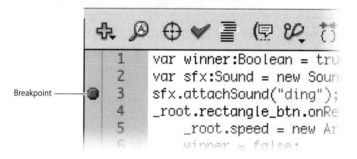

Figure 95a A breakpoint is indicated by a red dot in the left margin of a script. You can set breakpoints in the Actions window or in the Code View pane of the Debugger.

(continued on next page)

To see your breakpoints in action, select Debug > Debug Movie. Your movie previews in the Flash Player as it normally does when you test a movie, and the Debugger—a collection of five panels—opens at the same time (**Figure 95b**). In the Code View panel, you can see your script displayed as it is in the Actions panel. A yellow arrow moves from line to line as the script executes. When it gets to a breakpoint, the execution stops.

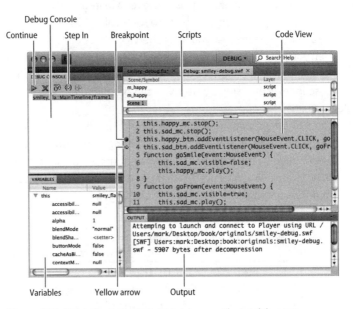

Debug Console

Continue Step In Breakpoint Scripts Code View

Variables Yellow arrow Output

Figure 95b This is the ActionScript 3.0 debugger. The 2.0 debugger is laid out differently, but has many of the same features.

From the breakpoint, you can step through lines of code, one by one, by clicking the Step In icon, or you can click Continue to resume execution of the script.

To return from the Debugger to the normal Flash environment, choose Debug > End Debug Session.

CHAPTER TWELVE

Using Components

If you use Flash frequently, there may be symbols that you've found yourself using over and over—a button, for example. There's no point in recreating the symbol and its accompanying ActionScript if you can reuse a symbol and script that you've already made.

Flash takes that principle a step further: It provides ready-made, pre-scripted symbols, called *components*, that you can use in any movie. You can find them in the Components panel (Window > Components).

The ActionScript inside these components is thorough and robust, so you can depend on them to work properly in every situation. In addition, because the ActionScript has been compiled (see #83), the scripts run much faster and make fewer demands on the computer than scripts you'd write yourself.

To make the best use of components, you have to be able to write scripts that will integrate them into your movie. Like the previous chapter, this chapter doesn't attempt to teach the level of ActionScript you need to know, but it does provide a few examples that will allow you to use components in simple ways.

Because ActionScript 3.0 and 2.0 are mutually incompatible, Flash comes with two different sets of components. If you choose ActionScript 3.0 as the scripting language for a FLA file, the Components panel shows the ActionScript 3.0 components; otherwise, it shows the ActionScript 2.0 components. The ActionScript 3.0 components are uniformly faster, lighter, and easier to use than those for 2.0. For that reason, we'll focus here on the ActionScript 3.0 components, although some of the techniques you see here will apply to earlier component versions as well.

#96 Getting to Know the ActionScript 3.0 Components

Gimme More

If the components that came with Flash aren't enough to satisfy you, there's a way to get more: In Flash, choose Help > Flash Exchange, and your Web browser will take you to the home page for Adobe Exchange. Formerly a place where users could upload and download extensions for Flash, Fireworks, and Dreamweaver, the Exchange has expanded to include tutorials, clip art, filters, and other downloadable accessories for all of the products in the Creative Suite. Choosing Flash on the Exchange home page takes you to Flash Exchange, where you'll find a variety of components and other files that you can try, buy, or use free. Clicking the name of a file takes you to an information-and-download page.

Although the page includes a Browse by Category list, Components isn't one of the categories; the files are classified by function rather than by type. If you want a Flash component, click Advanced Search (which is above the list of categories); then enter *component* as your keyword

(continued on next page)

The ActionScript 3.0 components that come with Flash CS4 fall into two categories: user-interface (UI) components and video components. The UI components (**Figure 96a**) are familiar elements that allow users to interact with programs and Web sites: buttons, menus, sliders, check boxes, and so forth. The video components (**Figure 96b**) allow users to control video that's playing back as part of a Flash movie.

Figure 96a The Components panel is shown here displaying the ActionScript 3.0 UI components.

Figure 96b. With the exception of the FLVPlayback component, which Flash deploys as part of the video-import process (see #69), the ActionScript 3.0 video components shown here require familiarity with ActionScript.

To add an instance of a component to your movie, drag it from the Components panel onto the stage. Two items are added to the library: the component itself and Component Assets, a folder of supporting files. To use additional instances of the same component, drag them from the library, not from the Components panel.

Note

If you use more than one type of component in a movie, only the first will add the Component Assets folder to the library. Additional components will share the same set of supporting files.

Adding a component instance to your movie presents the same problem as adding a button (see #27): The component functions properly in your movie—a check box is clickable, a slider is slideable, and so on—but it doesn't accomplish anything. To make a component useful, you have to write ActionScript code that monitors each instance of the component and responds to changes in it. You'll see an example of this kind of script in #100.

and choose Flash as the exchange to search.

Pay attention to the version of Flash that the component is intended for: If it's Flash 8 or earlier, the component will work only in Action-Script 2.0 documents. Also be aware that most of the add-ons in Adobe Exchange aren't supported by Adobe, so you use them at your own risk.

#97 Customizing Component Instances

While using off-the-shelf components is convenient, the components' default designs won't always seem appropriate in your movie. Flash addresses this issue by providing several ways to modify the appearance of ActionScript 3.0 components:

- **Use the Properties panel.** As with standard movie clips, you can use the menus on the Properties panel to change the color effect (see #25) or blending mode (see #38) of a component instance.

- **Use the Free Transform tool.** Transforming a component instance doesn't always yield the results you'd expect. Depending on the component, scaling an instance may change one dimension, both, or neither, and it doesn't affect text size at all. Skewing or rotating an instance works fine on the graphic part of the component, but it makes all text—labels and data—disappear. You can avoid this problem by embedding a font (see #99).

- **Edit the component.** Double-clicking an instance on the stage puts it into symbol-editing mode, but with a difference: *All* of the states of the component are shown (**Figure 97a**). Double-click one of the states to edit it as you would a standard symbol. (If you want a particular change to affect multiple states, you have to edit each one individually.) You can change the graphic portion of the component (**Figure 97b**), but you can't change the appearance of the text—that can be done only through ActionScript.

Tip

To change an edited component back to its original appearance, drag another copy of the component from the Components panel to the library. When you see a dialog box telling you there's a conflict, choose Replace Existing Items.

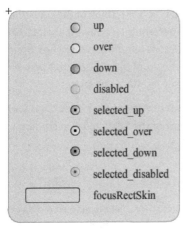

Figure 97a When you edit a component (in this case, the Radio Button), Flash shows you all of its possible states. To apply a change to multiple states, you must edit each one individually.

 **Brown**

 Blue

Figure 97b The Radio Button component has been edited to look like an eye (when selected) or an oval (when not selected). Think twice before you make significant alterations to a user-interface element; users may fail to recognize that these are radio buttons.

Hazel

- **Use ActionScript.** Although you can't use ActionScript to make radical changes in a component's appearance, you can change attributes such as its size and visibility. You can also make changes in the font, size, and style of the component's text. For an example of how ActionScript is used to set these parameters, see #98.

#98 Setting Parameters for Component Instances

Although the line between them is fuzzy, you can think of the *properties* of a component instance (see #97) as referring to outward characteristics such as size and color, and *parameters* as referring to more functional aspects. Each component has a different set of parameters, but here are some of the more common ones for user-interface components:

- **Label** and **labelPlacement.** A *label* is the text that's associated with an instance. The standard placement of the label varies according to the component (**Figure 98a**).

Figure 98a A label is typically placed to the left of a text field, to the right of a check box, and directly on a button.

- **Value.** When a user makes a choice from a menu or from among a group of radio buttons, the information that's reported back to Action-Script is called the *value*. The value is often the same as the label, but it doesn't have to be. For example, if a user chooses "Yes" in response to "Do you want a sales representative to call you?" the value (unseen by the user) might be "sucker."

- **Selected.** This parameter, which can be set to "true" or "false," determines whether an instance is already selected when it first appears on the stage—for example, whether a check box initially has a check in it.

- **Enabled** and **visible.** Selecting "false" for the enabled parameter causes an instance to appear dimmed on the stage; selecting "false" for the visible parameter causes the instance to disappear entirely.

There are two ways to set an instance's parameters:

- **Use the Component Inspector.** You can open the Component Inspector panel by choosing Window > Component Inspector. When you select a component instance on the stage, the Component Inspector displays a table listing all of that instance's parameters. A default value is filled in for each parameter, but you can make changes by typing new values into text fields or choosing them from menus (**Figure 98b**).

COMPONENT INSPECTOR

☐ Button ☆

| Parameters | Bindings | Schema |

Name	Value
emphasized	false
enabled	true
label	SUBMIT
labelPlacement	right
selected	false ▼
toggle	false
visible	true

Figure 98b In the table shown here for the Button component, the value of the `label` parameter is editable text, while the value of the `selected` parameter is chosen from a menu.

- **Use ActionScript.** The instance whose parameters you want to set must have an instance name (see #90). The ActionScript code for setting parameters takes this general form:

```
instanceName.parameter = value;
```

For this example, assume we have an instance of the check box component called *checkbox1*. To change the instance's label and put a check mark inside, we could put the following code in a frame 1 script:

```
checkbox1.label="I use Flash";
checkbox1.selected=true;
```

Writing this script doesn't change anything in the authoring environment; it takes effect only when you test or publish the movie (**Figure 98c**).

Figure 98c On the left, the check box instance as it appears in the FLA file; on the right, the same instance as a SWF file in Flash Player.

The simple syntax shown here is useful only for the parameters that are listed in the Component Inspector. Changing other characteristics of an instance requires more elaborate scripting, as you'll see in #99.

Help with Help

It's not easy to find out which parameters you can change with ActionScript and what the syntax is for changing them. Going to the Help panel (see #4) and searching for keywords such as "components" and "parameters" doesn't get you very far. The best thing to do is choose ActionScript 3.0 Components from the menu on the upper left of the Help panel; then expand the All Classes category. You'll see a list of items such as CheckBox class and RadioButton class. Click the class corresponding to the component you're using. All of its scriptable properties and styles (among other things) are displayed in a series of tables in the right pane. Also take a look at the UIComponent class, which includes properties shared by all the user-interface components.

#99 Formatting Text in a Component Label

Usually, the first thing you want to do with an instance of a component is change the appearance of its label. The label's small size and unexciting font don't go well with every movie.

Changing the label properties is tricky, because the label is actually a separate entity: In ActionScript terms, it's an instance of the TextFormat class inside an instance of the component (see #87).

To demonstrate how this works, let's continue with the example from Figure 98c. Assume we want the label for checkbox1 (the I Use Flash check box) to be in 16-point Gill Sans italic. We start by creating a new instance of the TextFormat class, which we'll name niceText:

```
var niceText:TextFormat = new TextFormat();
```

We can then set the properties of that instance:

```
niceText.font="Gill Sans";
niceText.italic=true;
niceText.size=16;
```

Finally, we set the style for checkbox1. The specific style property we're setting is textFormat, and the model we're using is the instance we called niceText.

```
checkbox1.setStyle("textFormat", niceText);
```

The finished script is shown in **Figure 99a**; the result of publishing the movie is shown in **Figure 99b**.

```
1  checkBox1.label="I use Flash";
2  checkBox1.selected=true;
3  var niceText:TextFormat = new TextFormat();
4  niceText.font="Gill Sans";
5  niceText.italic=true;
6  niceText.size=16;
7  checkBox1.setStyle("textFormat", niceText);
```

Figure 99a The finished script (including the two lines we wrote in #98) is displayed in the Actions panel.

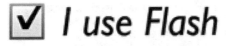

Figure 99b The check box instance looks like this in the final movie. Compare the enhanced label to the default version in Figure 98c.

You may choose to embed the font that's used in a label. Embedding a font isn't required, but it's good insurance in case the user's computer doesn't have that font installed. It also keeps the label from disappearing if the component instance is rotated or skewed (see #97). The only drawback to embedding a font is that it increases the size of the SWF file.

To embed the Gill Sans font that's used in the label for checkbox1:

1. Create a new font symbol by right-clicking (Windows) or Control-clicking (Mac) inside the library and choosing New Font from the contextual menu.

2. In the Font Symbol Properties dialog box, name the symbol gillSans (or whatever name you prefer) and choose its font, style, and size (**Figure 99c**). Click OK.

The font symbol appears in the library.

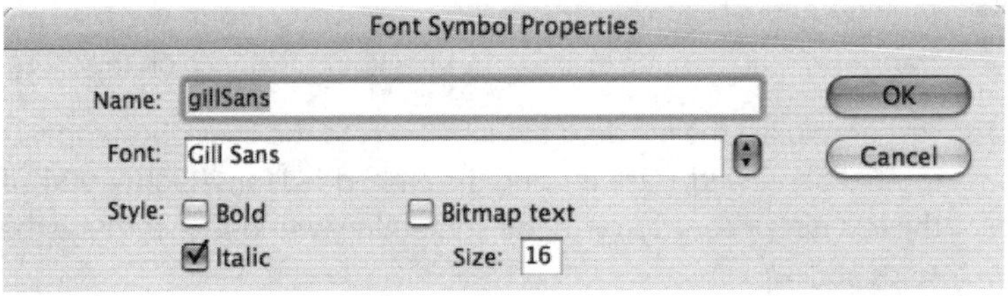

Font Symbol Properties	
Name: gillSans	OK
Font: Gill Sans	Cancel
Style: ☐ Bold ☐ Bitmap text	
☑ Italic Size: 16	

Figure 99c The Font Symbol Properties dialog box is set for 16-point Gill Sans italic.

3. Right-click (Windows) or Control-click (Mac) the font symbol and choose Linkage from the contextual menu.

4. In the Linkage Properties dialog box, select Export for ActionScript. Flash fills in the Class and Base Class fields. The information in these fields allows ActionScript to recognize the font symbol.

(continued on next page)

5. Write down the name that Flash put into the Class field. Click OK.

If an alert box appears, click OK again.

6. In the Actions panel, add the following line to the top of your frame 1 script.:

```
var embeddedFont:Font=new gillSans();
```

This creates an instance of the font symbol and gives it the name embeddedFont (or whatever you'd like to call it). The word after *new* is the class name that you wrote down in the preceding step.

7. Go to the line in which you formerly specified a font for the niceText instance. Delete the font name and rewrite the line as follows:

```
niceText.font=embeddedFont.fontName;
```

(If you used a different instance name in Step 6, use it instead of embeddedFont.) The revised code tells niceText to use the embedded font rather than the one on the user's computer.

8. Add one more line to the end of the script, giving the check box instance permission to use the embedded font:

```
checkbox1.setStyle("embedFonts", true);
```

9. To make sure Flash really is using the embedded font, use the Free Transform tool to rotate or skew the checkbox1 instance on the stage.

10. Test or publish the movie. If the label next to the check box appears rotated or skewed, Flash is using the embedded font (**Figure 99d**). If the text disappears, you've done something wrong—go through the steps again.

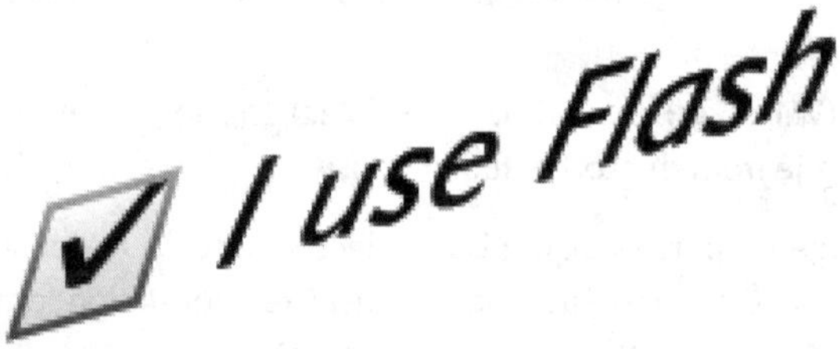

Figure 99d Embedding a font allows a component's label to be rotated and/or skewed.

#**100** Scripting User Interface Components

The component instances we've created in #97 through #99 look good, but they don't do anything useful. To make an instance respond to user input, you have to know two things: First, what event do you want the instance to respond to—for example, a rollover, a mouse click, a key press? Second, what do you want to happen as a result of that event?

For this example, let's combine the check box from #99 with the happy-sad face movie that we made in #90. What we want to happen is:

- When the check box is selected, the face becomes happy (**Figure 100a**).

- When the check box is deselected, the face becomes sad.

Figure 100a When the I Use Flash check box is selected, the face becomes happy (left); when it's deselected, the face becomes sad (right).

Let's start by laying out the timeline. It looks similar to Figure 89b, but the first frame has been deleted. There are now two segments: "happy" from frames 1 to 10 and "sad" from frames 11 to 20 (**Figure 100b**).

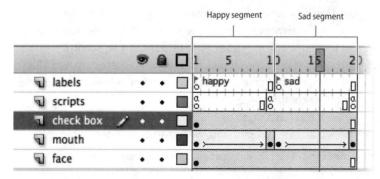

Figure 100b The timeline has a happy segment and a sad segment, with a stop script at the end of each segment.

The instance of the check box component—which we'll call just the *check box* for short—is placed where the Happy and Sad buttons used to be, and it remains visible throughout the movie. In frame 1 of the Scripts layer, we paste the script from Figure 99a. (For simplicity's sake, we're omitting the embedded font.)

If we test the movie at this point, the check box looks and works just as it did before. Independently, the face starts out neutral, becomes happy, and stops.

Now let's tie the movement of the face to the events in the check box. When the movie begins, the check box is selected and the face becomes happy: That's exactly what we want to happen. When the user clicks the check box to deselect it, we want the face to turn sad. To make that happen, we can add the following function to the frame 1 script:

```
function mouseResponse(event:MouseEvent) {
  if (currentFrame<11) {
            gotoAndPlay("sad");
  } else {
            gotoAndPlay("happy");
  }
}
```

(The function here is named mouseResponse, but you can name it anything you like.) You may not understand every detail of the code, but it should be clear what's happening: When the user clicks the mouse, if the playhead is anywhere in the happy segment, it moves to the beginning of the sad segment; if it's anywhere in the sad segment, it moves to the beginning of the happy segment. (We cheated here and used a frame number instead of a frame label, but doing otherwise would have made the script too complicated.)

We want this function to be triggered in response to a mouse click in the check box. To accomplish this, we use an event listener (see #88):

```
this.checkbox1.addEventListener(MouseEvent.CLICK, mouse
Response);
```

This line of code adds an event listener to checkbox1 that waits for a click of the mouse. When it "hears" one, it activates the mouseResponse function.

The finished script (**Figure 100c**) produces the results that were shown in Figure 100a. It doesn't do so in the most polished or foolproof way—for example, the script doesn't know whether the check box is selected at any given time—but it should be simple and clear enough to get you started with writing your own ActionScript scripts.

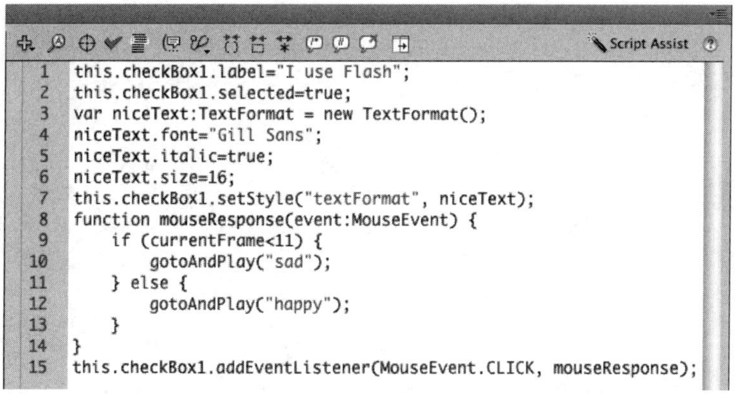

```
1   this.checkBox1.label="I use Flash";
2   this.checkBox1.selected=true;
3   var niceText:TextFormat = new TextFormat();
4   niceText.font="Gill Sans";
5   niceText.italic=true;
6   niceText.size=16;
7   this.checkBox1.setStyle("textFormat", niceText);
8   function mouseResponse(event:MouseEvent) {
9       if (currentFrame<11) {
10          gotoAndPlay("sad");
11      } else {
12          gotoAndPlay("happy");
13      }
14  }
15  this.checkBox1.addEventListener(MouseEvent.CLICK, mouseResponse);
```

Script Assist

Figure 100c The finished script contains an event listener and a function that's triggered when the event occurs.

Index

Numbers

3D Rotation tool, 50–52
3D Translation tool, 50–52

A

AC_RunActiveContent, 204
ActionScript, 217–246
  Actions panel in, 220–221
  animation converting to, 237–238
  Debugger in, 245–246
  for event-handling scripts, 228–230
  external files of, 239–240
  formatting scripts of, 241–242
  for frame scripts, 224–225
  interactivity in, 231–233
  object-oriented programming in, 226–227
  overview of, 217
  Script Assist in, 222–223
  for scripts controlling movie clips, 234–235
  testing interactive movies in, 243–244
  validating scripts in, 241–242
  versions of, 218–219
Activation screen, 2
Add a Hit frame, 78–79
Add Anchor Point tool, 40
Additional Rotation control for motion tweens, 120
Adobe
  AIR, 4, 213–215

Creative Suite. *see* Creative Suite
  Exchange, 248–249
  Fireworks, 146–148
  Illustrator, 140–143
  Media Encoder, 191–192
  Photoshop, 140–145
ADPCM Sound Properties option, 169
Advanced option in Color Effect, 73–74
AIFF audio file format, 158
AIR (Adobe Integrated Runtime), 4, 213–215
Alpha blending mode, 102–105
Alpha slider in Color Effect, 73
anchor points
  Pen tool for, 39
  reducing number of, 55
  selecting, 46–47
  Selection tool vs., 20–22
Angle in filters, 130
animations. *see also* motion
  blending modes for, 101–105
  converting to ActionScript, 237–238
  editing in timeline, 94–95
  frame by frame creation of, 90–91
  frame rates of, 88–89
  masking in, 99–100
  onion skinning of, 92–93
  overview of, 85
  scenes and, 106–107
  in symbols, 97–98
  synchronizing sounds to, 166–167
  testing, 96

  timeline of, 86–87
anti-aliasing, 57–58
applications, standalone, 212–215
Apply Recommended Import Settings option, 140–141
arguments vs. parameters, 222
armatures, 133–136
artwork, importing, 137–156
  autotracing bitmaps after, 155–156
  using bitmap properties after, 150–152
  breaking apart bitmaps after, 153–154
  Bridge file-manager viewer and, 138–139
  DXF files, 149
  file formats, miscellaneous, 149
  from Fireworks, 146–148
  Free Hand 7 through 11, 149
  from Illustrator, 140–143
  overview of, 137
  from Photoshop, 140–143
audio. *see* sound
audio codec for encoding videos, 194
Audio Event setting in Flash Player, 200
Audio Stream setting in Flash Player, 200
Auto Format in ActionScript, 241–242
autotracing bitmaps, 155–156
axes in transforming objects, 50–52

Index

Index

Index

Index

Index

Index

Index

Index

Index